# *THE TELECOMMUTERS*

*To*

B.M.K. and B.M.K.

# *THE TELECOMMUTERS*

**Francis Kinsman**

JOHN WILEY & SONS
Chichester · New York · Brisbane · Toronto · Singapore

**Library of Congress Cataloging-in-Publication Data**:

Kinsman, Francis.
The telecommuters.

Includes bibliographies and index.
1. Telecommuting. I. Title.
HD2333.K56 1987 331.25 87-25413
ISBN 0 471 91789 3

**British Library Cataloguing in Publication Data**:

Kinsman, Francis
The telecommuters.
1. Technology—Social aspects
I. Title
303.4'83 T14.5

ISBN 0 471 91789 3

Typeset by Woodfield Graphics, Fontwell, Arundel, West Sussex
Printed and bound in Great Britain by Biddles Ltd, Guildford

# Contents

# Foreword

For years people have been saying that faster communications and smarter information systems will end the need to work from impersonal office blocks in crowded city centres.

Most of us see this as a rather distant prospect. But for the telecommuters in this book the future has already arrived. F International celebrated its Silver Jubilee in 1987, and ICL's homeworkers have been operating for 18 years.

We sponsored Francis Kinsman to research this book because we believe that telecommuting is not just the curiosity described in some anecdotal articles. It is the precursor of a new way of working, in tune with the networked or federated organisation structures which are becoming increasingly common. It is in the mainstream of the social and economic developments brought about by the convergence of communications and information systems. As such it deserves serious study.

Inevitably, new ways of working pose new management challenges, but the difficulties are more than offset by rewards such as the telecommuter's positive attitude. In contrast to many conventional office workers, they do not see work as merely something to do when they would rather be doing something else. And they live and die by their ability to communicate. They put to shame many organisations whose staff occupy the same building.

Indeed, the telecommuters are children of our age. Their success depends on enthusiasm, communication and good management, and they have plenty of all three.

NINIAN EADIE
MRS STEVE SHIRLEY OBE

ICL

F International Group plc Silver Jubilee 1962–1987 25

# Introduction and Acknowledgements

This book is about a hope. A possible release, a way out, a new deal — which is now available as an answer to a whole range of business problems, as long as people have the vision and the stomach to ditch them and to take on change instead. Its potential will become increasingly evident with the passage of time, the application of technology, and the tide of social development. Meanwhile, it is already here and will more and more clearly be seen to be here.

In writing about it I have drawn on the intellectual, technical and human support of a large number of people. Foremost of these must be the two panels of respondents whose interviews provided me with such a powerful stimulus of enthusiasm and ideas. Their names are listed in the Appendices but neither a mere roll-call such as that, nor anything I can say in extension to it here will indicate the full value of their contributions. Their experience and approachability have been for me the most striking and rewarding aspects of this whole exercise.

Many of them belong to the workforces of F International and the CPS homeworking unit of ICL. To them and to their managements a particular debt of gratitude is due — not only for their total openness and co-operation but also for their generous sponsorship of this research.

In trying to encapsulate the past, present and future of the telecommuting phenomenon I have also been enormously dependent on the wealth of publication on the subject to date. Some of this I have referred to in the text in quoted form, and here I must acknowledge the kind permission that has been granted for its quotation from the following authors and publishers:

BCS Computer Newsletter, *Meet the People,* March 1987; Controller, Her Majesty's Stationery Office, 'Pamphlet IR56', Inland Revenue, May 1986; Controller, Her Majesty's Stationery Office, *IT Futures . . . It Can Work,* National Economic Development Office, 1987; Professor Ralf Dahrendorf, 'Dahrendorf on Britain', BBC TV 1, 9 January 1983; Eosys Ltd and the Highlands and Islands Development Board, *Opportunities to Promote Remote Working in the Highlands and Islands,* 1984; Phillip Judkins, David West and John Drew (Clevedon Management Services) *Networking in Organisations,* Gower Publishing Co. Ltd, 1985; Miles Kington and *The Independent,* 'Life in the Fast Lane', 4 April 1987; Tom Lloyd, *Dynosaur & Co.,* Associated Book Publishers (UK) Ltd, 1984; *Management Today,* 'Old Boy Network', February 1987; Spencer Stuart & Associates, *The New Agenda,* Francis Kinsman, 1983;

Xanadu Ltd, *The Way Forward*, 1986; Rose Deakin, *Women and Computing: The Golden Opportunity*, Macmillan, 1984.

In other instances I have gained encouragement and insight from a general review of the text concerned. Since this acknowledgment also applies to the above works which well merit further reading in their entirety, I have combined the bibliographies and references at the end of each chapter for the convenience of the reader. I should also thank those who were kind enough to grant me telephone interviews and send me details of their research, in particular: Colin Bowers of Avis Management Services; Tom Bowling of Bell-Northern Research; Dr Ken Eason of the Human Sciences and Advanced Technology Research Centre, University of Loughborough; John Frank, freelance consultant; Sir John Havey-Jones, erstwhile Chairman of Imperial Chemical Industries; Michael Houser of the School of Oriental and African Studies; Ralph Jackson of the National Federation of Self-Employed and Small Businesses; Eberhard Köhler of the European Foundation of Living and Working Conditions; Werner B. Korte of Empirica GmbH; John McCann of the Information Technology Division of the Department of Trade and Industry; Mavis McLean of the Centre for Socio-Legal Studies, Wolfson College, Oxford; Bengt Sahlberg of Nordplan; John Sellers of International Oil Insurers; Peter Senker of the Social Policy Research Unit, Sussex University; and David Sumner-Smith of British Telecom.

Finally, there is the immeasurable contribution of Gilly Cannon, Carole Henley and Anne Porter who triumphed over technological disaster, impossible demands and a horrendous time schedule to produce the final text. How they did it, I know not, but they did. To them, and to all my friends — especially Judy Smith — who have had to endure my creative absorption, a big hug.

FRANCIS KINSMAN
*Bath*
*July 1987*

# 1
# Is There Anybody Else Out There?

## COMMUTING OLD AND NEW

A visitor to Highgate in the 1830s complained that his sleep was ruined from 4.30 a.m. onwards by the constant tramp of workers' feet making their way towards employment in inner London. A Dickensian picture, but there are still echoes of those footsteps in today's metropolis.

*The Financial Times*, 12 May 1987, noted in its 'Men and Matters' column that stockbroker Charles Edmunds, aged 37, had broken out of the punishing life-style of the city of London without having to take early retirement—by switching employers to start up an international securities dealing operation in Edinburgh. He had been getting up at 5.45 a.m. in Guildford to catch the 0650 train to London, which usually failed to provide him with a first-class seat but just got him to the office in time for the 8 a.m. conference call with Tokyo. He set back on his journey home at 6 p.m. if he was very lucky, and never saw his house in daylight for half the year. In Edinburgh he hoped to live a few minutes' walk from the office; in the wake of the City's Big Bang there are signs that more financial specialists are emulating him by moving from London to Edinburgh than going the other way.

One can hardly be surprised. There comes a moment for everyone when the daily commuting grind finally becomes so unbearable that something snaps and the search is on for an alternative. Further, there is likely to be a continued reduction in the hours of most white-collar working weeks, while commuting time remains unchanged or even increases. As the contrast becomes more apparent, more and more people will start wondering why they commute at all. Unlike 150 years ago, however, there are alternatives at hand, and one of them is working electronically from home—or what is beginning to be termed telecommuting.

The original commuters were so called because they commuted their daily travel payments into a lump-sum in advance to buy a period railway season ticket at a discount. In this sense the word is now used only in connection with pensions and death sentences, which are commuted to cash and life imprisonment respectively. The telecommuter, however, besides carrying overtones of the telecommunications that makes him possible, has in a very real sense commuted the distance (*telos)* and time involved in the trek to and from work into the much shorter distance and time involved in working at or near home.

Of course, the hard-pressed commuter has other options, too. There is already a widespread movement towards many different styles of working. Fewer days with longer hours is one alternative, job sharing another, and flexitime a third, where the ultimate has to be the employment contract at Dutch State Mines. Here, the employee must put in 200 days work per annum, but subject to the agreement of his immediate boss and his team colleagues, these can be any 200 days in the entire year.

Much of this variety in working patterns stems from the general trend towards flexibility, individuality and small scale in business. The vast majority of people used to work within large corporations and institutions. Today, more and more work is in the small business sector, the size of which comes right down to the individual freelancer, and even within large organisations the entrepreneurial spirit is gradually becoming more prevalent. Again, people increasingly work for service organisations rather than in manufacturing and agriculture. As the information-handling aspects of office work are automated, the office itself can be decentralised into branches or into neighbourhood work centres where people from a number of different organisations congregate on a regular basis. Workshops, business centres and office bureaux also provide a range of facilities *ad hoc* or on short-term hire, while the traveller can also obtain office support at airports and in hotels. In other words, this is the era of mobile, remote and flexible work styles, uplifting the quality of the finished product as well as the quality of life.

## WORKING AT A DISTANCE

Many occupations traditionally do or can already involve work at home —not only the sweated labour of garment outworkers, but designers, architects, accountants, lawyers, researchers, journalists, authors, insurance agents, language and music teachers, exam markers, therapists and psychologists, specialist consultants, art dealers, farmers and investment managers.

> The technology will make homeworking more and more generally possible. In the financial world there are individual fund managers—private practitioners—who now have their kit anywhere. I have a friend who lives in Palo Alto and is a fund adviser appointing and monitoring the performance of other fund managers who look after tranches of the fund. He is responsible for the strategy but does no dealing himself. The fund totals five billion dollars and he oversees it from a garden shed.
> (*Michael Josephs, Director, Point Consulting*)

Many others, particularly those engaged in new types of work, could also be home-based if they realised it. These include tasks that require few direct personal transactions such as data entering and retrieving, typing, invoicing, order processing, stock control, distribution or operational research and book-keeping; and tasks that sometimes require peace and quiet, such as research, personnel, planning, policy formulation and organisation design.

> Secretarial bureau work is going this way, too. At the moment it has to be shunted round with dispatch riders, but given a reasonable network printing can be done centrally to good effect. Here, fax is also a great and hitherto underestimated weapon. As long as it is economic to equip a secretary with a £1250 machine (though this level is coming down rapidly, of course) it is economic to send manuscripts through fax.
> (*Michael Josephs*)

As an aside, it should be explained that Michael Josephs was one of a panel of twenty-one expert commentators who were surveyed for this book and whose views and experiences are incorporated here. Their names and attributes are shown in Appendix C.

Telecommuters sometimes inspire others of different disciplines to follow their example, by giving proof of the attractions of this working mode. This can have a knock-on effect, as with the business consultant's secretary who left her full-time employment to start a family in 1974, and then worked on a part-time fee basis on audio-tape, gradually acquiring additional business from other sources which necessitated taking on another homeworker as a sub-contractor in 1979. By 1987, the business has become a full business centre, with a staff of eleven of whom five work at home. Clients are mostly redundant ex-employees who are taking advantage of various government enterprise and retraining programmes to start their own businesses, which they are also able to do from home since the centre gives a comprehensive support service without their needing to set up a formal office. Homeworking is thus rippling out to become one of the most characteristic features of the small business sector that governments are so anxious to foster. But to some extent telecommuting is becoming more prevalent in traditional industry, also.

> It is a concept I've always been very keen on—we do it very successfully with our salespeople, who exchange all their information and their mail electronically. This has proven advantages both to them and to their customers. I am convinced that distance working is the way of the future, especially internationally. We are moving experimentally in this direction also—we have a worldwide fax system and are soon introducing teleconferencing between major centres after a successful trial.
> (*Sir John Harvey-Jones, erstwhile Chairman, Imperial Chemical Industries*)

The details, according to Ken Edwards, of ICI's strategic information technology department, are that in the UK all 100 sales managers and 700 of the 900 sales representatives now have electronic mail facilities. The former have dumb terminals or pcs, accessed directly into the mainframe, and are capable of upgrading what are already sophisticated negotiating procedures on site—obtaining complex information, comparative quotations and the like. The sales reps have simpler videotex viewdata equipment which transmits information to and from the local centre. The fact that they operate from home and have no office saves dramatically on overheads. Before they visit a client they can access information on sales availability of products, technical data and the like, all at their fingertips without having to go into the office.

Salespeople are by nature self-motivators and self-starters; but they also need conscious management and must on no account be left out in the electronic cold. Edwards therefore adds that ICI is now making dramatically increasing use of bleepers and cellular radio throughout its operations. The growth of both cellular radio and fax in business has taken everyone by surprise; nobody was prepared for today's explosion in demand. Britain now has more mobile telephone subscribers than any country except the USA—160,000 (and this could double by the end of 1988) as against 13,000 in France and 25,000 in West Germany. There has recently been an agreement among fifteen European nations to create common standards before the introduction of the new digital cellular system so that it can be used throughout Europe. Two rival equipment suppliers, Plessey and Racal, have joined forces to exploit this booming international market. In short, this aid to distance working is becoming very much a part of the British commercial scene.

People are now therefore able to use a car or a van as their office; already thirty London taxicabs have telephones. Birkenhead steel stockholders, Robert Smith Steels, have equipped three Renault vans with telephones and computers, and been able to close four of their six regional offices as a result. In effect, they are putting a conventional office on the road. The area manager out there is in constant contact with head office—he can use the telecom service to send telexes from his vehicle, the computer to keep tabs on stock and the fax to get information for himself or the sales prospect.

In a hilarious commentary on the whole mobility trend, columnist Miles Kington of *The Independent* imagined the ultimate legal consequences of it:

> *Counsel*: On October fourth last year, at 4.50 p.m., you were sitting in a black C reg BMW in a street off Aldgate. Is that correct?
>
> *Defendant*: That is correct.
>
> *Counsel*: As it was a forbidden parking area, a traffic warden started to write out a ticket, at which you jumped out of the car, shouting: 'Go away, I'm trying to get some work done.' Am I right?
>
> *Defendant*: Quite right.
>
> *Counsel*: Could you explain this strange outburst?
>
> *Defendant*: Certainly. The black BMW is the place where I do most of my work. I am in it over eight hours a day, phoning, dictating, writing and checking world prices. It is my office. You cannot book an office for illegal parking.
>
> *Counsel*: ...if you claim this BMW to be your office, does that mean you have no car?
>
> *Defendant*: No. I have one in Chelsea. It is 33 Fairfax Road.
>
> *Judge*: Do you mean, it is *outside* 33 Fairfax Road?
>
> *Defendant*: No, your honour. I am the owner of 33 Fairfax Road, a three-storey structure, which I have had registered as a motor car.
>
> *Judge*: What on earth is the purpose of that?
>
> *Defendant*: Your honour, the BMW is a very small office, so my rates are very low; 33 Fairfax Road is large, but as it is now a car, I only have to pay road tax and insurance on it, not rates. I am trying to cut costs without breaking the law.

Back in reality, SWEB, the South-Western Electricity Board, have had a computerised meter reading service since 1985. They have a mainframe computer in Plymouth, from which information is pumped up the line to their smaller computers in area offices. The meter readers load up their mobile mini-computers with this information, which gives them details of what they have to do and where they have to go next day. Their machines have shoulder straps and weigh eleven pounds, the heaviest part being the heat-printing mechanism. As they read the meters they key in all the details and leave the householder with a computerised print-out invoice. The machine retains the information and is unloaded every evening back in the office at the same time as being reloaded with information for the next day. Meter readers took a little time to get used to the process but now they can service 200 customers daily—far more than before—and declare themselves happy. The next phase, of course, will be for them to access the mainframe from their home telephones.

According to Roy Dibble of the government's Central Computer Telecommunications Agency, the British Civil Service has equipped its departments with several thousand Thorn-EMI Liberator portable word-processors. These unique machines are three-quarters of an inch thick and the length and breadth of an A4 sheet. Anyone can use them with a few hours' training and they are deployed throughout the Civil Service so that people can utilise their travel time effectively. The user can, for example, type minutes on the train coming into work, which are held in the memory and then dumped onto a mainframe computer in the office; or it can transmit the message by means of an acoustic coupler. It is basically an LCD display with twelve lines of 80 characters each, which folds back to reveal a keyboard. The early enthusiasts were computer-literate, but now it has been developed to a very user-friendly basis, suitable even for mandarins.

The purpose of describing all these different developments in some detail is to show that the home is just one element in the new overall trend towards the location independence of work. Any peripatetic worker, salesman, field engineer, maintenance man or social worker can operate in this way, either at home or on the hoof. Telecommuting in its widest sense is going to involve not only the home-based but the home-plus-vehicle-based. In IBM (UK), NOSS, their national office support system, enables an employee to sit at a terminal anywhere in the company, call up his electronic mail, reply to it and action it. Again, the next step will be to be able to do this from a home and/or a car terminal. Already the company has experimented successfully with up to 60 management and professional staff in four sites being provided with a second telephone line and company personal computer at home, so that they can undertake home work in addition to their normal working week.

## NETWORKING AND THE EXTENDED TELEPHONE

The technical trends applicable to telecommuting are cellular radio and feature-rich telephones; the continuing miniaturisation of electronic equipment, especially fax; the encyclopaedic memory of compact disks; telecommunicating software; the move to electronic publishing; and the general shift towards increasing compatibility in equipment. But above all its spread depends on an effective and efficient telecommunications service.

Here, an important boost to the homeworking phenomenon is that in spite of continuing difficulties with the technology, British Telecom is at last beginning to think more imaginatively about the services it can provide to encourage the home subscriber to dial up. We shall therefore get used to doing all kinds of things with our home telephones which we might not have considered before. There is indeed a group of people including several from BT looking at every electronic aspect of 'the home of the future' under the auspices of consultants, Taylor Nelson Applied Futures.

BT launched 'Talk About' in 1983—a service which allows up to twelve strangers to converse together on random topics of common interest, with human monitors listening in to cut off callers who swear or attempt to give their surname, telephone number or address. The average length of talk is four minutes and 50 million such calls have been made since 1983. But in addition, the thinking person now gains satisfaction by interacting electronically. Arpanet is an international messaging system where one can develop a group intellectual rapport on specialist academic subjects without ever actually meeting colleagues. Like radio hams, its users have worked out communication techniques for getting on together without personal contact. It is possible—after all, in *84 Charing Cross Road*, the couple never met each other either.

Meanwhile, 'Boulevard' is a BT experiment to encourage the use of the telephone for upmarket teleshopping, an exceptionally glossy quarterly give-away magazine. Teleshopping has not been particularly successful here, in France, in the US, or in Japan. BT believes that one reason is the general fear of new technology among consumers. Until photo-videotex is available in five to eight years' time, this will continue to be difficult. Youngsters are familiar with computers but the vast majority of older shoppers are not, so the only way of hitting them is through a familiar medium like print. Hence BT also makes the front end of the teleshopping mechanism as approachable as possible—there are no tapes, just trained individuals from Telecom Tan, their large core handling station with 450 staff. The third user-friendly ingredient they have incorporated is the familiarity of the stores advertising in the magazine.

The number of items purchased per call, from the first two 350,000 issues distributed in London and the inner home counties, was about equivalent to normal mail order experience. But volume was low, partly because the retailers sometimes got it wrong. Thomas Goode advertised a vase at £11,000 while Dunhill were featuring gold lighters at £850. These are the kind of things you want to drool over and fondle lovingly before you buy, rather than just ordering them sight unseen over the telephone. Nevertheless it is a step in an interesting direction and could be very significant if it caught on a little further down-market with somewhat less exotic merchandise.

One can, however, be a little over-optimistic about home shopping. The technology for it has been around for ten years, but it hasn't taken off. There are still glitches. A colleague got into it through acquiring a Micronet 800 as an educational network for his children. This also happens to be a sub-set of Prestel, so by buying it he had the whole of Prestel at his fingertips as well.

> I am quite computer literate but I really could not find my way around the menu of 30,000 pages. I was trying to book an order with ASDA and suddenly, I'm not sure how, I found myself in the erotica section of the British Library and had no idea how to get back to the world of baked beans and strawberry yoghurt. With Prestel you can book an order with ASDA at any time—3 in the morning if you like—so that means complete flexibility, and they will deliver three times a day. It costs 15% more, however, and after this rather unnerving experience I never used it much.
> (*John Frank, freelance consultant*)

Other adaptations of networking and electronic communications show more promise. The University of Bradford is hoping to wire itself up entirely, with a micro-computer on every staff member's desk, the network also incorporating all the students' dormitories.

> It may end up that as a prerequisite of actually joining the University all students will have to bring their own computer. Several universities are already doing this in the USA—Stephens Institute of Technology in New Jersey was the first. At the moment there is just one pay-phone on the ground floor of each Bradford dormitory which is either occupied or unutilised because everyone knows people won't go and get somebody to the phone from the fourth floor. What is hoped, though, is that electronic mail will increase the sense of community in the University and encourage students to move into this whole work-at-home life-style, to search the library to see if books are in or out, to get lecture notes from the departmental workstation, to read the student union notice board or to ask each other to come out and have a curry. In addition they could gateway out through Bradford to JANET, the academic network to which all university computers are linked throughout the country.
> (*Professor Tom Stonier, Chairman of The School of Science in Society, University of Bradford*)

## OFFICE, HOME OR BOTH

There are now two magazines—*Office at Home* and *Homebase*—which claim to unravel some of the problems of working from home and appeal straight to the home-based professionals. And colour supplements are beginning to detail the equipment and furniture that is not only suitable for office use but attractive enough to be considered for the home environment. Meanwhile, there is a growing undertone of criticism about the office environment itself.

A survey commissioned by Reed Employment and carried out by Nielson Consumer Research found among a sample of 500 office workers a mammoth list of ailments including back problems from inadequate chairs, eye strain and headaches. Half of those subjected to fluorescent or strip lighting complained of regular headaches, compared to only a quarter of those who worked under tungsten lights; only 23% enjoyed the luxury of working by natural light. Air-conditioning was said to be a source of stuffiness, breathing problems, headaches and the drying of skin and eyes, as reported by 'Office Life' columnist Alan Road in *The Observer*. According to a two-year study funded by the Health Promotion Research Trust, and carried out by former government scientist Sheena Wilson, building sickness (non-specific symptoms associated by sufferers with their place of work, and now recognised as a syndrome by the World Health Organisation) was experienced by 80% of over 4,000 office people canvassed. As Alan Road points out, the high-tech/high-tat office is actually bad for your health.

Those who complained of these multiple symptoms estimated that their productivity was reduced by at least 20%. In contrast, as we shall see, people working from home report increases in productivity of between 20% and 50%. The fact that employers get less rather than more out of employees by crowding them together like battery chickens is bound to be recognised in the end, and sometime the penny of distributed work is bound to drop.

> A certain amount of isolation is marvellous and it does cut out the terrible office politics. One reason that people like high-tech working methods is, according to a Henley study, the fact that all the office aggro is cut out. People hate being blamed for things they haven't done, though they don't mind being blamed for things they have done. With new technology there isn't the stupid argument about 'who took the file' because the information is there and the VDU will show clearly who has said and done what.
> (*Sheila Rothwell, Director, Centre for Employment Policy Studies*)

Further, the cost of commuting may be borne by the individual worker but is indirectly passed on to the employer and thence also to the consumer in the form of higher wage and product costs. Professor Jack Nilles of the University of Southern California, researching 2,000 insurance company employees in Los Angeles, found that to carry the results to their conclusion, if one-eighth of urban commuting had been replaced by telecommuting the United States would have saved 75 million barrels of oil in 1975, and completely eliminated the need to import any from abroad.

Architects are now recognising that there is something to be made out of the fact that some people would genuinely prefer to work at home. Conran Roche is a new type of architectural practice which embraces planning design and economic consultancy. Involved in the Milton Keynes Central Business Exchange and Infotech Exchange developments, it has designed and set up a number of advanced business centres and 'office-shops', or shared neighbourhood work centres, including a serviced office suite for BT's 'Network Nine' in Aberdeen. But it is now also starting to design the home/work unit, a building which is a house/flat/studio/workshop all under one roof, for the self-employed and for small or distributed companies. This will be holistic living space—the technological equivalent to living over the shop. One problem until now has been the restriction of planning consent, but in 1987 the regulations governing the definition of home usage are likely to be relaxed. This is a Department of Environment change, but for any specific development the local planners must also of course be convinced.

There is another development of this nature in Hammersmith/Fulham, a double-sided building with the house entrance on one side and the business entrance on the other. East Lothian District Council has also built a group of four houses incorporating a 400 square foot workshop facility, with three bedrooms and a groundfloor room that can be used either as an office or a dining room. And at South Woodham Ferrers, Essex County Council has erected a group of craft and studio homes, each with up to 1500 square feet of workshop or studio. In Bath, Conran Roche planned to put up a riverside terrace of homework units with studio network services and a central resources centre common to all, behind the residential development and containing all manner of high-tech facilities. Unfortunately, a takeover bid for the site's vendors has knocked the plan on the head for the time being, but the concept remains and will doubtless have another airing somewhere else before too long.

## DISTANCE LEARNING AND TELECONFERENCING

At the same time that working-at-home and living-with-work are taking root, so also is another closely related concept—distance learning—as pioneered by the Open University, and now, of course, taken up by the Open Tech and the Open College. The early plan was brilliantly structured, with all materials packaged in such a way that the course could be completed entirely at home. Unfortunately it fell flat on its face.

> Experience showed that there was often a problem surrounding the question of family attitudes. The OU found that distance learning was particularly difficult for many women because they failed to negotiate a contract with their family about their right to work at it. Then there was also 'the loneliness of the long distance student.' The Open University had to provide opportunities for human contact. Not only tutorials but a hot-line to a tutor—sympathetic as well as technical—then regional study centres to meet other students and compare notes, and finally a summer school.
> (*Peter Templer, management and organisation development consultant*)

The Henley Distance Learning MBA course is similarly organised, and the college is very much involved with training its trainers to bring distance learning into the pattern of things.

> We have regional counsellors all round the country, and also a hot-line into Henley itself which because people mostly study at night is equipped with an answerphone. We generally reckon to get a message back in 24 hours. People seem to ring up not so much for psychological support but over technical problems. We try either to get groups of people from the same area to work together, or recruit people from the same organisation so that someone is able to keep a watching brief on them in-house.
> (*Sheila Rothwell*)

People do want a greater degree of control over how they work or study, but they also want human help. They need to be trained to learn at a distance, just as they need to be trained to work from home.

> In IBM training, they found there was a real need for some hand holding after the distance learning process. Once people had been trained and got back to the real thing, it was recognised that within an hour or so they would have made a couple of mistakes and there was always the possibility that they would then say—dammit, I'm going back to the old method. At that moment they need someone to peep round the door and ask whether they are OK.
> (*Michel Syrett, Editor, Manpower Policy and Practice*)

Human contact is, for most of us, an extremely important aspect of our working lives—and there are particular parts of our working lives in which it is crucial.

> There are different forms of communication. With a telephone one can swap information, issue instructions or seek instructions. But to persuade

someone, to get to know an opinion, to obtain guidance, to develop an idea, with qualitative things like this I always find I have to meet somebody and talk to them face-to-face. The phone is frustrating in this connection.
(*Bob Pell, Director, Conran Roche*)

Some people are better over the telephone than others—indeed some are better over the telephone than they are in person—thus the video signal is not always necessary for successful teleconferencing, and indeed can be misleading or disadvantageous for other reasons.

I had the experience of working with a group at Henley who were interviewing 'candidates' as part of a management exercise. Those who were watching the interchange on video lost information which in some way was filtered out by the artificiality of the system, compared to what came through to the real interviewer. They did not get the measure of the person as well as he did.
(*Sheila Rothwell*)

There is substantial resistance to video-phones. For example, I work quite a lot in bed and do not particularly relish the idea of taking video-calls in a rather torn pair of pyjamas. In addition I like doing alternative things during boring calls so that I can save time and pretend to be listening—this activity would be impossible with video-phones.
(*Tom Stonier*)

Teleconferencing is, nonetheless beginning to be used. At the 1986 CBI conference a thousand delegates were addressed from Washington by Dr Richard Lesher, President of the US Chamber of Commerce. Ford Motor brought forward the launch of a new model by three months through regular video-conferencing between small groups of technicians in the UK and West Germany. Glaxo, the pharmaceutical group, added more than £525 million to its stock market value after a two-hour satellite question-and-answer link-up between the company's board and brokers in London, Paris and New York.

Photographs, slides, flipcharts, diagrams and working models can be shown and discussed at a distance, while fax terminals in conjunction can provide hard copy if necessary. Teleconferencing saves time and money on travelling, naturally; but the telephone time is still expensive. For a while, at least, this and the sense of unfamiliarity will preclude it from catching on to any great degree. Until the majority of people at a meeting are at a distant location and there is no alternative to teleconferencing, people simply will not bother to learn the techniques involved, fearing that they might make mistakes or in some way be wrong-footed in negotiation. The artificiality of the split screen was said by some to be rather daunting, too.

James Martin (*The Wired Society*) blames the innate conservatism of the British here, pointing out that the Institute for the Future conducted research on the psychological effects of teleconferencing and estimated that 85% of a business traveller's requirements could be satisfied by video-conferencing and fast facsimile transmission. Furthermore, of the users of a video-conferencing facility at Bell Laboratories, 91% said they would rather use it than travel 50 miles to a face-to-face meeting, and 51% said they would rather use it than travel 15 miles. The fact remains, however, it has not caught on very much more in the US than in the UK. The technology is expensive and still not adequate to overcome the lack of human contact where there is emotional involvement, as in the negotiation of deals or the resolution of arguments.

> Information technology has revolutionised management but hasn't yet touched such things as counselling, negotiating, motivating, or interactive skills. Electronics cannot be a surrogate for face-to-face reaction. In teleconferencing, body language and facial subtleties are missing. However, it is an intermediary between home and office which fits in well with the adhocracy of the consultancy mode which will be so much in the ascendent in the future. This kind of highly focused expertise is very well positioned from a home base.
> (*Dr Graham Milborrow, Director of Professional Management, British Institute of Management*)

What does this all imply? We have covered a somewhat roundabout route so far, first extolling the virtues and the potential of homeworking and being encouraged by some of the technical advances we accept in the broad field of communications to and from home, but then being brought up short by some of the inadequacies of the distance learning and teleconferencing processes, which may throw an obliquely negative light on homeworking itself. This route was deliberately chosen. It symbolises the marvellous potential of the working mode but does not shrink from the admission that there are still difficulties to be overcome.

## SOCIAL AND PSYCHOLOGICAL FACTORS

Some indeed of these difficulties are technological, but the vast majority are attitudinal. First, here, is loneliness and the lack of human interaction both real and imaginary. It really can be a case of 'is there anybody else out there?' for remote workers, unless both they and their managers make an effort to communicate. For many people, pure social chat—over and above any technical working content or the enjoyment of being part of a team—plays a great part in the working life, and for them homeworking would be a disaster.

I knew of one factory where the employees were pushing for a shorter working week. New machinery was installed which enabled them to have their hours reduced from 9–5 to 9–3.30. However, the women operatives stayed on for the extra hour-and a-half to chat to each other rather than going home, or going and doing something constructive with their time. It was need for the social element that led them to push for shorter hours.
(*Christine MacNulty, Chief Executive, Taylor Nelson Applied Futures*)

Though many women gain satisfaction from executive roles, others don't necessarily want to participate in management or be brought into things in the business. They want to earn pin money from their work *and* they want social exchange and chat from it. Also, people either lead episodic or continuous lives, and those who want episodic ones need changes of pace and venue. For the latter, the problem with homeworking is that psychologically there is no difference between the working environment and the leisure environment. One needs a change in *obsession* here; to go out and do something totally different. With me it is flying; with my grandfather who was a wheelwright and lived over the works, it was growing roses.
(*Graham Millborrow*)

As we shall see, there are many for whom telecommuting is the answer to a prayer, however, and where the ability to integrate work with leisure or with other kinds of work provides an enormous sense of freedom and release. These are people who set a high value on the flexibility of being able to plan their time and activities to their individual requirements. For others who are less resourceful and/or who feel themselves forced into working from home, there can be problems of claustrophobia, introversion or withdrawal symptoms due to lack of social contact, stress and overwork due to lack of distractions and other interests, health deterioration due to lack of physical activity, and even child abuse. Even for the initiated, there are rules which need to be followed.

The first difficulty about working from home is self-management. When you are in the traditional system you are driven along by it with its objectives, its deadlines and its management. Now, who is the manager? Suddenly, you are your own manager and this can be an occasion for panic. Time management is of the essence here and techniques to help with this are very useful—disciplines for managing time and effort by defining key objectives and then translating them into tasks.

The next difficulty is isolation. Personally, my best work has always been done in a small creative and committed team which builds on the total contribution of the group, so that one ends up having done it and saying *we* did this. Who contributed what is forgotten, and everyone owns the end result. Here the whole problem of social interaction is crucial, and it's not surprising that so many freelance consultants network among themselves, subcontract with each other, and generally huddle together for warmth.

Finally, the home can mitigate against sustained work. One has to switch off one's home and for some people this is very difficult to do. The reverse also applies too, though—one has to switch off one's work when home matters are uppermost, and the way the two things slide into each other can be a problem for other members of the family. It is also a part of time management. One can suffer from a sort of creeping disease whereby gradually the week comes to consist of seven Mondays and no Sundays.
(*Peter Templer*)

Finally, there was another gloomier respondent who felt that the element most characteristic of our culture was personal competition, and that here homeworking was completely inappropriate.

People who are attracted to this kind of work are psychologically of a type who don't mind contracting out and are happy to be solitary. But males, more generally, have been educated to socialise, to engage in human politics, to read faces and to do all these things in order to climb up the ladder in a highly competitive world by trampling on other people. The emphasis is on the political, on dealing, fighting, one-up-manship, whatever you like but it all means interaction and is therefore against the trend towards homeworking. Committees are in a sense a mass post-war invention but now form a way of life and a very good reflection of this whole problem. They are male inventions. Women don't like to play at them, except over single and specific issues. They would rather steer than politicise—the majority therefore opt out of the in-house competition. The computer business is like this too, which is why women working at home on computer based business work so well, but permanent homeworking would not necessarily succeed more generally with men or with non-computer related business.
(*Rex Malik, Contributing Editor Intermedia*)

It is a valid comment, but as we shall see later, there are signs that society is changing, and so is technology—both combining to push future events in a more positive direction. It is certainly a fact that in its most successful form, telecommuting has so far been the province of women and/or computer workers. Designing micro-processor circuitry is a somewhat introspective occupation—one goes off into a mountain-top and comes back with the tablets of silicon. Programmers are primarily task-oriented —absorbed in their work and happy to give it full attention without supervision. But more and more of business in general is becoming computer-related just at the same time as it is going to have to exhibit a more human face. Tomorrow's workforce, it will be shown, is going to require both. Suddenly, everyone is going to be far better emotionally and socially attuned to the idea of the best elements of telecommuting than they are now, once high-tech and high-touch are paramount.

As a foretaste, before the City of London's Big Bang, the floor of the Stock Exchange was a steaming cauldron of personal interactivity. With the changes of structure and operation that took place in October 1986, the market became internationalised, working as intermediary between the time-frames of Tokyo and New York. The cosy direct interchange was overtaken by an electronic function, which after a few transient hiccups became such a thundering success that even the most old-fashioned of dealers left the floor to update their practices in front of screens. So much so, indeed, that six months later, the Lloyd's insurance market decided to emulate the Stock Exchange and other financial markets and go electronic also. Thus some of the most traditionalist of institutions in our society welcomed on board the electronic future, simply because it was necessary to do so to survive and flourish. One may be sure that so will others recognise the thrust of market forces in this way.

There are necessary techniques for remote working, however, as has been mentioned. The wife of one of the survey's expert commentators is a space physicist, and does a great deal of work at home. She frequently corresponds through JANET, the university academic network, with a particular colleague in Cambridge and makes sure she includes chatty comments when interacting. Similarly, the social graces have been found to be important as between the remote consultant and his remote secretary —'joke of the day' is a crucial part of the high-tech transmission, plus details of all the marvellous sales prospects in the offing. In fact, given care and commitment, communication at a distance can be even better than what sometimes passes for communication in our civilised state. Urban Man cannot communicate properly with everyone, maybe with anyone. Working from home in the country, however,

> ...you have to relate to people and live together with them as neighbours, whether you like them or not. In fact you may detest them, but in order to get by and live in hope you have to cut the corners off each other. If you don't meet and do things with other people you stereotype them, and the imagination hardens this stereotype into iron, so making human contact impossible. Such isolation we may consider as effective defence but it is personally crippling. Ultimately you can't rely on technical devices that fictionalise people—even now large numbers of people are psychologically crippled by the substituting of informing devices like the newspaper and the computer for human communication.
> (*Professor Denis Pym, London Business School*)

Neighbourhood relationships can become enriched, but communicating with other homeworkers requires unfamiliar skills—two facts which we will return to in due course. Communication between telecommuters and their managers can also be difficult, but not as difficult as either might think. The British management attitude to the subject tends to echo the remark made by former French President, Georges Pompidou: 'There are three ways to ruin yourself: gambling, women and technology. Gambling is the fastest, women are the most pleasurable, technology is the most certain.'

## TELECOMMUTING AND MANAGEMENT

However, it is important that British managers should come to terms with telecommuting, because for them to do so soon is essential for its success, and its success will be vastly beneficial to them in the long run.

> In general the view is that there are three fields of interest about homeworking—(a) what is the attitude, commitment and support that the organisation provides? (b) what is the preference and nature of the activity of the individual? (c) what is the technical capability to provide it? Here (b) and (c) are more or less OK, and it is (a) that is the key issue—the willingness of organisations to experiment in organisational development with an open mind and a full commitment.
> (*Dr Jim Cowie, Director for Strategic Issues, British Telecom*)

For a transitory period, a great deal of exploration will be needed, and both organisations and individuals must make experiments. Each new way of using the home as a workplace will create new exposures and require new methods of management approach; but alas, most companies are prepared to finance R and D on products but not on concepts—and this is what is really required here. For example, in the City of London, people claim they have not enough time to get involved in this; they are too busy dealing with the day-to-day. In their competitive world this is a very understandable attitude. However, they are like athletes, whose techniques get stale if they are in a continuous racing mode and have no time to visit the gym to train. They need to experiment with new ideas to try to see if they can improve their future performance. This is all to do with organisational adaptability; what is required is a greater and more widespread use of 'imagineering'.

Thus in government, the principle of moving work is already much on the technological agenda because of the historical pressure for dispersal from London, not necessarily in the form of homeworking but in the form of remote communications between outlying offices and the centre. There is currently a fashionable counter-argument in favour of maintaining the London presence of the Civil Service at its existing levels, but this seems unlikely to prevail in the long run. Homeworking is not particularly easy for civil servants, as so much of their work consists of interfacing with the general public. However, there are functions that they could and now increasingly do fulfil remotely, as we have seen, and this concentrates the official mind.

In many organisations the practice is growing of occasionally permitting senior employees to work from home via a computer terminal, when they are recuperating from an illness or otherwise disinclined to travel for personal reasons. A senior employee is also sometimes allowed to take a terminal home to work on a report for several days where few interruptions and maximum concentration are demanded. Leading from this, some managers have installed home terminals which allow them full access to information and the facility to act upon it when they are unable to be present in the office.

> The role of the office is changing, and today's question is which functions are best undertaken in which location. The office is a place for interaction, the home for reflective work or a base for the peripatetic. There is therefore a spectrum of home-possible tasks.
> (*David Firnberg, Managing Director, Eosys*)

> But there is a generally negative attitude in traditional organisations about the control of freelancers. Most of the cost control of subsidiaries or divisions or departments is done through head-count. Freelancers are frowned upon, as there is an assumption that one is getting round corporate controls. The question is whether to do it formally, or let it happen by benign neglect.
> (*Ninian Eadie, Director, ICL*)

Talking here is an expert, the ICL director in charge of CPS, their main homeworking unit. He recognises that this whole new mode of working will need unusual co-operation between and within organisations, which may well be resisted from the traditionalist management point of view. But as far as he is concerned, ICL has seen the future and it works—given certain provisos.

> Homeworking is suitable for fulfilling a task that is the whole of something that takes no more than six months for an individual to do, where it is a part of something that can be very well defined and measured, or where reputation demands that it is done as well as is conceivably possible.
> (*Ninian Eadie*)

As a computer manufacturer ICL has a highly appropriate reason for having got into this whole telecommuting business—to retain the rare skills of women it has trained but who then leave to have families. So also has F International, which founded an entire organisation on this concept;

in addition there is the Department of Trade and Industry scheme where disabled people are able to be retained or retrained to provide valuable skills from home. Rank Xerox, the other organisation examined in detail in the following chapters, has used the technique to ease its people out rather than welcoming them in. All different management problems, all different management solutions. We shall see in the future a mass of such experiments, and a thousand flowers will grow according to each organisation's characteristics. And as time goes on more and more of this will involve every job being broken down into those aspects which are best conducted either at home or at the common place of work.

## THE EXPERTS—THREE SCHOOLS OF THOUGHT

Writers on the subject of telecommuting tend to be one of three types, the enthusiastic, the pragmatic and the pessimistic. Leader of the enthusiastic school of thought is American futurist Alvin Toffler, who in *Future Shock,* and even more in *The Third Wave,* gives us a picture of a society where what he terms 'the electronic cottage' increasingly becomes the place of work, to the great benefit of a population whose concern for and involvement in their immediate neighbourhood is thus magnified. Another who paints a positive picture is a British writer, James Robertson, in *The Sane Alternative* and especially in *Future Work.*

Robertson extends Toffler's thesis that the mode of work dictated by the Industrial Revolution may well turn out to have been an aberration, a mere 200-year blip on the curve of time. We used traditionally to work at home, in family units or sometimes in groups of families, until the Industrial Revolution overtook these home crafts and cottage-based industries with production methods that required massive capital equipment and the concentration of the labour force in one place. Pre-industrial and post-industrial societies have more in common with each other than with this intermediate period, goes the argument, as we see now that information technology has removed many of the reasons for centralised operations.

Charles Handy (*The Future of Work*) has also established the need to rethink work along these lines, pointing out that if groups or individuals do not need always to be in the same place, they do not need to be in any particular place at all. The success of the dispersed organisation spells the slow death of the gathered organisation—'the works' or 'the office'—he claims, with the process being given a gradual but inexorable impetus by the move towards consultancy, self-employment and the new individuality of the professional. The enthusiasts' picture is strongly borne out by market research and this is examined in some detail in Chapter 9. It is also borne out by Institute of Manpower Studies forecasts of an expansion of employment, especially self-employment, in non-professional business services, while trade unions also predict a growing casualisation of employment with an increasingly large periphery of flexible workers without security of tenure and a shrinking core of full-time, on-site workers. However, the upshot is that even so, full recognition of the advantages of telecommuting may not be generally current until the next century, by when both the technological infrastructure and the social change needed to ensure its acceptance will be in position.

Until then the pragmatic view will pertain, as exemplified by Richmond Postgate (*Home—A Place for Work?*), and by Eliott Stern and Richard Holti (*Distance Working in Urban and Rural Settings*), who were researching in the context of the FAST (Forecasting and Assessment in Science and Technology) programme of the EEC. They define several types of distance working—homework; shared facilities in a neighbourhood work centre; satellite branch offices; remote working enterprises where the customers are located at a distance; distributed business systems where a number of separate units involved in different stages of production are linked electronically; and mobile work. These working modes have in common the fact of communications technology. They also have in common the fact that they can be seen as playing some positive social or economic role in the new 'wired society'. The objectives are varied—the liberation of women with young children through remote work; the economic development of disadvantaged regions such as the Highlands and Islands of Scotland, and of depressed inner city areas; the integration of home and working life for senior male executives; the ability of disabled people to fulfil a valid working function. Using these techniques and delivering these results will ensure a future for telecommuting, they suggest.

Pragmatists Stern and Holti are quite prepared to accept that the whole homeworking concept carries with it the dangers of exploitation. However, the pessimistic school of thought dwells particularly on this aspect, looking back to the experience of the manipulated outworker, rather than forward to the future benefit of the released and enabled one, as perceived by the enthusiasts. For them the tyranny of working wholly at home is more likely to be destructive than the tyranny of working wholly away from home.

The Low Pay Unit and the European Foundation for the Improvement of Living and Working Conditions are the principal protagonists of this view, with authorities such as Ursula Huws and Simon Crine writing under the banner of the former. They point out that homeworkers, like all part-timers and women in general, can find themselves vulnerable to low pay, poor working conditions and unemployment as they try to reconcile their growing financial demands with their continuing domestic responsibilities. Huws and her allies admit that homeworking is unlikely to pose problems for top-level professionals with rare skills who can be sure of a continued supply of well-paid work. However, they point to the propensity of employers to exploit homeworkers in low-status working sectors just because they have few employment alternatives open to them. These are the ones likely to be hardest hit by interruptions in the supply of work, while opportunities for their training and promotion are notoriously inferior, and collective organisation to protect them is also difficult.

In *The New Homeworkers*, Ursula Huws updated a report commissioned by the Equal Opportunities Commission and carried out in 1982, involving 78 homeworkers concerned with the use of new technology—mainly computer professionals. This stressed the above points, and also revealed that average pay levels were significantly lower than equivalent on-site rates; that permanent workers' benefits were also more extensive in comparison to those accorded the self-employed; and that isolation was found to be a major problem in most cases—many citing this as the most important reason for preferring on-site work should circumstances permit it.

On the other hand, 35% of the sample preferred homeworking to on-site working and a further 41% felt that they could not give a categorical preference either way, considering the flexibility involved and the alternative of being tied with young children. Given that the sample was self-selected via a press release inviting them to participate (and the possible bias towards dissatisfaction as a consequence) this seems a more positive result than might have been expected. The report makes some valid recommendations for the consideration of national and local governments, though the suggestions for a code of practice in the employment of homeworkers are determinedly restrictive towards employers. Her feeling for the subject is a feminist one, according to John Chris Jones in *Futures* Magazine, in that men favour homeworking for women because to men the home is a centre for leisure where they are serviced by women; whereas for women the home is a place of never-ending work. As he has it, she sees telecommuting as the return to a life sentence from which women had begun to escape through the availability of work outside the home.

This argument may or may not find favour with many potential telecommuters. A more likely brake on the homeworking phenomenon is the development of other alternatives for the retention of the skills of child-minding mothers. With options such as statutory maternity leave before and after childbirth, plus the fact that employers keep their jobs open and that there is some increase in the provision of corporate nurseries and crêches, many of the more ambitious women tend to go back to original full-time work. National Westminster Bank go further, allowing a five-year break in mothers' careers during which they can bring their children up and return to where they left off. They are kept in touch in the interim with monthly information packs, they come back to work for a minimum of two weeks every year, and they attend an annual seminar and other get-togethers. Oxfordshire County Council also has career-break provisions, with a working parents' network, which is being copied by other local authorities. Thus homeworking is just part of the drive towards flexibility—an important part, but by no means the only one.

> Homeworking is only one aspect of the general decentralisation of work that's going on. People are working fewer hours, more flexible hours, more jobs per person, a shorter working life—all these are variants on a theme. And F International encapsulates some of these and demonstrates in a way that no theory and no business school can do, that it works economically—because in each stage of our growth, we've done it.
> (*Steve Shirley, F International*)

Like Ninian Eadie of CPS/ICL, Steve Shirley of F International is a doughty and persuasive protagonist in the cause of telecommuting. We will be hearing much more from both of them and their colleagues in the chapters that follow.

## SOME STATISTICAL MEAT

In a key feature of the February 1987 *Employment Gazette*, 'Homeworking in Britain', Catherine Hakim, Social Science Branch, Department of Employment, gives statistical teeth to the debate. The report updates the findings of a specially designed national survey of home-based workers carried out in the autumn of 1981, and among its major disclosures:

- There is a small but steady growth in part-time jobs generally—from 4.18 million in 1981 to 4.48 million in 1985 (19.7% to 21.7% of all employees).

- There has been a much stronger growth in self-employment, mostly single-person businesses. From 1981 to 1984 the self-employed grew by 440,000 to 2.6 million (9.2% to 11.2% of total employment).

- There was an even more dramatic increase in temporary work, from 620,000 to 1.3 million jobs between 1981 and 1985.

• Some of these three groups overlap in part, and all can contain home-based workers as well. By extension, therefore, there has been a steady decline in the 'permanent' workforce from 70% to 66% of all in employment between 1981 and 1985, with 64% forecast for spring 1987. The aggregate 1985 figure for 'temporary' workers comprised just over 8 million people, roughly 3 million men and 5 million women out of a total workforce of 26.6 million.

• Out of this, the 1981 estimate of homeworkers in England and Wales was 1.7 million or 7% of the labour force. This figure was expected to have increased to 10% by 1985.

• Other than those living at work, people with live-in jobs, in construction and road haulage, childminders and family workers—230,000 were working at home (70% women) and 400,000 were working from home as a base (70% men). This 2½% of the workforce constitutes the hard core of the homeworking phenomenon.

Homeworkers do not differ much from the labour force as a whole as regards health, income or unemployment record. They are more likely to be married and have dependent children at home, and much more likely to be owner-occupiers with a mortgage. They are far better educated and qualified—one third of homeworkers have degree-level qualifications compared to one in seven in the whole working population. Homeworking jobs are very diverse, but those in manufacturing are in the minority. 160,000 of them are in selling. Two-thirds of the men work full-time, and two-thirds of the women work less than 16 hours a week and therefore have particularly low earnings. Three-quarters of all homeworkers were satisfied with their pay, however, and about 10% of them have been doing this kind of job for over 20 years. Many of them are confused as to whether they are of employed or self-employed status.

The 1981 survey shows that the worst fears of the pessimists about telecommuting—that it is generally done by women with small children, unskilled, low paid, exploited and suffering from health problems—are broadly groundless. One should not be totally complacent about the dangers of exploitation, but the strongest inference to be drawn is that the pessimistic scenario is over-concerned, the enthusiastic scenario is on track but will not burst through for some years, and that the pragmatic—which recognises telecommuting as a growingly important and generally most advantageous mode of work—is just about in balance for the time being.

Statistics can incorporate a spurious sense of certainty into an analysis of future prospects, because so often a mere extrapolation of today's curve is a poor guide to the shape of tomorrow's unknown territory. It is perhaps better to depend on the weight of informed qualitative opinion than on the quantitative evidence of the past—hence the reliance here on a panel of the expert and the experienced. None the less there are plenty of figures that should encourage trendwatchers who look to telecommuting to provide an interest in the 1990s and beyond.

- In *Overcoming the Career Break—A Positive Approach*, Carole Truman mentions that in 1974 the British Telecom long-range intelligence unit identified 24 occupational groups comprising some 13.5 million workers which could contain potentially home-based jobs.
- In *The Remaking of Work*, Clutterbuck and Hill cite that 40.8% of a survey said that they would prefer to work from home for all or part of the week if they could do so, though admittedly only 16.8% said that they thought it was possible that more people would work from home in the next decade.
- According to 1986 Department of Employment figures, the numbers of women starting up on their own rose 42% in three years and a quarter of all small businesses are now run by women, who are particularly attracted to the idea of telecommuting.
- If the information sector is defined to include the whole of banking and insurance, central and local government and education and training, 40–45% of the UK workforce is involved in processing information. 97% of households have access to a television set and 76% to a telephone; 28% have a VCR; 18% have a home computer; 9% have a teletext set.
- 'The Institute of Employment Research at Warwick University estimates that by 1990 there will be over 24 million people in paid work and only 14 million in full-time jobs. Similarly Max Geldens, head of McKinsey in the Netherlands, estimated that by the year 2000 70% of all jobs in the OECD will be "cerebral" with 50% of the workforce moving outside the organisation—a total reversal of the position 100 years ago. The movement will be given added impetus by IT, by which means jobs will be able to be organised remotely.'
(*Professor Charles Handy, Visiting Professor, The London Business School*)

The rest of the book is now devoted to exploring the telecommuting phenomenon in detail through the words of its practitioners, authorities and commentators, and to projecting its future development through the rest of this century and into the next. Is there anybody else out there? Answer–yes.

## BIBLIOGRAPHY AND REFERENCES

Anon., 'Men and matters', *Financial Times*, 12 May 1987

Anon., 'Meetings: miles apart' *The Administrator*, March 1987

British Institute of Management, *New Technology Homeworkers*, Information Notes and Topics, Vol. 2, No. 8, May 1987

Brown, Malcom, 'Putting the office on the road', *Sunday Times*, 1 March 1987

Clutterbuck, David and Hill, Roy, *The Remaking of Work*, Grant MacIntyre, 1981

Crine, Simon *Forward to the Hidden Army*, Low Pay Unit Pamphlet no. 11, 1979

Deakin, Rose, *Women and Computing: The Golden Opportunity*, Macmillan, 1984

Hakim, Catherine, *Employers' Use of Outwork*, Dept of Employment Research Paper no. 44, 1985

Hakim, Catherine, 'Homeworking in Britain: key findings from the National Survey of Home-based Workers', *Employment Gazette*, February 1987

Handy, Charles, *The Future of Work*, Basil Blackwell, 1984

Huws, Ursula, *The New Homeworkers*, Low Pay Unit Pamphlet no. 28, 1984

Huws, Ursula, *The Potential for Decentralised Electronic Working in the Banking, Insurance and Software Industries*, Empirica UK, 1986

Jones, John Chris, 'Letter to the author: a review of Alvin Toffler's *Previews and Premises*', *Futures Magazine*, April 1987

Kington, Miles, 'Life in the fast lane—or how to counter the charge of parking with intent', *The Independent*, 4 April 1987

Lucas, Martin, Wilson, Kim and Hart, Emma, *How to Survive the 9 to 5*, Methuen, 1986

MacRae, Norman, 'The future of independent businesses', *The Economist*, 22 January 1972

Martin, James, *The Wired Society*, Prentice-Hall, 1978

Moran, Rosalyn and Tansey, Jean, *Telework: Women and Environments*, Irish Foundation for Human Development, 1986

Organisation of Work Panel of the BIM Economic and Social Affairs Committee, *Managing New Patterns of Work*, British Institute of Management, 1985

Postgate, Richmond, *Home—A Place for Work?*, Gulbenkian Foundation, 1984

Road, Alan, 'Work can damage your health', *The Observer*, 15 March 1987

Road, Alan, 'Sweatshops of the 1980s', *The Observer*, 24 May 1987

Robertson, James, *The Sane Alternative: A Choice of Futures*, revised edn, 1983

Robertson, James, *Future Work*, Gower, 1985

Shirley, Steve, 'The distributed office', Presentation to the Royal Society of Arts, 16 February 1987

Stern, Eliott and Holti, Richard, *Distance Working in Urban and Rural Settings* Tavistock Institute of Human Relations, 1986

Toffler, Alvin, *Future Shock*, The Bodley Head, 1970

Toffler, Alvin, *The Third Wave*, Collins, 1980

Truman, Carole, *Overcoming the Career Break: a Positive Approach*, Manpower Services Commission, 1986

# 2
# The Practitioners (1)—DTI and RX

So then, homeworking is alive and well and living in the UK. As we shall see, it is emerging elsewhere in the world as well, but one thing differentiates Britain from anywhere else. It is only here that we can find examples of the successful management of the homeworking phenomenon on anything but a small scale.

There have been, in fact, four major British initiatives which have now passed the experimental stage, and established themselves as models upon which a common foundation for the future development of this working mode can be built. They are, respectively, a government-backed scheme that transforms the disabled into the enabled; the evolutionary development of a company's intrapreneurs into freelance entrepreneurs; the budding-off of a homeworking group from the main stem of a traditionally structured organisation; and finally, the creation and growth of an independent remote working software house from scratch.

## THE DTI REMOTE WORK UNITS PROJECT

The Remote Work Units Project was set up in 1982—'Information Technology Year'—as part of a Department of Trade and Industry initiative to apply information technology to a wide range of needs including the requirements of disabled people. The pilot project involved six of them employed from home, who were supplied with a micro-computer to help each in their particular job. This met with such success that the Department extended their number tenfold, so that during the following two years another 58 were kitted out in a similar way with support from a number of IT consultancies. An experimental project such as this demanded very broad parameters so that as wide a range of employers as possible could be involved, as well as a variety of jobs and disabilities. Thus the general criteria were that,

- the employee's mobility was already affected in some way; and
- the job involved otherwise normal conditions of service, required no less than 20 hours a week, was computer-based, had long-term prospects, and generated pay in line with similar work.

The lessons of the project's first experimental phase of some 60 units were formally evaluated and then applied in a second-phase project, which ran from 1984 to 1986 and comprised a further 40 units managed by IT World Ltd. Again, the DTI provided funding for equipment and consultancy, but this time with matching support from the EEC's European Social Fund. The aim of this second phase was to develop guidelines for a permanent scheme whereby hundreds, and even thousands, of disabled people could eventually be helped to find fulfilling employment from home. This involved the Manpower Services Commission whose Disablement Resettlement Service was active at both head office and field staff levels providing help with recruitment, training, special aids and general support. As from January 1987 the MSC finally took over responsibility for the whole concept which is now operated by its Disablement Advisory Service on a nation-wide basis.

Table 1 RWU Project: number of units per size of company

| | SMALL (up to 25) employees | MEDIUM (up to 250) employees | LARGE (over 250) employees | TOTAL UNITS |
|---|---|---|---|---|
| Phase 1 | 32 | 17 | 6 | (55) |
| Phase 2 | 13 | 8 | 19 | (40) |

Table 2 RWU Project: number of units per type of employer

| | INDUSTRY light | INDUSTRY heavy | Retail | SERVICE Public sector | SERVICE Professional | SERVICE Other | VOLUNTARY ORGANISATIONS | TOTAL UNITS |
|---|---|---|---|---|---|---|---|---|
| Phase 1 | 5 | 2 | 10 | 2 | 7 | 19 | 10 | (55) |
| Phase 2 | 9 | 1 | 17 | 9 | 3 | 1 | 0 | (40) |

(Source: DTI and IT World Ltd)

Originally, as Tables 1 and 2 indicate, considerably more units were set up in small companies. They found the scheme relatively more attractive, free equipment on a first trial being a greater incentive than to the larger company, where in any event procedures tend to be more complex and regarded as unsuitable for remote work. However, in the second phase, more large companies were involved, it being successfully emphasised that they had already established a greater penetration of IT equipment with which suitable jobs could be created in an extension of technological usage. Hardly surprisingly, given the computer basis of these jobs, service and voluntary organisations were found to be more suitable than industrial ones.

Employees included some who had already been employed and had then become disabled, but where the employer was keen to retain their skills and experience. In such instances some retraining was frequently necessary—say, to enable the employee to do the same or an allied job on a personal computer, connected via a telephone to the company's mainframe computer on site. In other instances, when the employee was already experienced in IT, the transition did not need to be quite so elaborate. But in either case the technique also enabled employers to recruit new people who would otherwise have found it impossible to work for them.

A total of 32 different types of disability were involved in the two phases, including amputees, cerebral palsy, epilepsy, multiple sclerosis, muscular dystrophy, osteomyelitis, poliomyelitis, rheumatoid arthritis, Parkinson's disease, spina bifida, spinal injury (paraplegia and tetraplegia) and sensory disablement (sight, speech and hearing).

The success of the experiment will give encouragement to a host of people in similar situations. It is an integral part of the DTI's new initiative, 'The Concerned Technology', launched in 1986 by Geoffrey Pattie MP, Minister of State for Industry and Information Technology, to create an awareness of IT applications among people with special requirements. The emphasis has been to encourage handicapped and disabled people to ask 'what do I need?' rather than simply 'what is available?'

As well as covering jobs like word-processing and programming that one would normally associate with computers, these participants have taken on a wide range of tasks—copy-typing, typesetting, tachograph analysis, financial management, book-keeping, accountancy, invoicing, credit control, payroll administration, estimating, instrumentation engineering, viewdata editing and presenting statistics as charts and graphs. As John McCann of the DTI's Concerned Technology Section put it:

> There are all kinds of success stories. A school teacher who broke his back in a swimming-pool accident and now produces creative educational software. A programmer working for a County Council who uses electronic mail to overcome problems of poor speech. But what we find really exciting is that this way the handicapped can even have first bite of the cherry nowadays.

> We are beginning to be able to demonstrate that it can be *more* advantageous to take on a disabled employee rather than less so.

This is no idle boast, as the following case studies will show.

Gerry P. worked as a mechanical engineering draughtsman for a large fabrication company in the North-East. In his late thirties, Gerry had been with the company for ten years but his multiple sclerosis was becoming increasingly debilitating. He wanted to join the project and work from home, but because the necessary *ad hoc* discussions with the on-site design team were going to be difficult to co-ordinate, his employers decided to retrain Gerry to do an engineering programming job. Gerry was new to computing, so needed a high level of support both from the company itself and from ITEC, the MSC's national network of IT training establishments. Determination and commitment on the part of both employer and employee, plus the MSC's continuing involvement in training and general support, have been key factors in the successful development of this unit.

Beverly A. obtained a BA in Development Studies at the University of East Anglia, and then spent several months looking for work near his home. He is a thalidomide victim and joined the British Computer Society as one of the six employees on the pilot scheme of the Remote Work Unit Project. He now works as an examinations assistant from the conservatory of his home in Suffolk which is fitted up with a micro-computer and a printer. He has evolved a system for storing and producing tabular information about various exams and then word-processing the necessary paperwork, as a result of which the running of the exams has been formally transferred to his address. He spends his working time in contact with BCS headquarters and liaising with course tutors and examiners, arranging examinations. Beverly comments:

> The most enjoyable facet of the job is my contact with the examiners and tutors, all of whom are polite, co-operative and welcome voices on my phone. I don't know how many of them know I am disabled. It is satisfying that it makes no difference.
> (*Computer Newsletter*, March 1987)

The evaluation of the original 60 experimental units was undertaken by the DTI and prepared with support from info-tech consultancy, IT World Ltd. In the published evaluation study for the first phase (*Remote Work Units Project for Disabled People*) they describe how employers raised a number of questions when they were considering whether or not to become involved, such as:

- How do I get work to the employee?
- How do I supervise him/her?

- How can I ensure confidentiality?
- What other remote jobs have been successful in the project?
- How do I know a disabled person can cope with the job?
- What about training—cost? provided by? where?
- Can I be sure the technology will fit into my plans?

That these were by and large satisfactorily answered is borne out by the fact that of the 100 employees who originally took part, about 75 are still operating—mostly on a one-to-one basis with a single employer. A few of them, however, were set up as self-employed, which on occasions failed to gell. With hindsight, IT World feel that if some of the people had instead been put into formal employment, they would have stayed the course. There were a small number of redundancies and sadly, others had to give up even this mode of work because of their deteriorating health.

It must be remembered here that the experiment comprised a cross-section of jobs, ranging from very simple work like data input to the complexities of systems analysis. Thus there were some low-skilled individuals who would have been incapable of managing themselves without considerable support anyway, and who furthermore when they failed to get it, would not necessarily see their own working problems as due to their employer's inadequacies. Remote management does demand a higher than average degree of empathy and of effectiveness, but as Breda Robertson, IT World's project co-ordinator, underlines:

> This is the largest database of mixed homeworkers—as regards types of job, types of disability and types of employer—in the whole country. Given that, it is most encouraging that so many of the original units are still operating. It just goes to show what can be done when there is commitment and an understanding of what this kind of management really entails.

Remote working in whatever shape or form is not a well-tried concept—the 1981 Labour Force Survey estimated that only 114,000 people were undertaking work at home for a single employer in England and Wales. At present most people expect and do a job at a recognised place of employment rather than from their own homes. The idea of disabled people working from home, however, is a familiar one but these jobs have generally tended to be in the craft industries: basket-weaving and knitting being just two commonplace examples. In these cases payment is closely tied to output and the work has been neither highly regarded nor highly paid. Now, the advent of micro-technology is beginning to change all this. New and worthwhile jobs which can be done at home are being created as a direct consequence of the development of IT, and disabled people, especially those with mobility problems, are benefiting in particular.

The summary and conclusions of the IT World Evaluation Study put the points at issue into perspective by stating plainly both the upside and the downside potential of the genre:

## Disabled people

*Opportunities*

- Disabled people feel better if they work
- Disabled people are often highly qualified
- Disabled people have job expectations and career aspirations similar to those of other workers
- New home-based job opportunities for disabled people are being created by information technology
- Disabled employees can keep their jobs by converting from an on-site situation to a home-based one
- Disabled people with many different levels of skill and degrees of disability can be trained to work with computer equipment as effectively as able-bodied people

*Issues*

- The potential of disabled people with computer equipment is not always fully exploited by employers
- The training needs of home-based disabled people are not adequately provided for
- Remote management and isolation create problems for them
- Adequate financial rewards need to be assured them

## Employers

*Opportunities*

- Information technology holds many attractions for employers
- Costs associated with remote working are comparable to on-site costs, and may be even lower
- Productivity/output levels of remote disabled employees are good

- The potential for employers to employ remote disabled workers has not been previously exploited
- Employers are willing to embark upon remote employment, given funding incentives

*Issues*

- Remote management is not easy and expertise in this area needs to be developed
- Job and company induction training provisions are generally inadequate
- Employer support is crucial in achieving successful remote working
- Home-based remote working involving the use of IT is unlikely to be widespread in the short-term.

(*Source*: DTI and IT World Ltd)

In this context, IT World, proceeding from its experience of the original DTI and EEC projects, is now developing an innovative programme with American Express, the London Electricity Board and Plessey Major Systems for groups of IT-based remote workers and their on-site line managers. The programme is focused on training a small number of employees—both those who currently work on computer terminals at home and their on-site line managers. Special attention is being given to such skills as organising their time, their workloads and their home environment, and to the techniques of integration and motivation. As a result of these studies, two major questions have been highlighted.

> ...the first—what are the very specific skills needed by the employee and by the manager in this kind of operation? The second—how to train both of them, separately and together, in the acquisition of these skills to the required standard, by traditional and also by remote learning methods? In a series of further experiments we are cracking these two problems.
> (*Pamela Grice, Principal Consultant, IT World*)

Remote workers, it is now beginning to be appreciated, require a higher than usual ability to organise their time and resources effectively, since they lack the normal benefit of instant direction and support. The pilot programme is sponsored, once again, by the Manpower Services Commission, and its lessons and findings will undoubtedly be valuable in training other remote employees and their line managers.

> In homeworking, communication and management are major issues. The home-based worker rarely gets a chance to look at the company noticeboard and can soon get out of touch. We are now looking at what changes in

working operations need to be made to enhance the whole process. It is true to say that there is really no difference in the kind of management needed for this sort of operation, it is simply a question of better management. Training is basically the same, but it also has to be better. Working in a distributed manner highlights all inadequacies with painful clarity.
(*Frits Janssen, Managing Director, IT World*)

## RANK XEROX LIMITED

In July 1982 the *Financial Times* management page carried a two-part series of articles headed 'Why Rank Xerox is sending executives home'. They featured Roger Walker, a former personnel manager at Rank Xerox who had resigned his job the previous October to go solo and to form his own home-based company, which was supported in its early stages by selling part of its output to Walker's erstwhile boss.

Walker was the first of 55 employees with whom the company negotiated this imaginative and indeed revolutionary experiment. The main rationale behind it was that if sufficient people would volunteer to set up their own limited companies and yet continue to work for the company on a tightly controlled contract basis, Rank Xerox would be able to enjoy substantial savings on non-salary-related costs. Walker was Personnel and General Services Facilities Manager for the company, but had always wished, since leaving university, to establish his own business. Having carved out a reasonable career within Rank Xerox (who themselves tend to support the more entrepreneurial type of manager) he declared his intention to leave and try his luck in the open marketplace. Some three weeks before his departure, Rank Xerox offered him a network contract which involved him working from home with a micro-computer link into their headquarters in London, thus ensuring that his skills and experience were not totally lost to the company. Significant savings also accrued to the company in terms of facilities costs. As he remarked five years later in 1987:

> It wasn't meant to be any big deal, but it just mushroomed in terms of media interest. What excited people was a combination of three top stories all in one—new technology, small businesses and the change in work patterns.

When he was originally interviewed by Arnold Kransdorff for the *FT* article in 1982, he had left a £16,400 a year job with an attractive range of perks. Nine months later at the time of the interview, he had only an unaudited set of his own company's accounts, but estimated that his net income that far was probably similar to before—with no perks to brighten it up, however. At the same time, though, he felt there was a great deal more potential in it, despite the chill winds of risk that he would have to endure in the meantime.

By 1987 he has a business that has burgeoned from three—himself, his wife and secretary—to 65 people staffing a consultancy that specialises in recruitment and selection, career counselling, skill and aptitude testing, training courses, and the supply of temporary workers on a permanent basis. He is turning over at the rate of £3/4 million per annum and has 28 clients, all of whom are large UK-based multinationals. He is now in the process of franchising his business geographically on the same networking principle, and is receiving an encouraging number of replies to the advertisements that feature this opportunity.

The nuts and bolts of the Rank Xerox networking contract are that each networker forms his or her limited company, which in turn negotiates with Rank Xerox a contract of between one and three years' duration, for up to half the expected turnover of the networker's company. This generally comes to slightly less than the gross annual salary at departure. On top of this the company helps the individual to furnish his new office, and provides modern furniture and equipment including a micro-computer at advantageous prices. He is also given extensive counselling particularly on administrative and tax affairs.

Networkers are a varied breed, but most spend something like half their time with Xerox and the other half with a host of other clients. The least involved networker gets about 30 man-days work per annum from the company and the most, the equivalent time of 4 or 5 of his employees' output over a year. Rates vary from £80 to £600 a day, but on average they expect to make overall one third more than their previous salary in pure money terms by working for themselves. For its part, Rank Xerox has estimated that by using networkers it saves around £17,000 per head per annum in fixed costs, compared to the £1300 it costs to set up each one.

The Rank Xerox experiment has been chronicled in considerable depth by three senior managers who were concerned with the creation, development and management of the scheme. They are Phillip Judkins, David West and John Drew, the authors of *Networking in Organisations*. Judkins was Roger Walker's original boss, who guided the whole concept to fruition, and the book explores its progress in generous detail—warts and all. It explains that the initial motivation for the experiment arose out of an examination of direct and indirect employment costs. Taking into account items such as perks, pensions, canteen and sports facilities, office rental and rates, not to mention office furniture and equipment and secretarial support, Rank Xerox found to its horror that these could aggregate to another 2½ times payroll earnings for each executive in central London.

Most managers looking at the potential for cost savings might assume that salaries were the largest element of their departmental budget. In central London in 1982 however, they only amounted to 30% at Rank

Xerox's headquarters, the remaining 70% coming under three headings. First were facilities costs such as rent, rates, light, heat, security, maintenance, telecommunications etc., which mistakenly tend to be regarded as fixed by most of those who are responsible for them. Then there was internal support, divided more or less fifty-fifty between travel and data processing. Finally came the indirect costs of employment such as National Insurance, company pensions and benefit contributions of various kinds.

Judkins, West and Drew emphasise that at least as important as the scale of these costs is their nature. They are inflationary, out of the employer's control, sterile and non-motivating. Items like rent, rates and depreciation, maintenance, energy and security—all those costs involved in keeping an office building a fit place for heroes to work in—consistently rise faster than the Retail Price Index, as property-owners, local councils, utilities, and the like seek to gain a fatter return than the rising cost of living would warrant alone.

The facilities cost is also sterile—no value whatever can be added to a company's product from the 31% of the costs of a London-based office which relate to its facilities. Furthermore, they are beyond the control of the company; and finally, they provide no motivation for the employees. It is possible to demotivate people through an extremely poor environment, or maybe to motivate them slightly by an outstandingly good one. By and large, however, the environment and its costs are taken for granted by those who work in it.

Judkins *et al.* point out that Alvin Toffler perceived this very clearly, and correctly gauged its likely ultimate results in *The Third Wave*—that businesses would look for ways of farming out work in order to reduce and/or externalise these costs. Moving employees out into a home-based network is obviously not the only way of doing this. Relocation of offices and redesigning them are certainly two other ways, for, as long as the property market remains buoyant, the buildings in question will remain disposable. But for Rank Xerox there were two other features that influenced their decision. There was the tendency anyway for their most creative people to seek the ability to control their own work, rather than being controlled in smothering detail. Then, there was also the fact that the technology, in the shape of the micro-computer capable of transmitting data over telephone lines, was just at that moment becoming widely available at low cost.

The company therefore undertook its homeworking experiment as a serious attempt to investigate an alternative to traditional patterns of work. It was not a soft form of redundancy and all the individuals involved were still seen as valued members of the company. Networkers are not staff as the term is generally understood. Their companies act as consultancies in their specialist field and by all accounts the networkers themselves continue to show the same creativity and loyalty which they demonstrated when working inside the company full-time. As explained, however, they are encouraged and indeed trained to use the remainder of their time selling to other companies, or pursuing other interests as they so wish. *Networking in Organisations* has identified practical examples of the work of these networkers as including:

| DEPARTMENT | TASK |
|---|---|
| Marketing | Planning and running programmes for the launch of new products; identifying new markets; carrying out market research; analysing sales penetration, attrition, and compensation schemes. |
| Finance | Monthly analyses; specific cost-benefit studies; managing major capital programmes; analyses of competitive data; taxation and fiscal advice. |
| Personnel | Pensions; remuneration and compensation advice, development of training packages; personnel audit work. |
| Management services | Energy efficiency studies; operational research projects; safety and security advice; development of new computer systems. |
| Corporate affairs | Public relations; investor relations; public affairs; charities. |

(*Source*: Judkins, West and Drew, *Networking in Organisations,* 1985)

This is a substantial and wide-ranging list, and by no means exclusive as far as the future is concerned. But as the concerned manager or potential telecommuter will see in more detail later, there are jobs that either can or cannot be done from home, and there are also certain guidelines as to the characteristics of possible telecommuters. For example, counselling personnel cannot be undertaken on a remote basis, but Xerox have successfully networked the design of training courses, and recruitment at least up to the creation of a short list. Talking to Phillip Judkins in 1987, another interesting development that emerged was that RX were now also recruiting people from outside as networkers:

> Some jobs admittedly require a knowledge of the company culture and are therefore inappropriate for outside people. Opening up a new market would

not work on this basis, but for example negotiating the purchase of fleet cars works fine.

Judkins is quite prepared to admit that overall progress has been slow, however. In spite of the original plan to transmute about 150 key support staff fairly rapidly in this way, five years later they can only muster 61, of whom five are maternity networkers on full pay and will return to full-time employment once their period of initial childminding is over. However, the 61 in turn employ another 150 people, many of whom are operating on a networking basis themselves. The whole thing has indeed expanded in an organic sense, even if not in the shape or to the extent that was originally planned, but the figure of 150 remains as the top estimate for its extension in the near future.

The reason that development has been slower than anticipated is partly because many of the jobs concerned were, when it boiled down to it, inappropriate for homeworking; and partly because it was far more difficult than expected for the core managers to manage remote workers with whom they had not shared this experience, while themselves still staying totally locked into the central organisation and culture of the company. The distribution process was not on a large enough scale to demand changes in central management thinking. There was, for example, a sense of frustration among head office administrators who found that outworkers could not come to immediate meetings and so were left uninvited: the alternative of teleconferencing did not catch on. Once again—and this will be a recurring theme—it is clear that the homeworking mode does demand close management and highly empathetic people-skills for it to be successful.

> There is some kind of a mutation of the genetic code of an individual when, although he is still part of the company, he is working from home. Once people are out-workers they are different. Our main problem was that we trained the networkers to sell, but we didn't train the line managers inside the company either to relate to them or to buy. Compared to these new entrepreneurs our full-time boys were bereft of negotiating skills. The result was a score-line which read 'Lions 10, Christians zero', and we had to think again.
> (*Phillip Judkins*)

Given all that, however, it is remarkable that Rank Xerox have managed to conduct this experiment as successfully as they have done, and that the network, though small, is still flourishing. One major reason is that their networkers do possess a very high degree of independence. The company culture is aggressively entrepreneurial—one might rather say 'intrapreneurial' with employees virtually running their own semi-autonomous businesses and referring to colleagues as internal 'customers' and 'suppliers'. In Rochester, New York, they also have a corporate 'skunk-works' where other people's ideas are pulled to pieces and tested to destruction. Given this uncommonly free and independent background, it is perhaps not surprising that no other company has yet felt man enough to take the plunge and follow the Rank Xerox lead.

Even within RX, however, suitable candidates are rare. Roger Walker, the first networker, was an archetypal individualist and keen to set up his own business, anyway. But the next seven who were identified as having jobs which were potentially appropriate for this working method were not so enthusiastic—indeed, some were extremely reticent about it. All of them subsequently achieved success in their chosen fields, but the company realised that the scheme had to be contained within a completely voluntary mechanism, and their original plans for the more widespread distribution of work had to be curtailed.

It is now more the case for employees to come forward with their ideas of how to work individually from home, and for the company then to check them out, rather than the other way round. The individual first goes to his or her manager with a proposal which, if agreed at this level, is developed and put up to Judkins as a detailed proposition for his acceptance or rejection. About half the applications are turned down as providing no apparent benefit to the company, but even so Judkins still expects the network to grow slowly but surely in future.

Once accepted as a potential networker, the individual embarks on about four weeks of development and training activity, which can either be taken as a block, or spread over the final six months of full-time employment with the parent company. This consists of:

- Individual counselling on personal issues related to the start-up (mostly personal finance and taxation matters)
- The enhancement of specific skills
- The development of more general business skills, particularly in selling, small business management and micro-computing.

Meanwhile, the relevant core managers also require a specific training programme, covering three main areas over and above the new technological skills. First are contractual issues, particularly the definition of output and quality standards, and here the manager is trained to look at his own job in output terms and then translate that to the networkers under his control. Then come purchasing and negotiating skills, which are taught through role-playing and by formalising the brief-preparation and assessment of projects. Finally, the problems of motivating staff at a distance are helped by role-playing too, but also by training in closer and more positive business relationships.

However strong the continuing contact, though, in one very definite sense there has to be an arm's-length relationship between Xerox and its networkers, so that to the advantage of both they are accepted as owners of independent companies by the Inland Revenue and by the Department of Health and Social Security. They therefore have to register themselves as limited companies before they even join the network as such; the company contracts for work on a fee for a job completed, not pay for days worked; networking companies cannot commit Xerox funds; and they have to take out their own insurance against liability for damage to Xerox of up to £1.5 million—all of which in combination clinches their independent status.

But working at arm's length has its drawbacks. Having been lulled in the bosom of a large multinational, whatever the enthusiasm of the new networkers at the beginning of their change in career, it has been found that as time passes a sense of isolation sets in. Especially missed is the social side of working for a large organisation—not only the pleasant though maybe unimportant chat, but the informal supportive conversations with colleagues and the feeling of being involved in a team.

> ...the support given by people inside the parent company merely by being prepared to chat (or often even only to listen) apparently inconsequentially. Such actions give a substantial boost to the networker, who may need—as a result of the pressure of business—a second opinion, even sometimes a negative one; an overview of some new area of venture; a scanning of possible opportunities; or merely to relax in conversation after an otherwise unsuccessful or infuriating day. It is not easily possible to put a price on this emotional support, nor is it possible to arrange that such support will happen through a formal mechanism; but it is nonetheless important.
> (*Judkins, West and Drew, Networking in Organisations* 1985)

In order to reduce this isolation, Rank Xerox took pains to continue to identify its networkers as being associated with the parent company, and indeed they still feature in its departmental organisation charts. It is certainly far from true that networkers operate exclusively from home and never see, go into, or make any contact with the parent company other than through a micro-computer link. Most networkers regularly visit Xerox premises to meet their core manager for work reviews, briefings on projects to be undertaken, or the negotiation of contracts. At the same time, they take the opportunity to up-date themselves through their core manager, colleagues and support staff about the arcane world of organisational gossip, restructuring and office politics. This is to the considerable advantage of Rank Xerox since the networkers, with their deeper knowledge of the company, are able to supply far more relevant project work than would an outside consultant, who might produce a report with recommendations that are technically correct but incapable of being grafted on to the existing reality.

To begin with, the Rank Xerox core managers did not understand this, and failed to appreciate the implications of their networkers' new position. However, the subsequent training programme not only made for better working relationships but carried with it an additional benefit—that is, because the managers are now having to come to terms with these entrepreneurs, they themselves have started thinking in an even more entrepreneurial way. Networkers also bring to the party new ideas that they have successfully used with other clients. Since they are closer to RX than normal outside consultants and are reckoned to be 'one of our own' who know the policies and politics of the organisation, their new ideas are taken on board, being recognised as combining the advantages of both 'in-house' and 'not invented here'.

However, the Rank Xerox case history proves that setting up a distributed group does require a great deal of forward thinking at the top. There is need for a complete OD review, and all the implications and interfaces of the new structure must be understood and worked through in a very open and participatory manner. It must be accepted that there are bound to be these misunderstandings and problems between the new homeworkers and their core managers, and the colleagues who are still in the mainstream of the company. For example, there must be a scrupulously fair system of perks as between the homeworker and the fully employed on-site worker, since differences here inflame the counterproductive jealousies that lurk beneath the surface. This is one instance of how managers in this very different relationship need to display a more rounded perception, and muster a range of new talents of which empathy is not the least important.

Another fundamental aspect of the business support system is the setting up of Xerox's group of small businesses, known as 'Xanadu', the Xerox Association of Networkers And Distributed Utilities. This had been mooted as far back as 1979, but its establishment did not actually occur until early 1982, at around the same time as the launch of the networking scheme.

The relationship between 'Xanadu' and the network is a little complex, the former being open to everyone who has left the company to start their own business since 1977—five years before its formation. Ex-employee members do not need to have a contract with Xerox, however, and conversely networkers do not have to join 'Xanadu', which is an independent limited company of small business suppliers, the quality of whose members is known to Xerox which has an advantage in building on this familarity. Something like two-thirds of the networkers have joined 'Xanadu', but they are a minority among the total membership of around 250.

The purpose of Xanadu is threefold:

- to interchange business leads, services and information
- group purchasing of services

- to maintain contact between members and the parent company to the mutual benefit of both parties.

(*Judkins, West and Drew, Networking in Organisations, 1985*)

One important development has been the setting up of a number of local Business Support Centres for the 'Xanadu' membership, giving them access to facilities previously beyond their reach. The business and social value of this comprises more powerful information technology, a shared secretarial/administrative resource and an atmosphere of mutual support. Users create joint contracts for clients among themselves and encouragement is proffered to the less successful by those who are enjoying a good run. One of the first Business Support Centres was the office of the first networker, Roger Walker, a converted coaching inn at Stoney Stratford which is also used as a neighbourhood office by other networkers who live nearby.

Rank Xerox feel they have demonstrated a degree of social responsibility by making clear a positive belief in and support for these small businesses. They provide a limited amount of expertise which they feed to the association—such as details of the Budget's tax implications that are of specific interest to members, supplied free by their corporate economic section, and which would otherwise be expensive for individuals to acquire. However, in one sense, the relationship is less than the 'Xanadu' membership would like, in contrast with the formal contractual arrangements enjoyed by those who are also members of the network *per se*.

> An important factor in the relationship with RX is the perception of Xanadu by individual managers, many of whom are antipathetic even if they know of its existence at all. To change this view it is necessary for Xanadu to achieve demonstrable success in fulfilling specific and useful tasks... to remind line managers of our presence.
> (*Xanadu Ltd, The Way Forward,* Members Survey 1986)

It is beginning to become fashionable for large companies to foster such associations of their self-employed, retired or early retired, but few of them maintain even the level of contact that exists between Rank Xerox and 'Xanadu'. IBM (UK) initiated an early retirement programme in 1983, and thirty of its retirees joined Earlynet, a network of active IBM retirees described by its founder, Peter Templer, as 'grey panthers' in contrast to the traditional 'rose-grower' image of the pensioner. As a company, IBM is averse to partial commitments and rather suspects that questions of work definition, work measurement, instant availability and loyalty would pose difficulties in contracting with part-time professionals. However, Peter Templer has himself sometimes struck lucky, even so;

> They do actually buy work from me in the training field and this has now also happened to one or two of the other Earlynet members on a consultancy

> basis. In 1983, IBM were reluctant to get involved because they feared it might prejudice retirees' ex gratia payments if they were then seen to be working for them at home. A further early retirement programme in 1987, whose tax implications were negotiated with the Inland Revenue has run into the same problem.

Then also, in 1985 British Petroleum piloted the creation of an employment register for its pensioners, and two years later was joined by six other large UK companies in the formation of the Emeritus Register, a network of all their active pensioners:

> BP financed Emeritus for its first eighteen months, notifying 3,000 companies, government organisations and voluntary groups of the availability of this workforce. But matching jobs has not been easy. Of 600 responses, only 70 jobs were actually filled, primarily because of problems of geography or lack of appropriate applicants.
> (*Management Today*, February 1987)

In contrast to the Rank Xerox network, Emeritus members are only rarely engaged in contractual relationships with their ex-employers. But similar arrangements, where retired and early retired people are also working as home-based, part-time professionals, may in future embody more of the features of the RX networking experiment as the technology makes it easier and the publicity better known. Meanwhile however, when it comes to the distribution of work from internal intrapreneurship to external entrepreneurship, Rank Xerox still retains the palm for the time being. It has registered a success, though one which has been obtained through the difficult learning process that is common to every worthwhile pioneering effort.

On the other hand, it must be admitted that the experience has been gained almost exclusively among middle and senior executives, where motivation towards the project is strong, group dependency is low, and space and on-cost savings are high. There has been very little application of these concepts to support staff such as secretaries and clerical employees, although some of these have been able to work temporarily at home as maternity workers. The experiment is thus limited in the extent of its application, and the growth of the network membership to around the 60 mark between 1982 and 1987 only represents 5% of Rank Xerox's central staff groups in the UK and 0.6% of the total workforce in the country.

None the less, it is a significant development and Roger Walker, the only RX homeworker interviewed in the present survey, had some interesting points to make about it—even though a straw poll of one is hardly a statistically reliable sample, it must be admitted. He feels for a start that the emergent homeworker-entrepreneur needs not only new technology but a substantial increase in interpersonal, cultural and managerial skills.

> A lot of change has to happen inside the family. Everyone in my family has evolved enormously. My wife is my business partner now and has developed business skills which she never knew she had before. In the process, however, everything shifts and there is this complex interrelation of power and space. Questions keep coming up like, whose house *is* it? and, what should everyone's role *be*? The male homeworker who thinks that his wife is automatically going to act as his secretary could be in for a rude shock.

According to Walker, everyone has to adapt to each other, including the children, who now know much more about him than they ever did before. Indeed, he added, everyone in his family knows much more about each other than they ever did before. Initially, it was hard for his son to understand the new lifestyle; 'Are you never going to work again, Daddy?' was the nervous query. Now at thirteen, he knows all about the ups and downs of business, he knows how VAT works, and he knows how to take efficient messages on the telephone as one of the team.

One of the biggest dangers, complains Walker, is that he finds it all such fun that his body has no impulse to cut off. The pressure he used to feel at work was centred on his frustration at the internal restrictions of a large organisation. But now, pressure arises from the fact that there are no restrictions—it is all too much of a game. He has to make himself stop and exercise the dog or play squash, such is the compulsion of his enterprise. Because he has divided his time into equal thirds between working at home, at his neighbourhood work centre and at his clients' offices, there is plenty of variety, but behind that are the fears that he may therefore be kidding his body that he is not working as hard as he really is. But not only is the work/play syndrome symptomatic of running one's own business, Walker finds additional stress in the employment of other people. Again, this is part of the deal.

> You can't take half a risk, you have to go for it—but you have a responsibility for them, and it could all collapse tomorrow. Working absolutely on one's own is a much more flexible thing, but some people have to make their mark by growing a business. Those who work alone may gain satisfaction by being pre-eminent in a particular field, but others are not satisfied with this and have to create something new. For them the price of their responsibility for others is what they have to pay.

To him, there is also another kind of responsibility in the system—the responsibility of management for the homeworker, and here a great deal of imagination is required. Rank Xerox is a young company, delightfully free from sacred cows and accustomed to experimenting in management terms. Most corporations do not share this attribute, and are better at thinking of excellent reasons for not doing things than at thinking of excellent reasons for doing them. As Walker sees it, Rank Xerox's courage and imagination have paid off.

A wholly positive result for them has involved output measurement, the benefits of which are compounded by the stress that is laid at RX on the whole quality process. Managers there are in any event required to think in output terms, and this is even more essential to their relationships with the networkers. But other internal staff members are now also beginning to perceive their jobs in this way in consequence—defining the mission and then breaking it down analytically into the individual roles and the tasks involved. This is another instance of how homeworking and the need to organise it so concentrates the mind on effective management, to the advantage of the organisation as a whole.

## BIBLIOGRAPHY AND REFERENCES

Anon., 'Old boy network', *Management Today*, February 1987

Anon., 'Meet the people', *Computer Newsletter*, March 1987

Department of Trade and Industry, *Remote Work Units Project for Disabled People*, Information Technology Division, December 1985

Grice, Pamela, 'An introduction to successful management of remote workers', *IT World*, 1987

Judkins, Phillip, West, David and Drew, John, *Networking in Organisations*, Gower, 1985

Kransdorff, Arnold, 'Why Rank Xerox is sending executives home', and 'Life "out in the Cold"', *Financial Times*, 19 and 20 July 1982

Toffler, Alvin, *The Third Wave*, Collins, 1980

Xanadu Association Members' Survey, *The Way Forward*, 1986

# 3
# The Practitioners (2) —CPS and FI

The two homeworking entities with which this book deals in greater detail have one major attribute in common—the fact that the management of their distributed workforces is a far more involved and complex matter than it is with the two previous examples. For Rank Xerox and the organisations in the DTI scheme, the homeworkers constitute a minor though interesting anomaly, untypical of their main structure and its organisational thrust. But with CPS and F International, the principle of distributed work is their very *raison d'être*. They have been deliberately and wholly set up on a remote basis, and both managements have grasped the need to ensure that the concept is detectable throughout the entire concern.

## ICL—CPS AND PMS

This jumble of initials refers to the two homeworking business centres within the ICL group—CPS and PMS. Together they tot up to only 280 of ICL's 20,000 employees, so the scale of the enterprise is similar to that of Rank Xerox as a proportion of the total. However, there are substantial differences between the two operations. The first is that all ICL's homeworkers are fully employed by the company, unlike the Rank Xerox network, the members of which are contracted on a self-employed basis to work up to a maximum of 50% of their time; and secondly, the two ICL homeworking units have a predominantly female membership. This derives from the fact that they were set up for a totally different reason than the initial motivation which inspired Rank Xerox. For ICL it was not a question of cutting office overhead costs, but of retaining the valuable skills of employees who were, through force of circumstances, no longer able to work for them in the traditional mode.

The main, but not the only, reason for this is that ICL's homeworkers are almost all married women bringing up children. The story began in 1969 when Hilary Cropper, having had a baby but wanting to combine work with motherhood, was approached by her ex-boss who had moved to ICL as a divisional director after one of a series of mergers. ICL was at that time poised to introduce its new 2900 Series and in desperate need of software planners and analysts for it. So Cropper recruited a team of ten women who had previously been with ICL but had left to have families, and embarked on a six months' pilot scheme. The project was successful, with much support from senior management, and a period of further growth was initiated with the appointment of an additional manager, Janet Davies. Then as now, there was a sellers' market for high-grade programming and related skills, and this acute shortage combined with the value of the homeworkers' familiarity with the company culture encouraged ICL into letting the unit expand. Thus at the historical level, the whole concern was not the result of any elaborate strategic plan, but simply developed by capitalising on the pragmatic solution to an internal problem.

The core of what was once called Contract Programming Services thus started as the part-time software development branch of ICL's systems programming division, and its growth was steady but vigorous with numbers reaching around 60 by 1974. CPS gradually came to be known by its initial letters only as it began to recruit people outside the programming function and take on more sophisticated work. By 1974, because of its success, it was permitted to branch out into software support, technical writing and applications development.

It may be helpful to explain more fully these areas of work. Software support entails the diagnosis and correction of problems that crop up in systems software (such as operating systems and compilers) already supplied by ICL to customers. Technical writing, in 1974 anyway, involved the production of customers' reference manuals to accompany the system software. Applications development is the interpretation of a customer's manual system, or application, such as stock control or order processing, into a computer system. It involves fully understanding the customer's requirements; designing a system that fulfils these; the translation of that design into programs; and finally the implementation of the system.

In 1978 the organisation split, with the setting-up of a separate Product Maintenance Support (PMS) group to handle the software support function. About 100 out of ICL's 280 homeworkers now fall into this latter group. It is ultimately the responsibility of the ICL Mainframe Systems Director and is run in close collaboration with the whole mainframe business. It is therefore very much an extension of an existing department and its members are both more frequently home-based and more closely aligned to the traditional scheme of things than CPS, which has branched out in a far more independent manner since its division from PMS took place.

CPS, on the other hand, is run as a profitable business with a hard professional edge, not simply as a support—and it feels that way to the outside observer. Some of its work is in support of internal end-users within ICL itself, but it charges them for its services and indeed competes for their business with other independent software houses. Another difference from PMS is that CPS now sells itself outside the organisation, rather than relying on the ICL sales force—a factor the significance of which is explored later on in this section. For these reasons, CPS makes a better subject than PMS when drawing comparisons with the other major homeworking group, F International, as a free-standing software house.

Within ICL, CPS suffered from a low profile and lack of recognition in the early stages of its history. Although consistently gaining the support of top management, with those lower down the scale in ICL the going was tough—the Group's middle managers were reluctant to take these radical ideas on board, and some of them were actually gunning for the unit. The first issue of its newsletter in July 1975 carried a comment from Hilary Cropper, the departmental head:

> Janet Davies and I have repeatedly met reactions from prospective users which go something like this:- 'Oh, I know that x, y and z work at home but I didn't know they belonged to you.' 'Yes, I had heard of you before but I thought you had folded up.' 'Good gracious, I didn't realise that you were part of ICL.'
> (*CPS Newsletter, July 1975*)

Even now, although CPS is far better known throughout the group, it still has to live with a few areas of ignorance. At one stage, however, it was more urgently necessary for ICL's management to appreciate the worth and future potential of this small but feisty unit. In 1981 its very existence was threatened by pressure from ASTMS during redundancy negotiations. The union demanded that all contract and part-time staff should be dropped, but ICL successfully beat off the attack. None the less the shock of this episode convinced CPS that it had to jack up its credibility within the group as a whole. Survival itself was at stake, and depended not only on doing a first-class job, but also making sure that everybody else knew about it.

By 1980 CPS on its own numbered almost 70 staff, including a management team of four. Most employees were body-shopped; that is, hired out as individuals to users who themselves managed the project. There were, however, one or two other projects where CPS had responsibility for the total system and the project management of its own staff. Meanwhile it had also provided systems consultants to other parts of ICL on a few rare occasions, but projects and consultancy represented only about 20% of the total workload. At that time the users were still almost all internal to ICL, but even so there were gaps in the organisation where CPS was relatively unknown as a professional and highly efficient unit. Homeworking was not appreciated quite yet.

By 1985, CPS was 90 strong and the management team had been expanded by one to five. Pure body-shopping now accounted for only 40% of contracts, and many homeworkers had steadily increased their hours from the basic 16–20 per week to 25 and even 37, though the average was still around 21. They were asking for more responsibility and challenging work, which almost inevitably brought with it the need for greater mobility as well as for longer hours. On an individual basis this was in part answered automatically. Because of the reducing level of domestic commitments over time as their children grew older, there was less need for mothers to remain at home, giving them the flexibility and opportunity to concentrate more on their careers.

Another significant trend at that stage was the increasing involvement with ICL customers—CPS was now being invited to help prepare customer proposals by putting forward a software solution and then visiting the customer to present it. There began to be other occasions when CPS members helped out at a customer site due to temporary shortage of staff or the lack of a particular expertise, developing and implementing their proposed software system. There was also growth in end-user computing, primarily concerned with the local processing of the data available in large corporate systems, in such fields as office systems, personnel systems, local ledgers, conference booking and performance monitoring, for example. At the same time the nature of the work done internally was changing to incorporate a much higher design content. Gradually an enhanced degree of responsibility was being given to the group, more in line with the staff's capabilities and calibre. Due to the stringent selection process, staff come to CPS well proven, with at least five years' full-time experience behind them. In fact, the average experience across the unit is fourteen years. The potential of this very valuable pool of talented project managers, designers, programmers and authors was being realised through more varied and challenging work.

All this meant that staff had to become more flexible, more mobile, more commercially aware; and their response was that this was what they had wanted all along. The emphasis was changing from a home-bound system to a home-based one. More management effort was beginning to be required of the company—more project managing, planning and monitoring. Meanwhile, as the news travelled, ICL was regularly receiving requests for advice on setting up homeworking units from as far afield as Japan, France and Germany, as well as from major UK companies.

In late 1984 Ninian Eadie became ICL's Director, Office Systems, and called for a consultancy report to evaluate the potential of CPS, to investigate its current operation, identify good and bad points, and make recommendations to ensure the future success of the unit. One of the recommendations was the drafting of its Mission, a core statement of aims which has been formally accepted as a guiding principle for CPS by ICL group management itself, and reads:

> To be the preferred supplier of its professional services to end-users in our chosen markets, and a high technology showcase for home-based computer professionals; to continue to provide high calibre development and author resources to ICL's business centres.

CPS was given a glowing report by the consultants. The study found it to be a productive and efficient organisation which showed competitive growth and excellent financial performance. It was however short on marketing effort and had too high a staff-to-management ratio. The appointment of a marketing manager was recommended and the introduction of an additional level of line management, the area managers. At the same time it was emphasised that CPS had to shake off its cottage-industry image and display a more polished and professional aspect which more truly reflected the way it was actually operating in practice. In an informal postscript, the consultants added that if ever ICL wanted to sell, they would be interested.

From that moment ICL as a whole perceived the full value of this increasing asset. 1985 also saw a confirmatory step in this direction when, in November, Ninian Eadie promoted Diana Hill, by then General Manager, to report directly to him. This decision was made to raise CPS's status and give it the backing to exploit its potential for selling skills and packaged services—generally a more profitable activity than selling pure time in the body-shopping sense. The aim was for it then to become a self-supporting business centre in its own right with profit and revenue targets, and thereby to generate more opportunities for career development. The unit responded enthusiastically to its new status; evolving to cope with that growth, it was able to spend more on training and systems. Eadie imbues the homeworking phenomenon with a mixture of vision and pragmatism.

> At the top end there is the whole question of 'Management in the 90s', and whether CPS is going to represent a pioneering effort or merely be seen as an historical aberration. At the bottom end is the individual—coping with the human side, which is partly a matter for sociologists and psychologists to help us with. In the middle is the question of CPS as a business and whether the thing actually works right now. I think that the top end is probably more likely than not to be significant in future (though it won't be universal). At the bottom end I hope we've got it right but there is always room for improvement. As far as the middle is concerned, yes, CPS is a viable business—and more and more self-evidently proving itself to be so.

Eadie sees his role as a sympathetic mentor, guiding CPS through an evolutionary stage where it is now close to working out what its ultimate role and mission will be. This entails continuing the progression from an internal support to an extroverted free-market organisation. It has increasingly been working not only inside ICL but also for its customers, but one important constraint has always been that the actual selling has been done by members of the ICL salesforce itself. However, in 1986 CPS was granted a 'hunting licence' to sell direct to existing ICL customers through a sales force under its own control.

> This is a fundamental decision and probably the most important one that has been made for CPS in ten years. CPS is now learning to be a business and its people are learning to be business people. There is a gap in the market not served by standard software products or by big consultancies, or by the DP departments of big organisations themselves—CPS should and will be in there really bridging it.
> (*Ninian Eadie*)

Its market, then, exists within the quite substantial cracks that lie between existing larger markets. Basically, CPS is best at a craft job since it is difficult for it to undertake projects that require large teams. A small user, at the personal or small business end, can buy a package off the shelf. It may not be ideal but it is more or less satisfactory, and with trial and error a customer can get something fairly close to what he wants. At the other end of the scale is the vast mainframe computer where most of the work is done by an in-house data processing department. In between—and this is where they score—is the provision of working software programs for departmental computers, where there may be a small but crucial system needed and the in-house DP people are uninterested in setting it up. Here it will be a departmental manager in a big company, already a customer of ICL, who is most likely to use CPS. It has an existing connection, and the big consultants who are its natural competitors generally charge a higher fee because of their higher overheads, and can be beaten by the more nimble CPS workforce.

As an example, CPS has produced on a micro local tendering systems for drugs and surgical appliances on behalf of a health authority. Other examples are a stock control and order entry system on a PC for an engineering manufacturer, a specialised billing system on a mainframe for a public utility, and back office systems and procedural documentation for several large retailers.

One of CPS's advantages is that it does not have to worry enormously about any grand corporate strategy, since the board of ICL leaves it largely alone in its independence. The CPS management has been allowed to get on and prove itself without the powers that be breathing down its neck. Since 1985 the unit has had a clear remit to go ahead and build an exciting business, and permission to increase its headcount in line with business requirements. It enjoys the strong interest of the ICL main board, but within a framework of non-interference it is left to work on its own tactical and strategic development. This includes the division of its operation not only regionally but into the market segments of retail, finance, public service and manufacturing.

> We are now establishing market niches in our four chosen industry sectors, and satisfied customers are extending or renewing contracts—some for the fifth or sixth time. Really understanding the customer's business and his requirements are key features of the CPS approach.
> (*Diana Hill*)

General manager Diana Hill runs a team that consists of herself, four regional managers, the technical manager and the marketing manager. At the level above this, decisions are made merely by herself and the main board director, Ninian Eadie, to whom she reports. The organisation chart for the unit is shown in Table 3. This must by no means be seen as a rigid structure, but a passing representation of a stage in the unit's development.

At the sharp end of the operation, teams form and dissolve to match the project concerned. Under each project manager there may be five or six programmers, senior programmers and/or systems analysts, the latter having the job of devising a system to solve a given problem and then breaking it down into individual programmes which the programmers will write.

By now, in 1987, the middle initial of CPS should actually stand for 'professional' rather than 'programming'. Its 180 members provide all manner of professional services, from writing technical publications to consultancy, besides the programming and design of software and systems analysis. The technical authors' section, now numbering 35, has been in existence within CPS since 1973. Their job is to write definitive descriptions of complicated technical subjects in user manuals, both for ICL internally and for ICL customers and trainers. Mostly these guides are applicable to ICL products but there is also a small amount of specific customised writing, particularly for use in the retail sector. The authors work about 10% externally and 90% on internal ICL work at present, compared to an overall CPS split of 30/70 with an increasing external content.

There was an interim period during which the whole technical authorship process was concentrated in one unit embracing both on-site and off-site workers. But the unit suffered from high turnover until 1985 when a decision was made to move the off-site authors back into CPS. They proved to be much happier with the working arrangements and general ambience, and immediately the turnover problems disappeared. A crucial point, of which more later—there is something inherent in the shared experience of homeworking that is fundamental to good personnel relations.

> I was a technical author working with on-site managers, and homeworkers were very restricted as regards management potential. However, two years

Table 3 CPS organisation chart 1987

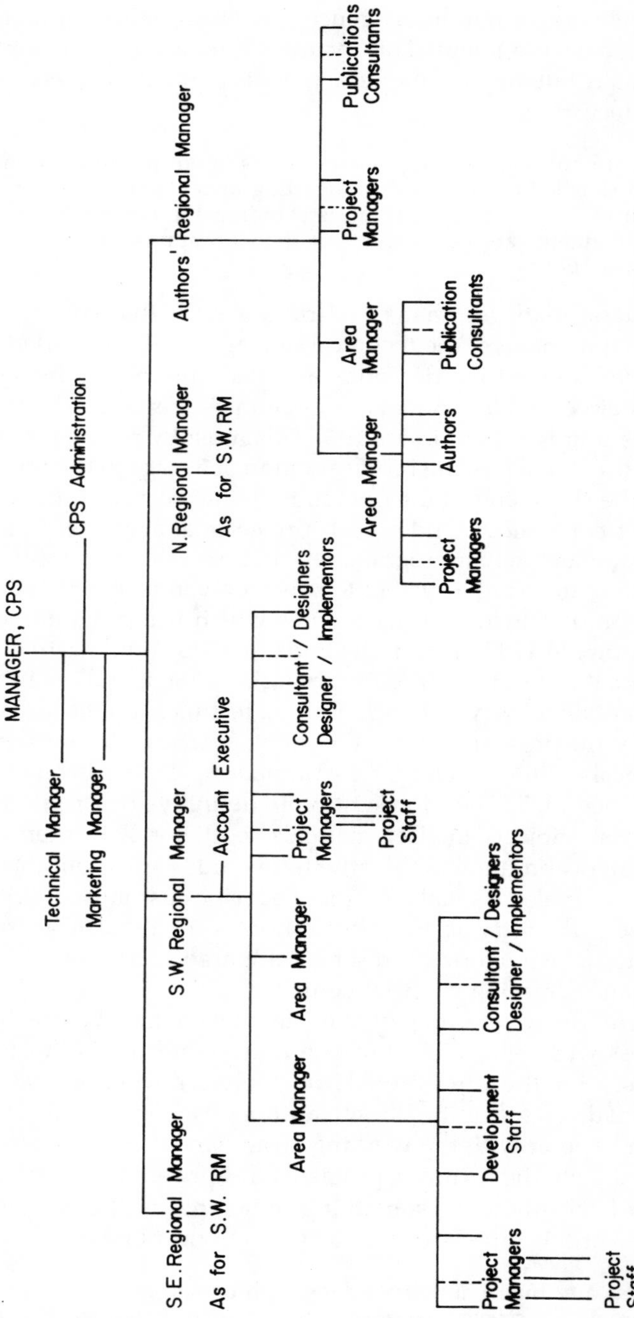


(CPS Standards and Procedures Manual)

ago the publications unit split and the homeworkers' side of it devolved back to CPS. I was a lot happier because I got into management, but it struck me that everybody else was happier too. We were all being managed by people who were also working home-based off-site and had this element in common. It leads to a greater understanding all round.
(*CPS Manager*)

CPS and PMS staff are full employees of ICL and therefore entitled to all the relevant company benefits. They are under contract for an agreed number of hours' work (minimum 16) per week as long as a job is available. CPS undertakes to provide a retainer of sixteen hours' pay per month if there should be none, but prides itself on the fact that this has only happened twice in 18 years. The rate per hour for these workers is the same as that of the relevant ICL salary scale. Everyone has a job description and a grade in ICL, whether part-time or full-time, and part-timers are paid the annual salary rate, divided by 52 weeks and 37 hours, multiplied by the number of hours they work a week. Site visits vary, depending on the work in hand, and range from one per month to four times a week. Homeworkers are paid a mileage allowance and their working hours are timed from when they leave home. All other travel expenses, postage, telephone calls, stationery and other consumables are reimbursed, of course.

They also have sick pay and holiday pay as pro rata of their full entitlements, plus the usual Bank Holidays. Holiday pay is incremental according to how long they have been employed in the group—thus original ICL personnel get more than those who join CPS from outside. Since 1986 CPS staff have also been provided with a portable pension scheme, set up separately from the ordinary ICL scheme (with which, in fact, it is not compatible). It is however comparable on a pro rata basis, the employers contributing 6% and the employees a minimum of 3%. The provision of the pension scheme has been symbolic in demonstrating the accepted professional status of CPS both to its own workforce and to other ICL colleagues. This, plus the direct reporting line to Ninian Eadie and the award of the 'hunting licence', finally leaves no doubt of their credibility within the group.

On induction, all new entrants are presented with a letter of appointment, a procedures manual and an 'auntie'—not a manager, but someone of their own standing to show them around. This has proved to be a useful new procedure, since the 50% who came from outside ICL (from its customers, competitive manufacturers and their customers, and freelancers) used to complain that being unfamiliar with the company culture they needed someone like this to hold their hand for a while.

Apart from the necessary project meetings and visits to site for testing programmes, CPS organises other opportunities for staff to get out of the house and meet one another. For a start, all employees have an annual appraisal meeting with their area or regional manager. Further, at least twice a year, special training sessions or seminars are organised, there is at least one purely social event a year, and finally there are biennial strategic conferences where the whole workforce comes together to look at future plans and share a vision of the future. Furthermore, a newsletter, *Contact*, is published two or three times a year, giving not only technical updates and official group news, but personal information and useful hints; such as the following 'super-person tips':

- most things (lamb chops, chicken, etc.) cooked in tomato soup and a pinch of mixed herbs taste delicious
- try to train your children to eat/like raw vegetables and fruit; these are good for them and it saves a lot of cooking
- convert to duvets; and buy enough underwear, shirts etc., so that you don't have to do frantic washing in the middle of the week
- photocopy shopping lists—list all items on one page (grouped in the order you go round your regular supermarket) and then just tick off weekly requirements. Saves time and also acts as an *aide-memoire*
- use waiting time to full advantage (at doctors, dentists, or waiting for children to finish swimming lessons) by taking material with you and catching up on reading, letter-writing, work etc.
- keep a spare car key in your handbag for when little Johnny throws your other one down the drain.

(*CPS* Contact *Newsletter, July 1984 and July 1985*)

Here is something of an insight into the distinctive style of CPS—the shared commonality of experience, the together but un-mimsy feeling that is very much a feature of both this and its other largely feminine counterpart, F International. These managements are approachable and friendly, but at the same time insist that administration has to be formal and efficient if a distributed organisation such as theirs is not going to fall apart at the seams. There are occasional moans from the homeworkers that too much paperwork is involved, but in practice it is an essential. Once again, an excerpt from the Procedures Manual gives the CPS administrative flavour—down-to-earth and perky, rather than bureaucratic or matronising.

**2.2 Forms**

*2.2.1 Payclaim*

A form that you fill in at 4-weekly intervals which is the source of your next salary. It details the hours you have worked/been sick etc. and for which you request payment. The form is sent to your Regional Manager unless you are told otherwise. The Manager checks and authorises it and keeps one copy for her records. The top copy goes to Payroll for calculation and payment of salary; the second copy goes to the CPS Administrator for her records. The fourth (yellow) copy is yours—if you don't want it throw it away and save the postman, your Manager and her dustman some effort.

There is *always* a deadline by which payclaims must reach Payroll if payment is to be made on the next salary date. If your form is late, either you miss a salary or other people have to go to considerable effort to ensure that you don't. Please do *not* assume that a 1st Class Stamp ensures next day delivery because it does not. Payclaims, etc. should be posted on the Payclaims Wednesday or the next day at the *latest*. If you have a really poor memory, check every Wednesday to make sure that it is not Payclaim day.
(*CPS Standards and Procedures Manual, 1986*)

All staff down to area manager level plus a few project managers and the sales executives, have an OPD ('one-per-desk'), i.e. a fancy telephone/wordprocessor/computer/electronic mailbox which transmits voice or data messages. It handles word processing, spreadsheets, database and graphics, and can also send files from one CPS station to another. It can dial into other systems on site, but so far has been used more as a management tool than for this purpose. An internal working party is now considering how to proceed further with this technology to satisfy all the functional and communication requirements of CPS. In addition, members of the network have answerphones and about 80% of them are supplied with their own individual PCs or small free-standing micros, more powerful than the OPD. Meanwhile, all authors have an ICL word-processor and some also have an Apple Macintosh micro-computer.

We shall be hearing plenty more about CPS from its homeworkers and their managers in the chapters that follow, but before then we must first also examine the history and morphology of F International and tease out comparisons and contrasts.

## F INTERNATIONAL

Professor Ralf Dahrendorf, in the last of a valedictory series of television programmes on his retirement from the post of Director of the London School of Economics, answered the question, 'Has Britain got a future?' in the following terms:

Some answers may be found in Party Manifestos. But the real changes are to be found where people live and work. . .F International has several characteristics which make it a model. It allows people to organise their own lives; it decentralises management decisions; it makes effective use of modern technology—and of course, it is successful.
(*'Dahrendorf on Britain', BBC1, January 1983*)

It is indeed extremely successful, but almost to its own surprise, at that.

> I look at some of the figures and I think, this can't possibly be us. Try dropping a couple of noughts off the end.
> *(Steve Shirley, 'The Company of Women', BBC South TV, April 23 1985)*

It has attracted a vast amount of publicity and interest both from the media and in business circles; it is in the forefront of the UK's software houses with a workforce of over 1,000; it is a public limited company with an eight-figure turnover; and it is cruising in stately fashion towards a market quotation. Furthermore, it was the first company to provide two finalists in the twelve-year history of the Veuve Cliquot Business Woman of the Year Award.

But home is where it started—to be precise, Derek and Stephanie Shirley's home—the original electronic cottage. Stephanie and her sister had been rescued from Germany by the Quakers just before the outbreak of war in 1939. Brought up by an English family near Birmingham, she obtained a BSc in mathematics and went into computing. An *entrepreneuse manquée*, she desperately needed to control her own environment, and reacted violently against bumblingly autocratic leadership. She resigned from all that to go freelance in 1962—with capital of precisely £6.

> We had no money—that meant it was impossible; we had no business experience—that meant it was impossible; and I was a woman trying to run a business—that meant it was impossible. I had to change my name to Steve from Stephanie in my selling letters before I got a single interview from a prospective client.
> *(Steve Shirley)*

It worked. By the time she had finished her first job she was 8½ months pregnant ('. . .how big is your workforce?' '. . . er, one and a half. . .'), but her fledgling company, Freelance Programmers, was up and running with a turnover of £700 in its first year. Sadly, it became apparent that her son, Giles, was seriously mentally disabled, but Steve Shirley poured energy into her business. When incorporated in 1964, FPL had four other workers, who expanded to 100 by 1970, 500 by 1978 (by then F International) and 1,000 by 1985—in which year company seniors won two of the computer industry's Recognition of Information Technology Achievement (RITA) awards. Steve Shirley was elected a Vice-President of the British Computer Society in 1979, and awarded the Order of the British Empire in 1980 and the Freedom of the City of London in 1987.

But this happy-ever-after story hides the reality of some tense and bitter moments in the interim. There was an early cashflow disaster which necessitated a second mortgage on their house, just at the same time as their son's handicap was diagnosed. Then in 1970, recession seriously curtailed their workflow, many clients went into liquidation, and worst of all her trusted partner left the company taking both homeworkers and desperately valuable business. Somehow she clawed her way back from the brink and into profit again by 1973.

> Management by women is not all just caring and support. One doesn't create an organisation like this without singlemindedness and some abrasiveness. You have to do something because you want to do it very much—that's the most important thing. And you may even make money as a result of it. (*Steve Shirley*)

> Steve's motivation was not money but a determination to prove a point, a desire to liberate women from some of the constraints of motherhood, a wish to be in control of her own destiny, a fascination with the science of computing, and the simple pleasure she took in playing a business game with skill in a world run by men.
> (*Tom Lloyd, Dynosaur and Co: Studies in Corporate Evolution,* 1984)

Since then the company has expanded and consolidated. The holding company, F International, was formed in 1974—the F standing, originally, for Freelance, but increasingly for Flexible and Free too, as more and more women discovered that 'Computer programming, since it needs only a desk, a head, paper and pencil, can be done at home', as Tom Lloyd put it in *Dynosaur & Co.*

A Danish subsidiary was set up the following year. Denmark has a high proportion of women in data processing, but growth was slow because the practicality of combining motherhood and normal work is already enhanced there by the country's supportive system of child care. Local managers proved difficult to control at arm's length, and one started up a rival operation on her own and obviously had to go. In 1986, the continued lack of progress resulted in a decision to sell the business to the local management.

Experience in the Netherlands has also been somewhat fraught, but progress is now being made. This subsidiary was created in 1976, and here again its long-distance management proved difficult at first. Furthermore, the local employment protection legislation stymied the F method of working and necessitated much fiddling about with short-term contracts and notice periods. There was also deep division between feminists and traditionalists about the woman's role in Dutch society, and F International found itself caught in the crossfire, pleasing neither side. However, determination has paid off, and there are now 35 or so working panelists and a total of some 50 who can be called upon when needed. Acceptance of the concept is becoming more general in the country, and the subsidiary contributes satisfactorily to group revenue.

The lessons learned from the company's 1978 American venture were rather different. It entered into a relationship with Heights Information

Technology Systems Inc. (HITS), licensing the home-based employment system and exporting the way in which the services were supplied rather than the services themselves. But the contract was a loss-maker, not renewed after its two-year term, and when, in 1983, FI acquired the organisation as a wholly-owned subsidiary, this failed to work out too. The market was too mature, the offices were in the wrong environment, the cultural differences were greater than had been foreseen, and the enterprise was going to take altogether too long to turn around. F International cut its losses and suspended the operation two years later.

The international aspect of FI is therefore now somewhat muted compared to the past, but at least Holland is now looking better, and the group is working away and keeping an eye open for investment in other EEC countries. However, here at home all has not been sweetness and light for it either, if one is to follow the course of events as chronicled by the Harvard Business School in its Case Study 9-486-118/120 of 1986.

In mid-1984, the group, having enjoyed a period of rapid growth which it foresaw was likely to continue, the bad news was that its management resources were close to snapping point. The cause of this stress lay partly in the highly decentralised structure, and partly in the need for additional talent from outside in areas which had been by tradition the bailiwick of organically-grown managers. These changes had to be made in order to ensure the company's survival, but at the same time the unique characteristics that distinguished it from its competitors had to be maintained as well.

The board agreed a proposal to add an extra layer of management to the organisational structure and to break down some of the existing functions. (Interesting, here, that the 1985 CPS management survey also evidenced the need for an additional tier of management.) This, however, had the effect of demoting most regional managers and inhibiting their access to the managing director. But at the same time it did bring new blood into the company in such areas as business development, personnel and training, sales and marketing.

These measures created a turmoil of controversy within FI, with many panel members voicing anger and astonishment that a decision with no input from below had been so abruptly communicated, in violation of the company's carefully nurtured image of openness and caring. However, it seemed at the time that before long most managers had got used to the change and indeed cashed in on the subdivision that had been effected, by developing an even greater sense of team spirit within the smaller groupings.

All was not quite as it seemed, however. Shortly after this, managing director Alison Newell resigned, her place being taken by Hilary Cropper who was headhunted from ICL's Professional Services Unit in July 1985. At about the same time it was also recognised that F International was not benefiting enough from the networking possibilities being opened up by advances in technology, and even more disturbingly, a City University Business School Survey of panel members revealed perceptions of:

- under-utilisation of skills
- desire for additional training
- long gaps between work
- isolation from the company's development
- lack of feedback about performance, and especially
- levels of fees

Determined not to make the same mistakes as last time, Cropper prepared her top managers for their second restructuring in a highly personalised manner, and they in turn communicated information to their staffs on a one-to-one or small-group basis. Since this second batch of changes was made in the light of panelists' and managers' feedback, co-operation was ensured in the main, though there were a few minor ripples of disquiet. The changes have entailed:

- The shutdown of the small business and consultancy divisions in order to concentrate on large blue chip business.
- An expansion of the client base, and its sales consolidation into three major sectors representing the main thrust of the company's business—financial services (banking and insurance); commercial services (leisure, food, drink and retail distribution); and the public sector (science and engineering—particularly the defence industry and secure establishments: and community—particularly health)
- The acquisition of outside marketing expertise and the establishment of a national sales force to that end
- The setting-up of a full electronic network, first on a pilot basis, but ultimately to link the whole panel together—to each other, to its offices, and to its clients' offices
- Further adaptation of the organisational structure to its 1987 shape. (See Table 4)

The result was a transformation from a production-oriented organisation with a heavy regional structure where the regions each ran their own rather ladylike marketing teams, into a technology and marketing-oriented organisation with a professional national salesforce. In addition there has been added emphasis on financial control and personnel development, with more training (especially of management) an individual assessment programme, and a concerted attempt to improve utilisation levels of both the skills and availability of the company's vital resource—its panel membership.

The immediate results were highly encouraging. In the year to end-April 1986, group turnover rose by 20% to £9.1 million with pre-tax profits up by 81% to £615,000. In the following year Hilary Cropper was promoted to Group Chief Executive Officer. Of the *Times* list of top companies, FI clients accounted for 25% in the top 500, 33% in the top 300, 50% in the top 100 and 8 out of the top 10. Here are some satisfied noises from them:

- High quality project management, programming and testing. (Sun Alliance)
- Combined friendly approach with mental toughness (London Borough of Islington)
- (We) have learned an enormous amount about the planning and control required to ensure . . . . . success. (Allied Breweries)
- ... a well-managed and skilled team of professionals. (Fiat Auto UK)
- ... work of the highest order provided within required timescales. (BICC)

(*F International Brochure, 1986*)

The current share profile of the company is that 58% of the equity is held by Steve and Derek Shirley, 13% by outside institutional investors, almost 25% by the FI Shareholders' Trust, and the balance by the past and present workforce including directors. It is therefore an unusual animal—a public limited company without a quotation which is also a close company—but it is the intention to take it to the appropriate market on the Stock Exchange in due course.

Something like one in four of the workforce hold blocks of shares in FI, having bought them as a gesture of personal solidarity as well as for profit, and in addition everyone was granted a single share on the occasion of the group's silver jubilee. Top management has an executive share option scheme and there is also the Shareholders' Trust which holds its 24.8% in common ownership on behalf of the workforce. Because the relevant legislation currently applies solely to employee trusts and so few of the workforce are employed as such, this raises a problem—the law, as usual, is lumbering on way behind the reality. So for the time being, the trust has to be couched in terms of employees only—though the trustees are also mindful of their responsibilities to the great bulk of the freelancers. The AGM of the company has its social as well as its statutory aspect—of the 250 members who held shares in 1986 over 20% attended, to the considerable amazement of the Registrar.

Finally, as an epitome of what FI stands for, there is the Charter, reproduced here, having been concentrated with much creative difficulty into a single page of text.

# F International Charter

F International is a group of companies which have sprung from seeing an opportunity in a problem: one woman's inability to work in an office has turned into hundreds of people's opportunity to work in a non-office environment. Because of its unusual origin, F International has a clear sense of its mission, its strategy and its values.

## MISSION

F International's mission is to stay a leader in the rapidly growing and highly profitable, knowledge intensive software industry. It aims to achieve this by developing, through modern telecommunications, the unutilised intellectual energy of individuals and groups unable to work in a conventional environment.

## STRATEGY

F International's strategy is to maximise the value of its unusual asset base by establishing a competitive advantage over conventionally organised firms, and imitators of its approach, through cost and quality competitiveness. This occurs by the development of a methodology which ensures quality and by establishing a company ethos which binds people who work largely independently and often alone.

## VALUES

People are vital to any knowledge intensive industry. The skills and loyalty of our workforce are our main asset. Equally important is the knowledge which comes from the exchange of ideas with our clients and their personnel. It follows that human and ethical values play a pivotal role in the way in which an organisation like F International conducts itself. This is even more true in a structure as open and free as F International. To maintain a high level of creativity, productivity and coherence in such an environment requires a set of high ethical values and professional standards that any member of the organisation can identify with and see realised, and reinforced, in the organisation's behaviour. F International has defined for itself such a charter of values.

### 1. Professional Excellence

Our long term aim is to improve our professional abilities so as to maintain a quality product for our clients. It is also our aim to develop fully our professional potential as people and to develop our organisation in a way which reflects our own individuality and special approach.

### 2. Growth

We aim to grow our organisation to its full potential, nationally and internationally. We aim to grow at least as rapidly as the software industry as a whole in order to maintain our own position as an attractive employer and a competitive supplier.

### 3. Economic and Psychological Reward

We also aim to realise and enjoy fully the economic and psychological rewards of our efforts resulting from the development of the unique competitive advantage of our structure and capabilities. We aim to achieve profits, reward our workforce, maintain the Employee Trust and provide an attractive return to our shareholders.

### 4. Integrated Diversity

We have a commitment to consistent procedures worldwide as a means of lowering cost, but aim to conduct ourselves as a national of each country in which we operate.

### 5. Universal Ethics

We respect local customs and laws, but see ourselves as members of a world society with respect for human dignity and ethical conduct beyond the profit motive and local circumstances.

### 6. Goodwill

An extension of our ethical view is a belief in the goodwill of others: colleagues, clients and vendors. We also believe that goodwill results in positive, long term relationships.

### 7. Enthusiasm

Finally we believe that enthusiasm for our people and our product, and the ability to engender that enthusiasm in others, is the most essential quality of leadership within the organisation. Enthusiasm promotes creativity, cooperation and profit.



F.S. 1/22

Steve Shirley

> The Charter is the glue that holds the thing together—boiled down to a single page. It arose out of a perceived need to sort out the myths from the facts, and became more clearly necessary as soon as not all the staff were centred on the same building. It has now become a part of everyday activity—a list of shared assumptions of what FI is doing. It is referred to in the evaluation of any proposed change or potential piece of business, and if that does not accord with the Charter it is not proceeded with.
> (*Steve Shirley*)

As has been indicated but not yet explained in full, unlike CPS whose workforce members are fully employed within the ICL group, FI workers are more often than not self-employed, indeed 75% of them comprise its home-based panel and operate on flexible hours. A further 15% are working part-time or flexitime on a salaried basis, and 10% are both salaried and full-time. The latter two categories are found mostly in management or on the sales and technical sides, and around three-quarters of these are home-based too—conventional office-based, full-time and salaried employees amounting to only 6% of the whole. These in effect provide the management, marketing and technical support which they, as it were, sell on to the freelancers in the shape of an invisible discount on the rate of pay they are awarded. An analogy is that of the French wholesale winegrowers co-operative where viticultural and agricultural extension services, transport, storage, marketing, etc. are provided by the co-op, and yet the great preponderance of the value added is in the brilliance of the wine.

There has always been some reluctance at FI to engage office-based people, with managers having to justify anything other than home-based recruitment. More salaried staff are now being taken on, though many workers avoid the commitment of being salaried and see their freelance status as a considerable advantage. FI's requirements for joining this elite are:

- four years' experience and/or suitable qualifications
- the ability to do at least 20 – 25 productive hours per week during a project
- the ability to undertake two or more local client visits per week, childminding arrangements being made accordingly where necessary
- a telephone and some kind of an 'office area' at home
- own transport or easy access to public transport
- high professional standards and the level of self-discipline required to work from a home base

Applicants may not qualify if they are:

- in full-time employment seeking additional part-time work

- between jobs
- out of touch with the industry as a result of a significant break

The paragon who possesses these positive features while avoiding the negative ones, may find that they represent the passport to the flexible working hours and flexible working arrangements that FI provides —whether home-based with on-site work as stipulated, or full- or part-time work with a higher on-site content (on either a salaried or a freelance basis). Tasks can include programming, systems analysis, consultancy, lecturing, training, administration, estimating and project management.

Like CPS, FI offers its workforce promotion prospects, with a variety of career paths and many opportunities for professional and personal development, through training in new technology and the chance to acquire new skills including management ones. Career development structures are available for part-timers and freelancers up to middle management levels.

The F International organisation chart (Table 4) should be regarded like that of CPS, as a snapshot in time—simply a picture of an evolving business at a given moment. Most of the jobs detailed on the chart are self-explanatory, but there are a few which may require some further explanation. For example, the resource co-ordinator co-ordinates jobs obtained from the sales department with the project managers, and chooses suitable panelists for them, bearing in mind experience, skills, availability by time and distance, etc. She also helps the resources manager, her immediate boss, select applicants for the panel.

The account manager will have a number of project managers working below her, and may also be managing a project team of her own, which can include business analysts and consultants. The project manager's activity consists of monitoring and scheduling the work that has been procured within the necessary financial budget, and then liaising with clients and managing the team of systems analysts and programmers beneath her. The systems analyst is the interface between the user and the programmer, working at a higher level of system but in less detail than the programmer herself. She is a generalist and defines what the problem is and how to solve it, designing and testing linked programs which are then individually farmed out to the programmers themselves. There is also a certain amount of user training involved in the job.

The testing of the program has to be done on the client's machine, unless the analyst has a terminal on-line at home, which is why people must be prepared to work on site away from home for two days a week. The salaried staff are vital to this formula, being on site for most of each week, and making it possible for the others to work off site at the same time. Contracts with freelancers are generally broken into short periods involving

Table 4 F international organisation chart 1987

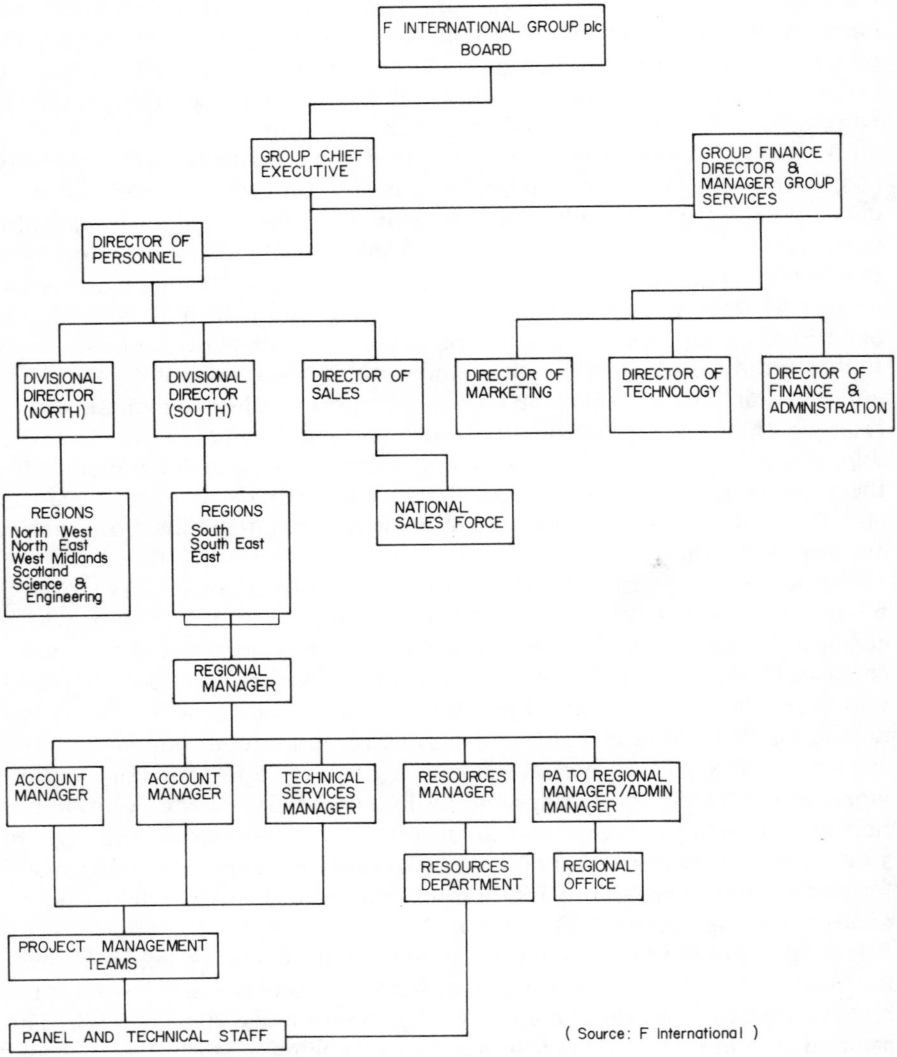


(Source: F International)

a minimum number of hours, but they are left to get on with running them as they wish within the agreed time limits. If a project requires more time than anticipated this is allowed up to a point, but workers are not allowed to let schedules slip badly. Experience shows that with contracts over six weeks, productivity tends to drop, according to Ursula Huws in *The New Homeworkers*. By dividing up the work in this way and closely monitoring its progress, F has achieved extremely high productivity levels—at the company's own reckoning about 30% higher than comparable work in an office, she claims.

Panel members are paid by the hour for their useful work and at a lower hourly rate for their travel time, though they do have a generous mileage allowance when using their own cars. While training, unless this is specifically required for the job in hand, they are not paid apart from a £25 daily allowance to cover childminding and other disturbance costs during group training sessions away from home. Rates of pay are structured by overlapping bands which progress upwards for each job title. The rates are less than an individual would earn on a purely freelance basis, since FI takes on the expense of marketing, management and other backup support. Rates are therefore set to correspond with something like the average for competing software houses, but there may also be bonuses for substantial commitment to working on site. Naturally, panel members are also reimbursed for all their direct expenses such as travel, telephone, postage and stationery, photocopying, lunch on-site and secretarial support.

Panel members are not employed under the terms of a contract of service, but engaged to provide services in connection with specific contracts. Unlike the salaried staff, they are therefore not granted employee-type benefits such as sick pay, holiday pay, or superannuation. They are assessable for income tax under the self-employed provisions of Schedule D, and also liable for National Insurance Contributions in line with their self-employed status. At one stage, FI had considerable trouble over the status of its panel members—first with the Inland Revenue and then, immediately afterwards, with the Department of Health & Social Security; but after protracted negotiation both contentions were resolved. If their taxable turnover exceeds the stipulated level, panel members are of course required to register for VAT. Many are registered as partnerships or companies. At the insistence of the Revenue, sales and senior managerial staff are all salaried.

In terms of insurance, FI provides personal accident cover to the homeworkers while at work. It also covers any of its equipment at homeworkers' homes but the panel members themselves have to cover their own transport. Since FI has one contract with the client and another with the homeworker to match it, it is unlike an agency where in most instances the homeworker has a contract with the client direct. FI therefore picks up the tab for professional indemnity, which is of no further concern to the panel member. Finally, as mentioned, a pension scheme is provided for salaried employees, while the non-salaried have access to a voluntary pension club, distanced from but approved by the company.

A large number of freelancers already own their own home micro-computers, but in the past these have not often been used in their work with FI, except where the equipment has been supplied by the client for a particular project. By and large, the only home technology has been the telephone till now, but this is changing radically. As a result of a successful pilot scheme, panel members are being offered the chance of purchasing or leasing from a selection of microcomputers under favourable arrangements negotiated by the company, with the aim of creating a complete electronic mail network. Salaried (full or part-time) workers will be issued with them, but in order to maintain the self-employed integrity of the freelance panel members, the investment in this equipment will have to be their own, though they will be paid for its use.

By the autumn of 1987, over 20% of the workforce enjoy this facility—all managers and about 15% of the panel—with the basic micros having a variety of different equipment tagged on to them. This electronic mail network, which uses dial-up lines, has already covered all the company's project managers and salesforce, who are now able to transfer text between users wherever they are located without delay, to improve the efficiency and speed of communications across the management team, and to reduce significantly the time previously wasted in telephoning. The opportunity to use the micro-computers for personal computing applications and for corporate and regional information systems has also been opened up in the process.

Now that this management network has been established, it will be expanded to incorporate use by the workforce for remote working on behalf of clients as part of the production process, so that FI becomes in effect a distributed software factory. The manager will be able to take a project, split it into chunks and physically move those chunks anywhere she wants. The workload will be evened out across the whole project through a proliferation of computers at home, plus low-cost, leased lines to clients' offices and between FI's own regional and local centres.

The third phase will be a complete mixed network—a combination of leased voice and data lines between offices and a web of management centres with full equipment, plus terminals in homes. FI's new focus on increased project size now makes this cost-effective, together with the enhanced speed of telecommunications installation and the diminishing cost of personal computers, falling at the rate of about 35% a year. The tools are now available for a rapid advance—sharing designs between homeworkers, amending them, and then feeding off each other. To date, FI has lagged somewhat behind CPS in the use of equipment from home, but this new development catches up with CPS's OPD facility. But in the last analysis networking itself is not enough—what will be needed in spades in tomorrow's world is the management of networking. Both FI and CPS will be there, pioneering it.

But in another human sense FI, like CPS, is a different sort of network as well—a network of people who communicate shared experiences and agreed strategies for the future, and thus perceive more clearly their role in the progression of the organisation. Informal meetings often provide a greater breakthrough than formal ones, here. There is thus a regular biennial system of 'Freespeaks' in FI, local gatherings which are extensions of team briefings and answer the need for everyone to know where they are going in relation to everyone else. Originally this gave rise to basic nuts-and-bolts stuff like the level of fees, the terms of service and so forth. However now, after a few years, it is business questions that come out of these meetings. A high proportion of the people truly understand and wish to become involved in strategy, and it is practical to involve those who do so. This is the measure of true participation in FI and it does not only occur when things are going well. For example, in the early 1970s the agreed strategy at all levels was to survive at all. Participation is indeed a salient feature of the company's ethos, and though there have been times in the past when it has been temporarily out of kilter, the essential characteristic still holds good, with tangibly positive results.

> When I arrived at F in 1985 the company was going through its quality audit for the Ministry of Defence. The auditor said to me, 'I have to tell you that this is one of the best software houses I have ever seen—but the other thing is, it is obvious that you all have such a lot of fun'!
> (*Hilary Cropper*)

As a final postscript to underline this spirit of participation, in June 1987 F International were presented with the third annual 'Team Excellence Award'. The winners of the first award, two years earlier, were the Red Arrows flying team, which gives some idea of comparative status. And with total appropriateness, the award's sponsors are none other than Rank Xerox (UK) Ltd.

To wind up this chapter, before proceeding with the common experiences of the CPS and FI managements and workforces, it may be useful to summarise the differences between them, and also the contrasts with the DTI and RX networks. Table 5 gives an outline of this.

As for the differences between CPS and F, there are fewer of them than there are similarities—which makes that much the more telling a combined analysis of the opinions of their workers and managers. Most of the fundamental differences stem in some manner from their unshared structural attributes of subsidiary status on the one hand and independence

Table 5 Summary of formal homeworking programmes in the UK

| ORGANISATION | WORK UNDERTAKEN | EMPLOYMENT STATUS | OCCUPATIONAL GROUP | NUMBER OF PARTICIPANTS | DATE COMMENCED | MOTIVATION | USE OF COMPUTER | USE OF DATA TELECOMMS |
|---|---|---|---|---|---|---|---|---|
| F International | Computer Consultancy/ Project Management | Self-Employed/ Contracted to F Intl | Professional/ Managerial | 1000 | 1962 | Provide Employ-ment/Utilise Scarce Skill | Moderate | Moderate |
| ICL (CPS, PMS) | S'ware Maint/Tech Wrtg/Proj Mgt/ Applications Development | Employees | Professional/ Technical | 260 | 1969 | Utilise Scarce Skill /Retain Talent | High | High |
| Rank Xerox (UK) | Various Consultancy | Self-Employed/ Contracted to Rank Xerox | Professional/ Managerial | 60 | 1981 | Cut Over-heads/Staff Levels | Moderate | Low |
| Department of Trade and Industry Work Units for the Disabled | Word Processing/ Database Manage-ment/Data Entries/ Programming etc | Employees | Clerical/ Professional | 100 | 1982 | Provide Employ-ment for the Disabled | High | Limited |

(Adapted from *Opportunities to Promote Remote Working in the Highlands and Islands*, Eosys Ltd, 1984) on the other, and were encapsulated by Hilary Cropper who is in the unique position of having managed both organisations.

> CPS is a satellite with quite a lot of freedom but not as much as FI—which is an independent business, able to decide exactly what is its strategy and where it must position itself in the marketplace. CPS has a relatively captive market in the shape of a high proportion of ICL users, while FI has to go out into the highways and byways for clients. My impression is that FI's work involves more sophisticated large scale projects—although CPS are advancing rapidly here, too. Finally, there is the obvious contrast that all CPS's homeworkers are employed whereas the vast majority at F are self-employed—and the various other personnel and allied differences that stem from this. (*Hilary Cropper, FI; late of CPS*)

From the viewpoint of an outside observer, FI appears to have been behind CPS on technology but is now growing faster; CPS has a golden chance to grow far more rapidly than in the past, however. F people are slightly more independent, but some are not quite as happy with their freelance conditions. CPS are somewhat more supportive, but F may be marginally more productive. You pays your money and you takes your choice. Those survey respondents who had worked for both respected the other but were happier where they were at the moment. They are both highly effective and stimulating organisations to have anything to do with, and together they are pioneering perhaps the profoundest revolution for working mothers since the pill—not to mention its even more widespread long-term effects.

## REFERENCES

Board on Telecommunications and Computer Applications, *Office Work-stations in the Home*, National Academy Press, 1985

Clutterbuck, David and Hill, Roy, *The Re-making of Work*, Grant McIntyre, 1981

*Contact*, CPS Newsletter, July 1975, July 1984, July 1985

*CPS Standards and Procedures Manual*, 1986

Deakin, Rose, *Women and Computing—The Golden Opportunity*, Macmillan, 1984

Eosys Ltd, *Opportunities to Promote Remote Working in the Highlands and Islands*, 1984

Franklin, Diane, *et al.*, *F International A, B and C*, Harvard Business School Case Study 9-486-118/120, 1986

F International Brochure, 1986

Hall, Adrian, *F International. A Management Report on Employee Relations*, The City University Business School, 1985

Huws, Ursula, *The New Homeworkers*, Low Pay Unit Pamphlet no, 28, 1984

Lessem, Ronnie, *The Roots of Excellence*, Fontana-Collins, 1985

Lloyd, Tom, *Dynosaur & Co.: Studies in Corporate Evolution*, Routledge & Kegan Paul, 1984

Lucas, Martin, Wilson, Kim and Hart, Emma, *How to Survive the 9 – 5*, Methuen, 1986

Marshall, Judi, *Women Managers: Travellers in a Male World*, John Wiley & Sons, 1984

Syrett, Michel, *Goodbye 9 – 5*, New Opportunity Press, 1985

# 4 The Homeworker's Tale (1)

## THE CONSTRUCTION OF THE SURVEY

In order to fathom the realities of active homeworking and its management, a second survey was set up involving homeworkers and managers from the two companies. There were five managers at the very top, Steve Shirley, the founder director of F International; Hilary Cropper, the FI Group Chief Executive Officer, and late of CPS and ICL's Professional Services Unit; and Penny Tutt who as F's company secretary had been with the Group for twenty years. From CPS came Ninian Eadie, the ICL main board director responsible for the unit, and his general manager Diana Hill.

There were then eight intermediate managers. The FI contingent consisted of the UK sales manager, a community sector manager, a regional manager and the UK personnel and training manager; while from CPS there were the technical manager, a regional manager, an area manager and an early manager of the organisation, Janet Davies, who had opted for a less central role in recent years. Under them were the homeworkers, 28 in number—15 from F and 12 from CPS plus one from PMS, making 13 in all from ICL. Though a small sample, its members felt their views to be representative of the whole, and indeed no distinctions of any moment emerged other than those between CPS and FI which have been explored in the previous chapter. The names of the participants are in Appendix A and the questionnaire they answered is shown in Appendix B. Homeworkers and intermediate managers were promised the non-attribution of their remarks which ensured that these interviews were totally frank and open. For the format of the homeworking panel, see table 6 opposite.

Table 6 Structure of homeworking panel of respondents

| | FI | CPS |
|---|---|---|
| Middle Manager | 1 | — |
| Project manager<br>Senior tech. manager | 4 | 2 |
| Systems analyst/<br>Tech. manager | 2 | 2 |
| Senior programmer/<br>Senior tech. officer/<br>Senior tech. author | 6 | 5 |
| Programmer/<br>Tech. officer/<br>Tech. author | 2 | 4 |

As mentioned, one manager from Rank Xerox was interviewed in addition, plus one member of the Rank Xerox network—Phillip Judkins and Roger Walker respectively. The CPS homeworkers were, of course, company employees but apart from the managers, all but four of FI's homeworking respondents were freelance. By and large, FI panel members worked somewhat longer hours. CPS requires a minimum 16-hour week and indeed this is par for the course at FI as well. However, only one in FI was on this level compared to four at CPS, where there were two on 20 hours compared to seven at FI; for longer periods up to full-time the differences were slight. Several respondents, particularly from FI, emphasised that these were minima and that normally speaking they would expect to work longer, the rate for any additional hours being the same as the normal contract rate in either case.

The contract, however, relates to a given project and there may be nothing immediately available or suitable for the homeworker once it is finished. Unlike FI, CPS provides a minimum retention of 16 hours pay per month in these instances for the maintenance of childminding and other domestic arrangements until re-engagement on another project is possible. However most respondents were generally kept busy—at CPS particularly so—and indeed worked more hours than the minima demanded in their contracts. Two FI panellists reported utilisation rates of only between 50% and 75%, however, and one CPS homeworker also mentioned some variability in workload, though pointing out at the same time that there were remedies.

> I work 25 hours, though this varies. One can lose working time between projects and in one four-week period I only did 55 hours instead of my availability of 100. On the other hand, it's normally fairly full. If you are out of work, it's your responsibility to let it be known and keep on letting it be known.

There was also variation in the number of projects being worked on simultaneously, but most respondents had one at a time, which if large would be divided up into bite-sized contracts lasting maybe six weeks or so. Some homeworkers had been working on the same project for up to six years, while others lived much more on a hand-to-mouth basis. The internal ICL contracts undertaken by CPS were often of very long duration, whereas external ones and those at F International tended to be somewhat shorter, although F was now clearly picking up a higher proportion of longer contracts. Systems analysts and project managers, although they too could find themselves with a single large contract, were more likely to be on a number of smaller concurrent ones.

Respondents' length of service varied between one and ten years for homeworkers and 2½ to 20 years for managers, but tended to be shorter for the CPS workers, the company having been in existence for only 17 years as opposed to F International's 25. Four homeworkers were on their second spell of work with their organisation; three FI homeworkers had been with ICL and one at CPS had been with FI; three of the FI managers had also been at ICL at one time or another.

All but three of the sample of homeworkers were women and Ninian Eadie was the only male manager interviewed, Rank Xerox apart. Only three homeworkers and one manager had no children, while of the remainder the majority had two, this being the average family size with a smaller but equal number having either one or three. After their first or their second child, several had interrupted their careers for between one and six years before returning to homeworking or taking it up for the first time. On the other hand, there were others who came back to work as little as three weeks after their child had been born, having made the necessary domestic arrangements. Those who worked shorter hours tended to have very young children, but as these grew up and went to school, the mothers were able to work for longer periods, especially during term-time.

The majority of homeworkers worked partly at home and partly on site, though of course at FI they had to guarantee to be available on site for at least two days a week. Some respondents from each organisation worked exclusively on site either because they were men or had no children, or because they were able to do so during term time. These tended to be on maintenance, debugging and enhancement contracts, or were auditing other colleagues' work for quality control. CPS workers worked more frequently from home; however, the balance could change somewhat once the FI electronic mail network is fully operational.

Some 50% of the CPS homeworkers originated from within ICL and had joined when they started a family, this being historically the main source of its recruitment though now more outsiders were being successfully sought. FI has always had to push harder to recruit its homeworkers, who had either heard about the company through the press or television; or through a friend or relation; had answered an advertisement; or had worked for a client themselves, (these other alternatives all also applying to a lesser degree to CPS.)

So much for the technicalities of the respondents' panel, then, and on to their opinions, which are rather more revealing. Here, interestingly, there was little difference between F and CPS, whose collective homeworkers have been described somewhat disparagingly by an outsider as 'very nice, middle-aged, middle-class ladies with handbags, who shop at Sainsbury's'. True or not, this by no means tells the whole story. Yes, they are almost all Anglo-Saxon, aged between 25 and 45, highly educated and articulate. But there is much more to them than this. For one thing, they are supremely positive.

## THE HOMEWORKING EXPERIENCE

> Smashing! Fantastic! Blissfully convenient... A gift from above... It has to be a terrific idea... It suits me down to the ground... I can't believe my luck...

Such were the characteristic responses to the question 'What are your broad views about your experience of homeworking?', overwhelming the questioner in a cornucopia of enthusiasm. One might nurture the cynical feeling that the sample could have been especially selected by the companies, but this unworthy thought was countered by two facts. First, as the interviews progressed a few niggles indeed emerged, assuming a fairly regular pattern that lent credibility to the genuine balance of the whole exercise. Secondly, as mentioned, apart from technical differences the interviewees felt that their attitudes were absolutely in line with those of their colleagues. Even with as small a sample as this, when one establishes such a substantial commonality of shared views, it must be counted as impressive evidence.

Clearly, the proof of the pudding is in its eating too—23% of its workforce have been with F International for more than five years, 10% have received the ten-year award and there are even a half-dozen who have been there for 20 years out of its 25. CPS, though a more recent foundation, envinces similar loyalty and long-serving employment: it only loses four or five people a year, and these generally leave for personal reasons such as husbands who have been posted abroad. Furthermore, although a few homeworkers had returned to full-time employment once their children had left home or reached an age where they could look after themselves, a far greater number had stayed on to continue their careers in the same fashion. The idea of homeworking may have been conceived as a bridge between two periods of full-time work, but those who have already worked in this way and need no longer do so evidently find it satisfying enough to carry on. Only one respondent declared that she would eventually work in an office again rather than at home, compared to the half-dozen who volunteered, unprompted, that they would never want to work full-time again. It is, as far as these people are concerned, an ideal atmosphere.

> Everyone I've met has been filled with enthusiasm and this in itself is incredibly morale-boosting.

Homeworking comes over as a very civilised way of work and a most sensible use of resources, but working remotely is clearly something that also takes adjustment and can create or intensify other pressures which have to be recognised and coped with.

> There is lots of opportunity and challenge. I feel driven by the demands of the work and of my obligations to other people. This sometimes pressurises me but I can generally stand back and sort it out. This is probably because I know it fits in so well with the rest of my life, my personality, and the training I have had.

They clearly feel a great sense of commitment, having opted to work when there is every reason for them not to have done so, given the other demands on their time. Having made that decision, they are determined to stick to it—possibly the more because of the general restraints society has put upon them as women, in addition to any personal difficulties that may relate to their own individual circumstances.

> There is an aura of feminism about it. We had to make a very strong case for ourselves within ICL. I remember a man saying, 'Career prospects? Married women haven't *got* any career prospects!' That made us all mad, I can tell you. Nowadays career opportunities are more generally available to women, but normally only as long as they are prepared to work like men. What we are doing here is another and a better way.

This sentiment was echoed by another homeworker, who had joined CPS with considerable relief from a different electronics company.

> I wasn't committed to working there because although I enjoyed it very much I was not getting enough merit and recognition, being a woman. I left in a rage and spent six months trying to get work but was always rejected because I was 26, just married with no children. Everyone assumed that I would disappear in a puff of smoke to have a family. Whether I do or not doesn't matter now—it suits me down to the ground being here with CPS.

At FI, they share these views to the hilt.

> Most women can cope with the big traumas—they get knocked on the floor but they get up again. The really draining stress is the on-going continuous thing that you can't manage, and for many women in work today one of the most debilitating aspects is the constant drip, drip, drip of sexist chauvinism. It's not as vicious as it used to be, or as callous—it's generally just unthinking and sometimes even meant kindly, but it's there. Some women go under, but others simply have to battle through, and in the best possible way our organisation reflects this.

Not that this is a frontal attack in the famous War Between Men and Women. There is no antagonism towards men here, they work happily within both organisations, which are most likely to recruit many more of them in the future. It is simply that today, the aspirations of capable women to demonstrate these capabilities in the face of a substantial residue of disbelief adds a sharp spur to their already keen interest in contributing to a successful business. They also revel in being able to follow a career in management while working based from home, and are encouraged by the hope that their example will enable other women to take up similar opportunities.

The whole question of the management of these distributed organisations is dealt with at some length in Chapter 6, so suffice it to say for the present that one aspect came through very strongly when comparing homeworking with traditional full-time employment—namely that here, managers understood their team members' domestic circumstances in the light of their own experiences, and were therefore able to make the relevant allowances where necessary.

> Before, I was always under stress about what I was going to do if my child got ill or something. Here in F most of the senior people have had children and understand exactly what it is like to try and run a home and work at the same time. On the other hand, it is a two-way process with give and take. One is expected to do one's best and not down tools automatically if there is a domestic problem.

The two-way process was also discernible to homeworkers in other respects. They too saw themselves as having responsibilities as a result of it.

> Because everyone is working remotely, I realise that management is more difficult. One therefore has to be most punctilious about reporting and I keep my manager very well briefed. One has to keep strict control of what one does and document the control for management information purposes.

Several comparisons were made with traditional work patterns, but these are largely dealt with under the following section which describes the advantages and disadvantages of homeworking. However, two other differences are better worth a mention here—the first being that between homeworking and the experience of lone freelance work, and secondly the comparison made between CPS and ICL by those who had worked in both—comparisons between CPS and FI having already been made in the previous chapter.

For those who had done it, unattached freelance work got the definite thumbs down as compared to homeworking within a distributed organisation; the latter providing greater continuity and larger projects. Admittedly, the actual hourly rate is higher for a lone freelancer but it was resoundingly clear that other aspects militated against this.

> You get a better rate but you need more hours to land the business. There is the pressure of doing one's own marketing and knowing one has to pay for the nanny whether one gets the job or not. It's better actually doing the work rather than chasing the work, and in CPS I know that the pay is regular anyway.

There was also a clear recognition of the career element in a properly organised homeworking business, together with the fact that the work concerned is more varied and interesting, in any event. Solo freelancing is unfulfilling when, as commonly, it primarily covers a small business clientele, whereas the kind of projects a large organisation can attract are that much more sophisticated and intellectually stimulating.

Intellectual stimulation is certainly felt to be a bull point in CPS as compared to mainstream ICL, though ironically there are still said to be suspicions in ICL that CPS offers no career prospects. In fact, CPS provides more variety and its workers have to be more versatile than the average ICL employee. They are generalists rather than specialists, which could have something to do with the fact that they are housewives, of course. There is also a strong measure of independence and an attractive *esprit*.

The management is better here—I am especially impressed with its quality. They made sure right from the beginning that I was happy, confident and had lots of communication in both directions. They and the whole team I'm in are most professional and experienced.

In ICL if one moves regularly one can get a salary increase and it is interesting to go off and do these different things. On the other hand, you can do it too much and get labelled as a rolling stone. With CPS one can move more freely and as often as one likes without any stigma.

## ADVANTAGES AND DISADVANTAGES

As always in life, the positive has in it the seed of the negative, and vice versa. It must be admitted straight away, then, that remote working has both its good and its bad points. However, given the imperative and the will to work in this way, most of the disadvantages can either be overcome or accepted as a trade-off, it appeared.

The word that kept on ringing through these interviews was 'flexibility'. With over half the respondents mentioning it unprompted, it is obviously the ability to organise their dual role as they wish to that most of all attracts these working mothers. From the start it is possible for them to bring up a family and meet deadlines at the same time, as long as they organise themselves to do so. Homeworkers claim they normally find it quite possible to fit their work round their home responsibilities, and furthermore to adapt it to circumstances as they change. They are able to alter work patterns to suit themselves to cope with Nativity plays, dentists' appointments, or more formidable commitments like sick children or school summer holidays. They can arrange their lives so that they still have coffee with friends and go shopping. They also have the choice of sticking their heads down and working at home, or visiting the office for a little working social contact. Homeworkers can change their work patterns day by day, week by week, or month by month. F International's freelance workers can refuse jobs they would rather not take if they conflict with their domestic circumstances, or if the travelling involved is too onerous. Furthermore, they can give notice of the fact that they want to take six weeks off in the summer.

When on holiday, if it's a short break I have emergency phone cover, or for longer periods I arrange cover from another project manager or my senior manager.

Even full-timers can adapt in a flexible way, all contracts being on a month's notice anyway, with plenty of leeway within that.

I have a core time but in theory I can do my 37½ hours whenever I want. I like to take a day or two off when it suits me since I am heavily involved

> with community theatre. With a traditional job I would be expected to be in the office from 9 to 5, though.

It is not only mothers with children, then, who value this flexibility. The above quote came from a man, and another homeworker without children had a husband who also worked on a flexitime basis so that they were able to take days off together for trips and leisure pursuits. Such convenience and the independence it brings is at the core of this working process. Respondents were able to attain a rounded and holistic existence working and mothering as they pleased. 'A lot of my friends aren't even aware I work at all,' as one of them said. Finally, although sometimes crises arose simultaneously in both a work and a home context, it was generally felt that there was less stress in the conflict between professionalism and the home than when in full-time work.

The dual role was immensely important to these people, though they were strictly mothers first and workers second. Being at home when the children were there, keeping mentally stimulated and enjoying an advance in status, albeit possibly more slowly than if they had been working full-time—this was the winning combination.

> I worked full-time in another software house, and my career path came to a grinding halt when I was having a baby. This does not happen here. To a large extent people are able to work in whatever way fits in with the rest of their life—maintaining and then developing their careers at the speed which suits them.

In the past, workers in both companies had sensed some lack of career opportunity. However, the subject had recently come very much to the fore; with CPS consolidating itself as a distinct entity within the ICL group and with the introduction of annual assessments by FI's new managing director, Hilary Cropper, the career path had suddenly become a motorway. CPS people stressed that they were now missing out on nothing that an equivalent full-time ICL job would provide, given pro rata pay and conditions and their new pension scheme.

In the enjoyment of stretching both their minds and their wills, homeworkers came over as distinctly ambitious, though in a very unusual way. What switches them on is an ambition to fulfil their own potential in the interests of the team, rather than the more common male motivation of individual goal-seeking. There is something almost Japanese in the lack of internal competition and the very strong group ethos of both these organisations.

> It is a self-propelling thing and there's less spur of competition; but on the other hand one can contribute to the whole at one's own pace without

> having to dovetail exactly in with others. This means that overall there is greater work output and a greater fulfilment for everyone.

Compared to traditional work, including that in ICL, the atmosphere was felt to be very much more relaxed. Even though deadlines had to be met it was altogether a kinder life. With less direct management contact, one respondent stressed that having to be self-motivated and organise herself more than in full-time work had improved her time management and her general effectiveness. This led on to the perceived advantage of deadline discipline as a feature of homeworking, and the fact that people worked harder and more effectively at home than in an office. It was pointed out by many panellists that the home with no distractions was a most stimulating working environment.

> There isn't the chat and one can therefore achieve more. 20 to 25 hours off site is equivalent to working a 37-hour week on site—the work is solid at home and every minute is accounted for. I went on site a week ago and it took me four hours to do what I expected to complete in two and a half. I was being interrupted the whole time and the people I wanted to see were also being interrupted the whole time.

Futhermore, chunking work into short, divided bursts of, say, two or three hours at a time tends to be more productive than spending a full 7½ hour day on it. The homeworker can work when freshest and most efficient and there is no waste of time. One respondent touched on an interesting peripheral point here, claiming that the ability to make every moment count actually cut down on her guilt feelings. Although not often mentioned in these discussions, sometimes the mask slipped and it was evident that more working mothers than are prepared to admit it do suffer from feelings of guilt both towards their family and towards their employers. Trying to do two things at once and not doing either of them properly is the spectre that haunts them, although to the outside observer most homeworkers would seem to have perfected the balancing trick in brilliant style. More on this in a moment.

Many of them emphasised that they worked harder than most of their clients' employees, taking a pride in producing as much in their 20 hours a week as the others did in their 35–37½. Though they have to work extra hard to get more done, the satisfaction is more intense.

> The work is harder. People don't mess about, they clock in, and then they clock off again as soon as they stop to do something else, even get a cup of coffee. It is dedicated time in every sense of the word.

The sense of pride had another positive psychological boost for some.

> When one is bringing up small children it's very much a long-term project, and sometimes it feels as if one isn't getting anywhere. In comparison it is really good to see the end-product of some work at the end of the day, and know that one has achieved something.

The variety inherent in the work was also a bonus, being mentioned unprompted almost as frequently as the flexibility. Either homeworkers were given a series of different projects or if on a single long project, it was divided up in such a way as to make it interesting. Furthermore, there was variety not only in the different kinds of projects, but in the different software used in them and the different people they met.

As for the disadvantages, many of them represented the same factor that others perceived either as an advantage or an extension of one. Such is human nature. Thus, the ability to work hard by oneself and get things done without interruption had as its negative corollary the feeling of loneliness and isolation. Some found this not too depressing as long as they went on site every so often. But CPS homeworkers tended to go out somewhat less compared to those at FI, who have to commit themselves to be available on site for two days a week, of course. There is, moreover, the general recognition of these problems of isolation among all homeworkers, which intuitively breeds a friendly atmosphere and a sense of immediate mutual acceptance even if people meet very seldom. Formalities and feelings of shyness are shed very rapidly as a conscious effort.

However, no matter how hard they tried to compensate in this way, for some there was still an emptiness. They were not great ones for gossip and chit-chat and by their nature wanted to get on with the job in hand, but they did miss office contact. Several felt that without this it was harder to keep in touch with the progress of events, though some added that on-site workers never knew what was going on either, so maybe it actually made little difference.

> I can feel a bit cut off sometimes, and I think collectively we are not sure we know everything we should know. On the other hand I have the telephone and can always contact or visit colleagues and my manager. But if nobody has rung for a few days one does wonder why.

It is not only the human social contact—there is the matter of problem-solving. A major complaint about remote working is that one cannot physically turn to someone else for casual advice, and that people are nervous about going to the lengths of ringing up to ask, for fear of looking foolish. What is missing here is being able to compare notes with the person at the next desk and interacting informally with them to get help.

> I miss not being able to lean over someone's shoulder to ask, and learning that way. You can't check up with someone at 11 p.m. when you are hard at it and get stuck. Some people don't try what's available because they are reluctant to bother someone else about it.
>
> I have had to grapple with a package on the micro and been floundering around with it wishing there was someone to hold my hand. You can sometimes do this over the telephone, though—luckily I could go over the same procedure with someone else who also had a micro on her desk and could copy what I was doing and vice versa.

On the up-side here, it was first agreed that colleagues were far more willing to share their knowledge than was normal in conventional employment. Nobody kept a competitive advantage to themselves by guarding a skill that others did not possess. Because everyone had the same difficulties and came up against the same realities they showed an openness and co-operation that helped to defuse the problem. Secondly, people at all levels were aware of the communications difficulty and conscious of the additional care needed to foster a climate of mutual help. Not only were colleagues quick to answer queries when asked, but sensed the need to offer advice and help even before it had been requested. Thirdly, homeworkers stressed the calibre of their respective managements and their instant availability to advise and support if needed (but without breathing down people's necks); and the standards, back-up procedures and guidelines of working practice that stood behind them.

The enhanced spirit of communication, both among homeworkers at their own level and between managers and managed, also took its toll in the shape of another disadvantage, however—the tyranny of the telephone. Networking and electronic mail will, of course, help with this in the future, but at present those at the receiving end of telephone calls, though they appreciate the need for them, are very much aware of the fact. Homeworkers get irritated if the person they are trying to get hold of is always engaged or out; but conversely managers are theoretically on call all the time in the evening and at weekends when, because of the homeworker's circumstances, she may be working, but they themselves want to concentrate on their families. One manager complained that it was impossible to get away from these demands even if one was off sick, and another that she could never have a holiday at home or take time to redecorate without interruption. There was however this overriding sense of obligation to be available, regardless of inconvenience.

> I find it hard to say 'no' when people ring late at night, as inevitably they will be in some crisis otherwise they wouldn't be ringing at that hour. One leaves it at one's peril because if one doesn't answer, the problem could compound itself. Interruptions in non-working hours are inevitable

> for a manager and this and the general culture makes it very difficult to turn one's back on work.

The question of answering machines is a moot one. A few FI managers have them, but all homeworkers are entitled to them at CPS, where, though most rely on them extensively, a few find them very far from ideal. Certainly best are those that enable one to hear the message without picking up the telephone, and therefore provide the option of answering or not according to an *ad hoc* judgement of the conflicting priorities.

Whereas there was no criticism about the levels and method of payment from CPS workers, at F International quite a difference of opinion can be found. One group protested that though F 'claims to look after you', the rates of pay are low compared to what a full-time freelancer would get. These were generally those who were necessarily in it for the money and stretched by their personal commitments. But others who had actually experienced lone freelance work were in no doubt how much they preferred working for F International by comparison. They recognised that FI fulfilled a marketing function for its workforce, the time, cost and management of which had to be covered, adding that the flexibility involved also bore a trade-off price which homeworkers had to pay. Finally, some accepted that F could undercut the competition by reason of its cost structure and *modus operandi*, and was therefore in a better position to provide work for them; and that in any event being employed in the traditional mode was not that secure any more.

There was, moreover, another large group who were working primarily for self-developmental rather than for purely financial reasons. These feel that the rates are good enough compared to most other forms of homework, and that panel members have to weigh up the other benefits of working in what is an unconventional environment. These people do not by any means feel hard done by, and some of them suggest that those who complain are being hard to satisfy.

> I'm not going to get rich on it but it's fair on the whole. Maybe they could be a bit more generous, but the overriding thing is one couldn't work in this style in any other way.

> I am not a greedy person and don't think the pay is unreasonable. It's swings and roundabouts. One gets the back-up and support and the marketing and I wouldn't be any good at selling myself.

But,

> I don't have to work for the money—I'm here on a developmental basis. Some certainly do, though, and I would be less enthusiastic about the fees if I were in that position.

The fact of work not being guaranteed was mentioned by four respondents:

> There may be a contract that lasts two to three months and then one gets used to the money. If there is nothing to take its place when it comes to an end this can hurt.

> We have generally kept homeworkers well supplied with work but there is not complete security. The managers know what work is coming but the individual doesn't and there is sometimes a sense of insecurity.

> The main complaint of F's panel members is this question of there being no guarantee of work. This is because they live in the wrong place, or can't provide the hours, or have the wrong skills for a given project. 60% of the panel are employed by F only, but we encourage people to go freelance elsewhere too because it is good for them to have this to fall back on—and it benefits us when they pick up different skills from other places.

As the reverse of the coin, two salaried full-time workers complained that the part-time freelancers had it better than they did in some respects. They themselves had to take any job that was offered even if the travelling was difficult, adding that they could not easily opt out of work to take a holiday, and that they had to travel for three-quarters of an hour a day in their own time. On the other hand, a freelance homeworker pointed out that she did not get paid if she was ill, like they did. You cannot please them all.

Travelling to and from site for long distances was particularly unpopular with a few, but one countered that working flexibly she could more easily drive outside rush-hour time. Another felt the strain of constantly having to walk into a new client's department with every new project and hype herself up to relate to a sea of new faces. Some found that they were not regarded as part of the client's team, but those in CPS generally preferred to work for a customer; work outside the group was often more interesting than working for ICL itself, even though they enjoyed more frequent on-site acceptance within ICL.

Another negative aspect of not working in a traditional way was the necessarily greater reliance on the postal service. This lacks the certainty of just ambling down a corridor and picking up the right piece of paper from a colleague. And along the same lines, homeworkers found that the repair of equipment took longer than in an office, which sometimes caused frustration and even serious hold-ups as they struggled on from day to day feeling maddeningly out of touch with practical help.

But for many these technical problems were minor compared to that of the guilt, already touched upon, associated with their dual role. There was mention made here of the strain of being on site away from home and not really knowing what was happening back at the ranch. For some, the strain was that domesticity conflicted with work, sick children being a particular difficulty, while for others it was failing to switch off the work that seriously intruded upon family life.

This relates also to other problems of being at the beck and call of one's project. For managers, and indeed for homeworkers too, the telephone always rings at the wrong time, but the task at hand is as demanding as the need to communicate about it. There is always that room at the end of the house where the conscience lurks, and even those who enjoy the adrenalin-inducing affect of the deadline admit that it has its down side.

> I'm obsessive about getting things done and I tend to be twice as professional as is necessary—it's so hard to leave alone. I am also inclined to cheat myself—when I am having a cup of coffee I turn off the meter. My project manager says this should be 'think time' and I should be paid for it, but I feel uncomfortable about that.
>
> If I'm ill—too ill to go into work, but not at death's door—it is actually quite possible to be working at home on the terminal.
>
> I always want to do that little bit more—it's immensely more-ish, like tapestry. My husband says I take on too much work, but it is virtually a hobby for me. It's all to do with the Protestant work ethic, I suppose. I do feel it's essential to enjoy work, but in fact I love my work so much it almost makes me feel guilty.

There we go again, guilt—one can't get away from it. Well, even if the there are elements of guilt about, for some people it seems almost more comfortable to feel it than not.

At the other end of the scale is the criticism that the work is sometimes more mundane and less intellectually demanding than the skills of the homeworker warrant. Others, however, welcome the fact that it is less stretching and more relaxed. As a manager explained:

> People frequently join at a lower level than before and then pick up speed as their commitments reduce at home and their confidence grows. They often start by saying 'I only want a little job' having been out of practice for two or three years, maybe. But basically, they are far better qualified than that, and with training and development they generally end up very satisfied as their career develops.

By and large, then, advantages well outweighed disadvantages, and there was almost a ribald response to the suggestion that this was anything other than a most fulfilling mode of work. Reality proved to be a far cry from the gloomy pictures painted by some of its theoretical detractors.

> To try and lump us together with sweat-shop garment-makers is a real combination of chalk and cheese.

## WORK PATTERNS AT HOME

There proved to be almost as many ways of running the demands of work and home together in harness as there were interviewees. No single given pattern emerged which could be recommended to all and sundry. In the main, though, it was agreed that trying to work with a very small child at home was especially taxing. Hardly surprisingly, some who had experienced it said they would never try again, while others had recognised the likely difficulties and decided to stay with the children till they went to school without working at all in the interim. Most people who had made the attempt, as long as the demands of the work's time and content were not too enormous, had just about been able to contain the situation successfully, but a 16-hour working week was the top limit.

> I didn't want to stop working in the computer industry for five years while my child grew up, but with the benefit of hindsight I probably wouldn't do it again.

> I tried to work three months after the baby had been born but it was too soon to guarantee 16 hours so I packed it in. After another nine months I had sorted it out, though, first with a nanny and then a childminder.

A further problem with the necessarily limited scale of work in these cases is that even while in touch with technical change, career advancement is often held up until the children are able to take care of themselves. But some were determined to look after their young children at all costs.

> I have been under pressure from my manager to get a childminder but I absolutely refuse to do this. I have to look after my son myself. It isn't easy though, and with the demands made by him and my work I have not had time to make many friends.

In contrast, there was the less avidly maternal type.

> My first baby screamed for a year and I simply had to leave her to the childminder and get away into work as a release. The second one was as good as gold so I didn't have quite the same impulse.

With childminding as the chosen method, time must be taken to make a good arrangement and then stick to it.

> The problem is that you're paying someone regularly but you can't be sure you will always want them. However I really learnt it was essential to organise childcare for more time than one theoretically needs, so that sudden crises can be covered.

Some mothers happily drop their children off at the childminder's home, but others insist on them coming over so that the children can stay in familiar surroundings. But whatever the details, good babysitting arrangements of some kind or other are essential. Some had full-time or part-time nannies, others had teenagers, others relied on parents or parents-in-law, aunts or neighbours or a combination of all of these. The vital rule is to make definite arrangements for 80% of circumstances, bearing in mind that though one can never plan for the other 20%, somehow things always work out.

> A good minding system is crucial and anyone who tries to do without is asking for trouble—and the arrangements must include cover for emergencies. If you aren't sure of this the conflict will nag at you—you must be able to walk away and leave it and get on with your work with confidence.

By the time children get to school a different pattern of demands asserts itself. While mothers with small children tend to work in the evening, or at weekends when their father can take the children away and out of her hair, once they grow up and start going to school evening work is at a discount. This is now reckoned to be family time, generally much to the relief of the husband who may well have been feeling neglected in his position of computer widower. By now however, the new imperative for the mother is to be there at the beginning and end of the school day ('...I counted them out, and I counted them back in again...').

Sometimes the husband will take and/or collect them or there will be a shared car pool, and it is then possible for the homeworker to be out almost every day during school-time. Term-time is generally easier for on-site work and for clocking up the hours, but holidays, particularly the long summer holiday, are much more difficult. Mothers try to organise more off-site work then, to rely on credits of hours worked during the term, to take their own holidays, or to send their children away to stay with grandparents or other relations for part of the time. In any event, somehow the system works—at some times better than at others—but well enough in the end.

> It is always changing and never the same—one has to be a juggler. I have a childminder for one day a week, which means that I can have an eight-hour crack at home or twelve hours if I am travelling. I work when the baby is sleeping in the afternoon and in the evenings too, although I insist on keeping my weekends free.

> I try to restrict my work to the children's school hours. This is because they each play two musical instruments and I haven't yet found a deaf babysitter who can abide the constant practising. Holidays are difficult but the boys understand.

> During holidays I do more work at home. I try and make it a five-hour day between 8 and 1 which leaves the afternoon and evening free. When one is actually working at home the holidays are containable, but it isn't as easy if one is working in the office or with a client.

All in all, the super-woman bit can be stressful and requires great organisation and thought. It is the same old conflict that exists because both work and home are important to the homeworker, and something has to give.

> As far as I am concerned it's family first, work second, and nowadays housework a very poor third! I probably used to be over-houseproud, anyway—homeworking puts things into perspective.

In talking to these women it was clear that almost all of them were exceptionally balanced and stable. We shall soon be coming on to their views of what makes a good homeworker, but stability was one characteristic they none of them mentioned, probably because as far as they were concerned it went without saying. This double-life is only bearable for those with a secure emotional and psychological base, making it possible to shut out either home or work with confidence while concentrating on the other for the moment.

Apart from the supreme need for good childminding arrangements, an essential underlined by almost all respondents was the need for a space dedicated to the work. Of course, the domestic situation and the work had to be kept apart in the mind of the homeworker but above that is the need to keep the workplace physically away from the rest of the house's disruptions.

> There must be an office—somewhere separate where one can't see the washing up. One must dedicate a room to work in and have a lock on the door. A cubby hole is not enough. One needs to keep the work away from sticky little fingers, and when they are older one also needs to keep oneself away from teenage demands for a while.

Ideally, one should be kitted out with a room of one's own but this does involve the loss of valuable house space. With older children it may be enough to have a smaller personal space as long as it is sacred and inviolate.

Panelists also emphasised how important it was to draw up a plan, a starting structure for the working pattern, even if it ended up differently in the event. There was a prime need to be organised, disciplined and a good time manager. Splitting down tasks, scheduling work and reviewing it on a continuing basis are necessary parts of this exercise. On the other hand,

> The main thing is not to worry too much. You find ways of solving the administrative problems that crop up. You might not even start at all, ever, if you thought of the things that can go wrong and generally do, but they all get solved in the end. If you want to do it badly enough you can. Once I was committed, I did it and I always enjoyed it—that was the pay off.

Other wrinkles that people found useful and/or necessary, using their own words:

- To ensure it is possible to get away from the house sometime, even for only one day a week—otherwise one goes mad
- To schedule colleagues so that except for dire emergencies they ring in at one's own convenience
- To arrange to be off work at half-term and really concentrate on the family; to make weekends and holidays special for them so that they come as a contrast to the working week. This creates a feeling of general excitement which is probably rather good for everyone
- To have a second car—a single car shared between husband and wife is a recipe for aggro
- Last but almost most important of all—to obtain one's husband's agreement and co-operation

## REACTIONS OF CHILDREN

Children broadly accepted their mothers working at home and were even quite interested in some cases.

> The children always accept working as a role their mother has. What I do is perhaps more difficult for them than my going out and working in a shop, but not as difficult as my being a doctor.

Five out of the 36 homeworkers and managers expressed mild concern that their children, or more often one particular child, felt or had felt a little abandoned by the process. These were inevitably younger ones, however, and out of five respondents the two whose children were now older said categorically there was no more trouble when the child concerned reached double figures and was able to create its own life.

> The first few times one leaves the baby with the childminder and looks back at that little tear-stained face crying 'Mummy, Mummy' it can be quite a strain. On the other hand, I started working when he was seven months and didn't get into an over-protective habit, so the period of distress lasted only a fortnight or so. Further, I don't feel guilty about it

> because I know perfectly well I would lose patience with him if we were together 24 hours a day, so the upshot of it is that I am a better mother. He is now two and perfectly well adjusted.

Apart from the occasional demands of the smallest children, the offspring of these homeworkers were generally at least able to tolerate their mothers' working habits, and sometimes downright excited to go out and visit various friends and relations. One said, 'I wish you didn't go out to work, 'cos if you didn't I wouldn't have to go out to school', and had to be gently disabused of her logic. There were occasional family difficulties but the mother could almost always make herself available when needed; moreover the message generally filtered through that by working in a fulfilling way she was happier in the home, and that by earning money she could provide more for them all to enjoy. One arresting anecdote came from Penny Tutt, a long-serving member of the FI team, and the assistant company secretary of the Group.

> It was interesting that after I had brought up two children on this basis, when my daughter was adult she said, 'I would like to do exactly what you've done—to have the best of both worlds and let the benefit of that rub off onto my children, too.' Both she and her brother assured me that they were glad I had done what I had because as a result they had a more interesting mother. We could afford extra things as a family, they had had to become more independent and they were more generally liberated.

Many of the older children were clearly interested in the whole computing scene, having been introduced to it already at school. The majority tended to get involved only in playing games and fiddling about with the word-processor, however—though in essence, this is positive in that it means that these children are at ease with the computer as a familiar tool, so that in later years they will automatically rely on it. Several mothers hoped and suspected that their children would become involved in computing as a career, particularly their daughters, but some girls and indeed also some boys were distinctly averse to computers and had completely different interests. Others, however, actually copied their mothers in their work.

> My children 'play at offices'—they get desks and use a stapler, labels, paper clips and so forth and send each other messages. They have an 'office activity centre' and play telephones that connect their rooms.

Some are even more advanced—generally the older ones, of course—but one homeworker's son who was highly computer literate had actually programmed a customer's job at the age of eight when his parent was working freelance. Others had typed in lists or done small jobs of this nature—tomorrow's equivalent of 'helping Mummy in the kitchen'.

This was evidently a generation the majority of which would be infinitely more at home with computers than their predecessors have been, and in this connection they were also being exposed to the fact that women can work with them as well as men do. However, the stereotyped message they are absorbing from their peers, from their schools and from the content of children's television programmes tends to militate against this liberal view. One mother was outraged to hear her twelve-year-old son say to her ten-year-old daughter, 'it's all right for you, you won't have to go out and work when you're grown up.' The mother slammed on the brakes of the car she was driving at the time and demanded, 'What on earth do you think I've been doing for the past eleven years?' 'Oh well, Mum, you're not typical,' came the reply.

Finally, the older children were sometimes required to look after their younger siblings on occasions, which they generally did quite effectively. In addition, some had also been trained to answer the telephone in a professional manner, though others were less reliable about taking messages, with one respondent remarking,

> You might as well lean out of the window and shout the message from twenty miles away as expect any of my children to deliver it properly.

Clients and colleagues will be glad to know that the answering machine is always on.

## REACTIONS OF HUSBANDS

Many husbands were in computing themselves, the couple having originally met at work. These in particular tended to be interested in their wife's activities, *au fait* with the technicalities, and thus able to share and indeed help with the disasters and triumphs of her work—though this was not always the case. However, it is perhaps unfair to single out the computer husbands as especially angelic, as there was much evidence from those with non-technical husbands that they too were pleased, proud, supportive and co-operative.

Certainly it was agreed that the husband had to be deeply involved in the decision for his wife to work from home in the first place, and that he must appreciate what this implied. Some homeworkers, particularly those with no children, were prepared to keep the household in order entirely themselves. However, when children arrived, almost inevitably the father had to accept his share of the burden. Some were in a better position to do so—those who worked flexible hours, were home-based themselves, had school holidays since they were themselves teachers, or had been made redundant.

Husbands mainly came over very well, earning bouquets such as 'highly supportive', 'exceptionally tolerant', and the like. Some, however, primarily those whose wives were working in the evenings and at weekends, occasionally felt neglected and in need of a little attention. One husband completely took over the household when his wife was working, even going so far as to do the ironing. Most of the others, though, restricted themselves to washing up, looking after children and so forth, but some only to such 'acceptably' masculine pursuits as DIY and car maintenance. Nevertheless, there was the impression that in almost every homeworking family, a more even distribution of the parenting roles benefited all concerned and increased the sense of family solidarity. Many wives claimed that their husbands much preferred them working from home to their having a full-time job, and had encouraged them to this end.

> My husband takes a very positive stance about the whole thing and was really the driving force who got me back to work, knowing that I would need this kind of fulfilment to be happy.

The partnership of a committed husband was, then, an important factor in the equation for homeworking success. None of those interviewed were in fact single parents, though it should be added that in both organisations there are some, and that they work to great effect. However one must infer that it is more difficult for them to operate without the support that a husband could provide.

One respondent said her husband thought she worked too hard for too little, but others appreciated the extra money coming in, and indeed one couple had made a deliberate decision to get a bigger and better house on the strength of it. Another was educating her child with the results of her work, and in general it appeared that the second income was regarded as a means of attaining a higher standard of living rather than simply as pin money for frittering away. Several husbands had commented that their wives were happier and livelier as a result of this work, and there was also the largely unspoken relief that if anything happened to the husband the wife would have a career to follow. Homeworkers themselves were glad of the money their work brought them and of their husbands' pleasure at it, but for most of them the main reason for working was self-fulfilment.

A few husbands were said to feel that their wife's work was entirely up to her, but demanded that it should not be allowed to disturb her wifely function. And for a last gripe amid all the euphoria, one of the three homeworking men interviewed did comment that some husbands were nothing like as tolerant as they were claimed to be, when caught at the other end of a telephone at an inconvenient time.

## REACTIONS OF FRIENDS AND FAMILY

Only three of the 36 interviewed had met any criticism from friends over their trying to work and run a home at the same time. These incidents, moreover, were all in the early stages of their homeworking careers, and had proved obviously unjustified. However, a small number were reticent about mentioning it at all in their immediate circle.

> As far as friends are concerned, I really play down the business of working at home. I'm afraid if I went into it at all they might say, 'is she neglecting the baby?'

But another respondent stressed that these responses were few and far between.

> My friends are divided into two camps—some believe that women should stay at home and others love going out to work. Most are in this category and would jump at my kind of working arrangement.

Respondents' friends who did work voiced consistent envy at their attainment of the best of both worlds: 'How can I get in?', 'I wish I could have that kind of a job'—these reactions were repeated throughout the survey. Many friends with part-time jobs were frustrated at the lack of any career element in what they did, while one homeworker had a friend who assembled camping equipment at home and was paid a pittance on a grossly unfair basis. Then there was another friend who went back to work having had her baby and was downgraded from a managerial to a depressingly menial position. Case histories like this made homeworkers much aware of their happy lot in comparison.

Friends who did not work evinced an amazement that homeworkers could actually combine two conflicting priorities and concentrate on both. 'It's all right for you, you're clever,' was their frequent comment. In contrast there were a few respondents who had to get over the 'home knitting' image, and tactfully put across the message that they were not totally mindless.

Parents and in-laws were mostly supportive towards respondents, though some were at first a little concerned that their grandchildren would be neglected. Homeworkers with mothers who had themselves worked a generation earlier enjoyed their strong backing and approval for what they saw as such an excellent deal compared to their own in the past.

# 5
# The Homeworker's Tale (2)

## CHARACTERISTICS OF A GOOD HOMEWORKER

Does a good homeworker tend to conform to a particular psychological type, or if one is an astrologer, to a particular sun sign, say? Further research may well be needed here, but the characteristics of a good homeworker, as suggested by the panel of respondents, did fall into a specific pattern, though they were too modest to assign it to themselves. These, then, are the attributes mentioned, followed by the measure of their support in brackets, out of a total of 36. The list should be read also bearing in mind the more formal requirements for acceptability by the two organisations, outlined in Chapter 3.

- *Self-disciplined* (25)

The outright winner. This requirement was defined as the ability to sit down and get stuck in even though other circumstances made it difficult. To know that there was a deadline or an expected finishing point, and to be able to muster up the will to meet it.

> It's amazing at the end of the day when you think you have been chained to the desk for eight hours, and you look at the worksheet and see how long you've taken off to do household things. You must try and ignore these distractions.

The ability to separate out the home and the working life was a crucial feature, allied with the need not to be too emotional and over-protective towards the children. One respondent pinned it down to being able to work in a room with an unmade bed in it, and then went on to explain that this brand of discipline was one common to many computer people.

> You are that sort of person because you are in computing—compartmentalising, separating, planning things, analysing the system—it's part of the occupational philosophy.

Others, however, felt that it was more the case of having been taught self-discipline during the process of higher education, pointing to the fact that a high proportion of homeworkers were in fact graduates.

> It might be more difficult for people who have not had to study a lot in the past. Graduates have had to learn the discipline of organising themselves, and even people who have only done A-levels have been exposed to this to some extent. But someone with three or four O-levels who left school at sixteen might not have ever imbued themselves with the will to get down to it.

> It is difficult for lower grades to work at home—they are not good at making action plans for three months ahead, and so on; but primarily it is because they don't have the commitment and self discipline. This may be a function of age, though, looking at the two on-site people with whom I am now having management difficulties.

- *Well-organised in time management* (13)

This quality goes hand in hand with self-discipline and involves the ability to plan effectively, to set standards and to stick to them. Many respondents emphasised how easy it was for time to melt away at home without a timetable to help organise oneself.

> When we have our get-togethers, there is so much talking crammed into the time that one realises how extraordinarily efficient people are with their time management, as a matter of course.

- *Dedication* (13)

Homeworking is not easy and one needs a sense of dedication to do it successfully. This is enormously enhanced by having a strong reason for doing it, and at least there must be some motivation beyond the mere wish to get a little job to fill the time. Homeworkers must be volunteers and extremely keen volunteers at that, committed to success either for financial or ideological reasons, liking the work and liking the lifestyle that goes with it.

> There are two sorts of people here; the first enjoy working but like doing other things too. The second are frustrated full-time workers who are filling a gap and keeping up to date until they can return to full time working. But both are dead keen.

- *Ability to work on one's own* (11)

This falls roughly into the same package—the dedication that leads to initiative and independence, and overrides the fact that there is no one else there to take the decisions. It embraces a sense of self-reliance which can survive having little personal contact other than on the telephone.

- *Confidence* (10)

One aspect of being able to work by oneself is the need for confidence in one's own abilities; but another is the confident lack of shyness to get in touch with someone quickly for the necessary information when things are going wrong, rather than sitting there for ever in a fog of incomprehension.

> If one tries to solve problems on one's own it takes a long time; one must get over the fear of ringing up a colleague and sounding pathetic.

- *Ability to communicate* (6)

This related quality has been frequently mentioned in the last chapters.

> You need to be able to communicate up, down and sideways—if things are going well, and even more so if they are not going well.

- *Technical experience* (6)

Although some may claim that a wide range of skills is not critical since one can always learn, obviously some degree of technical experience and competence is necessary. It was largely managers who brought this one up, but the likelihood was that most other respondents simply took the requirement as read and therefore never mentioned it.

- *Flexibility and adaptability* (5)

This involves the resourcefulness to turn one's hand to anything, as demanded by the variety of the work involved.

- *Trustworthiness* (4)

It goes almost without saying that anyone working at home with a timesheet must be faithful to their employer as to the amount of time they work. Both managers and the homeworkers themselves stressed that they were by any standard an extraordinarily honest bunch, and even did themselves down in order to contribute a full whack.

> People must have the maturity to be honest. I interviewed one applicant the other day who asked 'how would my manager know how much work I had done?', and that put the lid on it for her as far as I was concerned.

- *Professionalism with clients* (4)

Homeworkers must make firm and rapid contact with clients since they are not going to be visible for long periods like those who are working on site.

- *People skills* (3)

Being easy-going, humorous, tactful and able to get on with people obviously scores Brownie-points, both as regards clients and colleagues.

- *A quick mind* (2)

A good memory for a lot of little things at once and the ability to absorb, assess and relate them to each other quickly and effectively.

## MEN AS HOMEWORKERS

Some interviewees were determined that there was no psychological reason why men could not become successful homeworkers, though they admitted that many men's job structures might make this technically difficult. Men are gradually coming into the homeworking field, however, and it is by no means an exclusively female domain any more. ('We take men if they're good enough!' they say at F International.) With a changing social climate and friendlier technology, this trend is likely to accelerate, though first of all it will be necessary for men to accept that homeworking is now more than just a cottage industry. These who expected more male participation felt that homeworking demanded more an attitude of mind rather than a given gender.

> My husband has often said, 'I fancy a job like yours—you know how I have to bring home stuff because I never get a minute's peace at the office.' As far as I am concerned he could easily do it because he does have the dedication.

In contrast, the majority found something special about the largely feminine make-up of these two organisations. This school of thought felt linked by the team spirit and shared experiences that were clustered round the common need to combine these two jobs of work and home—a spirit with which by definition men could not easily identify.

> A woman has already had to make a mental adjustment to have children, and therefore she has to recognise that her life is going to change. A man doesn't think his life is ever going to change—he just drifts on and never has to face up to the shift in attitude that is necessary.

Possibly so in the past, but one could argue with this on the grounds of the major adjustments—redundancy not the least of them—that men are nowadays having to make. Meanwhile, the other main reason given as to why men would not adapt to homeworking was that it did not conform to their stereotyped self-image. They would fear they were being pushed out on a limb away from the organisation; the requirement of 'going out to work' is part of the male hunting culture; this kind of work style does not offer the security that men with mortgage pressures need; working at home would not satisfy the aggressive urge to be visibly competitive in the smoky world of office politics.

> It might be difficult if there were a lot of men. They need the security whereas most of us are just working for extra money. They would therefore probably find it difficult to enter into the spirit that we have created. Women here are so happy to have the job that they are prepared to put up with its difficulties to fulfil themselves within it. Our employer is orientated towards the feminine and understands us. With men it could well be rather different.
>
> The archetypal male unit is the platoon or the tribe. The archetypal female group is one of women working together—gathering, sewing or winnowing grain, rather than going out and killing a bison, which although it requires team effort also involves intense competition between members of that team.

Not all males are totally sold on the office politics bit, however. Working for a large organisation, it is by no means unusual to find that 80% of the time is taken up with worrying about three unknowns—Does my boss appreciate me? Are my subordinates letting me down? And are my colleagues stabbing me in the back? It is hard to believe that there are not myriads of men who share the longing to get away from this absurd rat race and focus their time and effort upon the work at hand instead. In comparison, there appeared to be blissfully little office politics in either of these organisations.

One male CPS homeworker confirmed that many of his ex-colleagues in ICL could be tempted to switch over and join him, but held back because the two pension funds were incompatible. Nevertheless they often envied the flexibility and autonomy of his lifestyle. Meanwhile both organisations are getting more applications from men in their fifties. CPS now employ twelve out of their total workforce of 180.

They cannot take retired men, being an employed network, but they can and do take on the early retired. One of FI's male homeworkers told how he found it there.

> Though younger men in client companies are glad to have full-time permanent jobs, a lot of them in their forties realise that they could do

> the same as me and are half-envious, but half-nervous too. Once one has broken the bond, one realises one could have done it years ago—but the bond is difficult to break. It's easier for the women because most of them haven't created a working bond with an employer before. They have not spent long enough with them before getting married and having children. This is another reason why it is easier for a woman than a man to take on this kind of work in today's culture.

Another male respondent still found it difficult to get across to people that he worked at home. But his reward was that he could help to look after his children and get to know them better, while at the same time they now understood more about both him and his job. On the other hand, several of the women respondents baulked at the thought that such lyricism might demonstrate a general rule. A woman homeworker had the house more or less to herself and could work as long as there were no interruptions from the children. Men, however, would also have to train their wives not to interrupt which might prove more difficult in some cases. Some wives strongly resisted the idea of having their husbands around at home all the time anyway—like the story of the American lady who complained, 'Honey, I married you for better or for worse, but not for lunch!' This sentiment was echoed by many respondents who said they would rather not have their husbands working at home since they both needed space and interests apart from each other, as well as what they shared together. Two respondents rather unfairly suggested that men who wanted to work at home could even have personality problems, or be after a soft option.

> Women join because they are ambitious, well organised, need the money and are prepared to work even harder. They have cast iron reasons for not joining, therefore the fact that they do join means that they must really want to. In contrast, men tend to join because they want to work less hard.

Another and subtler drawback: women, being generalists rather than specialists by nature, were reckoned by some to be better at thinking of a whole range of things at once; or rather, perhaps, keeping aware of them while still being able to focus on the one thing that mattered at the moment. One of the male CPS homeworkers saw the lack of this in himself.

> A lot of women in CPS manage this better than I do. They can pick up work, do it for half an hour, go away and do something else, and then come back to it again without checking their stride. In contrast I have to work right the way through. If I worked at home on a part-time basis I would have to decide that Monday, Tuesday and Wednesday were total work days and Thursday and Friday were free.

Normally, men are not expected to do a lot of different things at the same time. CPS women can be deep in a meeting one moment, then drop everything and dash off to collect their children from school the next. Most men need everything to be in order so they don't have to spend time considering all aspects and facets of the situation. Women do this on the run, as it were.

## POTENTIAL HOMEWORKERS

So there is a diversity of views here. There does seem to be something in the suggestion that women find homeworking easier than men, for a host of psychological and cultural reasons. But with the impact of ever-friendlier networking technology many more men will doubtless discover the urge to work from a home base. The movement in this country is now focused on mothers with small children, budding entrepreneurs who work part-time for their original employer, as in the Rank Xerox model, and the disabled. There are however a number of other categories of people—both men and women—for whom this mode of working practice is going to become increasingly attractive in future.

- Those on early retirement or who are retired.
- Those with an additional interest or hobby—the railway buff, the individual who wants to devote part of his time to good works, the musician with an irregular performance schedule, or the sportsman training for the Olympic swimming team.
- Those who already have a part-time self-employed business—a smallholding or a pottery, for example. In this category there is also the couple who ply a canal boat for hire all summer after which she works from home in winter. (One caveat here, however; both F and CPS have attracted applicants who are starting their own computing consultancies and here, of course, there is an impossible conflict of interest.)
- Those who are taking a degree or some other adult education course, or researching a book.
- Those who want to live in some remote and beautiful place but still continue to work.
- Those with elderly parents to look after.
- A married couple who want to share a job and both bring up the children. If they are both working for the same employer, they both have to be very good however, and things do not always work out that way. Success is perhaps more likely if the two are in different forms

of employment—as long as they are happy living in each other's pockets the whole time, of course.

## RELATIONSHIPS WITH OTHER NETWORK MEMBERS

Homeworkers from both companies shared the view that their relationship with other colleagues in the network was precisely that—as colleagues, not as personal friends. One reason was that people did not live close to each other and distance therefore precluded much social exchange other than at work. Only three respondents had become close friends with a particular colleague, and only one of these had created a relationship which also included their husbands—who in this instance shared the same profession.

Panelists agreed that work was the focus of common interest but that they would also chat sociably together if this was indicated. Firm working relationships were built up and people enjoyed their colleagues and got on well with them. Most did not hanker for any closer involvement since they had their own friends anyway away from work. However, one homeworker who had recently moved had deliberately made the effort to acquire local friends very quickly since she was likely to be away from home a good deal. Most of them were obviously quite skilled at building relationships on the telephone. It is, however, worth noting that almost all those interviewed were mothers with children who had already made friendships from other aspects of their lives, and were therefore less reliant on work for this. On the other hand, young people on their first job use the workplace as a means of meeting new friends and sometimes partners. For them homeworking will always be considerably less appealing, therefore.

F International used to have an annual disco until it grew too large to do so any more, but now there are regional panel briefings set primarily in a work context but with a social element (even more so with the CPS equivalent, known as *'get-togethers'*). In F, panel members in some locations also come together in 'contact groups' which are purely social evenings held about every two months at somebody's home or in a pub. Both organisations also have annual conferences, Christmas lunches and so forth, and for F the shareholders' AGM is also made an important social event.

Those who had worked full-time elsewhere felt that both of these organisations created more team spirit than they had experienced with mostly male colleagues.

> We feel we are an elite, so senior people treat us as professionals not as underlings. There is no feeling of Us and Them and our project managers never pull rank on us.

> There are not the tensions one gets in a male-dominated workforce—our people here are less status conscious.

This was echoed by two of the male workers—one from each company—who described the women that they worked with as being more considerate and less internally competitive, friendlier, closer, livelier, more content and happy with what they had achieved both in their work and with their families. The feeling of good relationships in these organisations was very strong.

> None of us are afraid of personal relationship problems and perhaps basically women are better at this. I have had a colleague request a meeting to sort out personal difficulties with me and everything then came out, after which we were able to work together much better. Men in contrast are often tremendously afraid of emotional upsets. They push them under the carpet and hope they will go away. My husband has had desperate problems like this in his work where people say one thing and do another. Men feel more anguished about it and more at risk since they are worrying about their responsibilities and daren't unbend.

## RELATIONSHIPS WITH CLIENTS

One difference between FI and CPS that has been noted already is that the latter obtains a good deal of its work from internal ICL end-users. However, as explained, the new sales facility is already bringing in more work from outside customers. In any event, relationships with internal and external customers are very much the same as far as the CPS worker is concerned. And indeed, although many ICL departments now know them and the kind of service they are able to provide, nonetheless a few still require educating in the same way as an outsider. Though now far better accepted than before, homeworkers are still occasionally left off circulation lists and can be made to feel less part of the team, compared to other on-site colleagues.

Both organisations found that a new client often felt some initial uncertainty, and that the first sale could be difficult to close. The fears were: Would communication within the team be more difficult? Would the turnround take longer? And would one of them drop the job in the middle and miss the delivery date? In the event, none of these problems ever amounted to anything and both CPS and FI were obtaining plenty of repeat business. It is difficult, though, for some customers to grasp either the philosophy or the effectiveness of the system—particularly middle-aged men—and sometimes the uninitiated do keep them on a fairly tight rein at first. However, they always relax when the professional and business-like approach becomes evident.

Homeworkers are well aware of the image they need to foster and the standards they have to provide, and they try harder as a result. They emphasise that they are not merely 'body-shopping' like freelancers from an agency—providing technical programmers for a problem that has been defined by the client—but delivering a quality product in the shape of a solution to their problems. Customers soon learn that homeworkers are highly productive, committed, under control and available even at unsocial hours.

> I have taken over jobs at 12.30 on Sunday morning and 8.30 on Tuesday night and finished them for start-up time the next day.

The client does not have people cluttering up his site and can thus save valuable space in city centre offices. Homeworkers do not go onto the customer's head count, and they tend to be more than qualified for any given job. Furthermore, it is possible to have two people working on a job, each for half their time, contributing qualities that would never be combined in any single person.

> We don't take up his desk space, we don't drink his coffee, we don't obstruct his team. I am there when he wants me, he is there when I want him. I can take my micro on a journey, I can push drawings from one end of the country to the other.

Occasionally customers worry about problems of security, but these fears are soon put to rest. Occasionally, too, panel members' true calibre is unrecognised.

> Most of us feel we are a lot more efficient than the client's employees—they don't seem to know what they will be doing next week, but we have to. So it was irritating in a recent project where we were almost regarded as tea girls when actually we were more senior than the on-site staff.

There are sometimes feelings of resentment or jealousy on the part of the client's analysts or programmers towards homeworkers, who may also have to be fed with explicit answers to what might seem to be time-wasting questions, simply because they are not used to the procedure. On a long contract, everybody settles down in the end, however.

In high technology, gender is unimportant. Over the whole software field there is more or less equal recruitment of men and women, but though the numbers are in balance to start with, the industry loses two-thirds of its women over the course. Inside offices, systems analysts average out in the ratio of about eight men to three women, so people are not unaccustomed to seeing women in this position. As women, they tend to score at getting to the nub of people's precise requirements, but they can sometimes miss out by not being quite assertive enough. Male customers may be over-protective towards homeworkers, but in contrast it is very rare for them to be manipulated at work.

Some clients are so interested in the homeworking process that they borrow the technique to retain their own people on maternity leave, but this has never yet been implemented on any large scale. However, the overall picture is one of considerable appreciation. Two client companies—Avis Rentacar, and International Oil Insurers—gave refreshingly positive assessments.

> We have a small staff and no data processing department as such, so brought them in to organise our DP. We are very pleased - there have been very few occasions when we could have wished that someone was on site when she was actually working at home.
> (*John Sellars, International Oil Insurers*)

> F International have provided a very good service to Avis over the past seven years. They have very well qualified staff with 5–10 years' experience whom we have used to supplement our own DP Department. We have found that they get on with the work and are excellent at meeting project deadlines and staying within the budget. They also have a very sophisticated estimating department. We try, wherever possible, to keep the business knowledge with our permanent staff, but on the basis of past experience are happy to involve their staff at all levels. We have encountered no problems with them being home based. The relationship has worked very well and they really look after the account.
> (*Colin Bowers, Avis Rentacar*)

## CHARACTERISTICS OF A GOOD HOMEWORKING EMPLOYER

In continuation, all the interviewees were asked what they felt were the characteristics of a good homeworking employer. The question of communication and support came very much at the top of the list, here. More communication was thought to be required than usual, with managers needing to be particularly sensitive over the telephone to avoid giving wrong impressions. Since the homeworker is generally not aware of any physical management, she or he must be reminded that it is there if needed, but not overbearingly so—the manager not checking up to see if they are doing the work, but checking up to see if they are all right. The network must look after those who are in want of support and react positively to a cry for help.

This especially applied to those in FI who were without work for a time. They felt lonely and anxious, but this presented difficulties for managers who found it hard to chat constructively to them if there was nothing very definite to say. Some suggested that links for those not on projects could be kept up through training, but there are always the problems of self-employed status to consider, besides which, unless training soon leads on to practical application, it proves to be largely wasted. Of more value are meetings with colleagues, both project and regional-based, including pep-talks and exchanges. Particularly when beginning work with a distributed organisation, the homeworker should be kept in close touch with management and colleagues so as to feel a full member of the group.

But the manager has to communicate not only support but a good deal of information also, when for example the client himself fails to supply it. Powerful communication is crucial, not only between management and workforce but among members of the workforce too—though once again technical advances in networking will greatly ease this burden. Nevertheless, above all this, it is knowing when to leave a homeworker alone and when not to—combined with approachability and a sympathetic ear—that provides the sense of true delegation, of autonomy laced with supportiveness, which is at the nub of a successful operation of this kind.

In its monitoring and control there has to be a grasp of problems even before they are likely to arise. Because there is less physical contact with the worker than normal, this entails a more intuitive style of leadership. Managers have to be aware of where people are coming from and be able to assess instinctively what is going on.

> They must read the reality of things even though they are unspoken—this being essential because one is working so much more on the phone, rather than face to face in an office.
>
> A good manager here needs a good ear—she needs to be someone who listens to what is going on below the surface. Problems can grow out of all proportion, especially if one cannot get back to the person concerned there and then. The manager has to pick this kind of thing up and understand why people are acting in a certain way.

The question also arose here—an echo of the previous airing of the subject—as to whether women tended to be better at managing this sort of workforce than men, because of their inherent feminine qualities. Certainly these managers had to be multifaceted generalists, and capable of seeing things systemically rather than mechanistically. This was felt to be a mode of thinking perhaps more common among housewives than among men, who are traditionally more at ease when called to perform as intellectual specialists. Two contrary views, and one in the middle, are expressed here.

> As far as my experience is concerned, men have been pretty sympathetic—only one was ever unsympathetic to domestic problems. But they are not often *au fait* with children's illnesses and childminding. If they worked from home themselves they would understand, but if they are not able to put themselves in that position they can't.
>
> Managers have to have been in the same situation as the staff under them. Men don't talk about these problems to each other in a work situation, so it would be very difficult for a man to run a homeworking network of women. When a man goes out of his front door to work, he's single again.
>
> Other women with home responsibilities appreciate how to run a network like this—like giving someone enough notice to make domestic arrangements. But this is not necessarily because these people are women, it is because they are parents. On that basis a man could manage us just as well as long as he took a substantial share of the bringing up of his children and knew what that was all about.

Much of the secret of good communication was argued as being to do with managers first understanding the realities of a mother's life, and not imposing a 9–5 regime on staff who needed to be flexible. This then necessitated a more caring approach and an interaction with the worker as a whole person while still maintaining a sense of discipline. It involved being prepared to speak to people out of hours at times not convenient to themselves, and encouraging considerable freedom while still setting very definite targets and deadlines. This in combination has to pervade the whole business as a philosophy of balance.

> At the very top of the organisation there has to be somebody whose job depends on the home-based thing working and that person has to understand the exact nature of the concept.

Obviously the manager has to instil a high morale and foster the belief that homeworking can work. It is necessary to engender a feeling of trust and fair play on both sides, so that people do not abuse the system and respond appropriately to the relaxed but distinct control that is imposed. Reasonable pay, conditions and fringe benefits are naturally essential here, since without them the engine would not turn over at all; but there must also be congruity between conditions for on-site and for off-site workers. Respondents demanded job satisfaction with well set aims and targets, and a system of assessment and career guidance that ensured that career opportunities for advance were as good as with a conventional unit. In the absence of office feedback, a system that invited the voicing of opinions was also important to them. But above all managers should have an especial feel for people, should back up, intercede, sympathise, be diplomatic and act fast on situations so that homeworkers could see that their needs were being met.

The desirability of sound and selective recruitment was also stressed by respondents from both organisations. Then, since so much depends on good personal interaction between homeworkers, a co-operative atmosphere has to be created in which people help each other without rivalry while maintaining their own ambitions. A good reporting system with well-documented, formal procedures was also emphasised, with reliable technical back-up and an effective process of damage limitation if things went wrong.

At the traditional level, finally, managers were also expected to be soundly based in the normal professional management abilities—getting priorities right, planning and estimating, budgetary control, administration, training, marketing and matching available skills with what had been sold to the client. However, it was agreed that they had to attain a higher ranking in all the talents of management than would normally be required. This is because although a 70% performance is generally good enough in an ordinary conventional organisation which bumbles on under its own momentum, the more mettlesome and finely-tuned distributed unit requires a 95% performance from its leaders. It is more difficult to manage, so it must be better managed if it is to survive at all. This, however, has its advantageous side. By its very characteristic of having to excel unless it is to fall flat on its face, the distributed organisation must automatically rank a cut above its competitors. There is nothing especially different in the type of management required; it just has to be more effective in every way.

## HOW FI AND CPS STOOD UP

Homeworkers were asked to what extent they felt that their own employers respectively matched up to this shopping list of ideal characteristics, and on the whole marked them fairly generously. In addition to the general question on the management of their employing organisation, respondents were also asked to comment on a number of particular aspects—communication, motivation, control and supervision, contact and support, training, fulfilment and development, and finally, the incidence of any manipulation or exploitation.

### Communication

Taking communication first, a massive majority on both sides found their managers entirely helpful. Few people had felt lonely, and almost all had been in contact with their manager every week or ten days, and on occasions almost daily. One lone protester had suffered in the past from a manager who made very little contact, however.

I felt that no one cared or showed an interest, and that I was left to sink or swim.

This apart, managers were thought to look after their staffs both technically and humanely, without too tight a control. Not only were good personal contacts made but the regular regional meetings, 'Freespeaks' and project meetings were appreciated as well. Occasionally respondents came across colleagues who far from welcomed being telephoned in the evenings or at weekends, but these tended to be systems analysts rather than the managers themselves, who were always said to be approachable. Managers in both organisations are accepted as 'one of us'; having, as it was put, come up through the ranks they have all shared the common problems of working from home, and are prepared to pool their experiences. Besides having an understanding attitude, both managements were reckoned to be efficient, due in part to excellent procedures.

My previous manager in ICL never really knew what I was doing. My present CPS manager asks how I'm doing, whether I have any particular problems, what the people I'm working for think about it, and so on. I have a much firmer feeling that my work and my opinions matter.

There is an opinion survey of all ICL group employees every year in which CPS always scores extremely highly on communications, appraisals and objective setting.

In the past there had been some criticism of FI's internal communication, its career structure, and the utilisation of its human resources; and some criticism of lack of recognition within ICL and of the induction process at CPS. However, it was felt these were outdated hangovers and that in the past twelve months or so, important lessons had been learned by both managements, so that now everything seemed under firm control and set for an exciting future.

## Motivation

Most panelists were much involved in their work, but some felt this was primarily due to self-motivation and motivation by colleagues, the goal itself rather than the company being what switched them on. A number amplified this by adding that the company motivated them indirectly by providing challenging project opportunities; but also by trusting them and giving them a route for their ambitions. Managers who were generous with praise were also particularly motivating but occasionally things went wrong, as when a homeworker felt demotivated by inaccurate estimates which led to deadline and cost problems for her, due to someone else's error.

Three CPS panelists had mild criticisms. Two did not feel that they were quite part of the ICL group as yet, and the third raised the problem of induction for homeworkers recruited from companies other than ICL—now solved, however.

> I wasn't an ICL person to begin with—the others were company people and they referred to things by initials and numbers and expected everyone would know what they mean. On the other hand, there is now a scheme for new recruits to be paired with an 'auntie' which gets over this problem.

### Control and supervision

There is an active attempt to control and supervise tactfully and with balance, neither too little nor too much. Quality rather than quantity is the managers' stated aim here, and recent improvements were noted in both organisations. Four homeworkers out of the 28 felt they were given too little control and supervision, and one that she had too much. Once again, however, it depended on the project, on the manager concerned, and on the personalities of and interaction between that manager and the homeworker. A minimum contact of once a week or so was needed to check on whether people were maintaining standards and keeping to schedules.

On the whole, those who felt they needed only a little supervision only got a little, while juniors just joining had all they required. There was general approval of the way managers carried out this function, communicating effectively by telephone and trying hard to get it right. A guiding hand was always available if people had problems, but on the whole they were allowed more autonomy than in conventional work. There was, however, a substantial degree of reporting back about what they were doing—to some, this meant rather more time spent on administration than they would have preferred, though they accepted it as necessary. Lateral communication and shared control was also good—this was enhanced, as was the effectiveness of management, by the common experience of working at home.

> People, especially with small children, need a lot of support but managers who have experienced this themselves can tell when to be tough and when to be gentle with the homeworker. This is not to say that men managers will inevitably be hard—indeed they may let the homeworker get away with far too much due to inexperience in the reality of her lot.

There was a vague feeling of concern within F International about the recent emphasis on undertaking large projects, due to some fears of re-employment difficulties for panel members at their termination.

However, management planned to defuse these problems by staggering the tailing-off process, and was in general giving considerable thought to the full utilisation of human resources.

## Contact and support

This aspect of management was also appreciated by panelists, those in CPS stressing that things had markedly improved, particularly in the number of get-togethers and meetings held. It was broadly agreed that somebody was always available on the telephone for personal support or technical back-up, the latter including a long list of technical contacts specialising in various fields.

> It took me a long time to find out how helpful people are because I was just afraid to ask. The amount of knowledge available within the organisation is staggering. Even though they may be ambitious, women are perhaps naturally more supportive and co-operative. They don't see their colleagues as a threat and recognise they won't lose something by sharing it. I have never worked in such a congenial environment.
>
> My baby was allergic to food additives and was quite ill in the early stages. This was all well understood and a contract I had been offered was willingly postponed. Everyone was aware I was getting too little sleep, and I was encouraged to stay the night after a training session so that I could get at least one night's rest.

Some concern was felt by two FI panel members that the new electronic mail network could mean less travelling and less social contact in future. However, most of their colleagues discounted the likelihood of being stuck at home altogether, contending that there would always be projects where personal contact was a significant feature.

## Training

To maintain their self-employed status, F International has to keep somewhat at arm's-length from its panel members over the matter of training. Members may be invited to training courses but there is no insistence that they have to attend. Thus, in the past much training has tended to be informal and/or undertaken by means of distance learning from manuals. Though distance learning was accepted as useful by homeworkers, both they and their managers realised that people learn more quickly face to face, and furthermore that group training has an important bonding function. Distance learners miss out on the sharing of problems and successes and on assimilating knowledge by comparing notes. For those who find it difficult to leave home for training sessions distance learning is extremely convenient, however, and now much improved through the use of A/V techniques. None the less, panelists missed the subliminal input of traditional work.

> Some subjects are suitable for distance learning, but one doesn't find out things as one goes along as much as in conventional work. Here, everything is very structured, and there isn't time, for example, to pick up a technical magazine and read it as one might in an office. One can't appreciate what's happening in the industry and absorb background material through the pores of one's skin.

There seemed to be considerable variation in the amount of training that F International panel members had had. Some contended they had been offered very little, while others had been on a number of courses. The majority felt they were rather left to acquire their own skills on the hoof, as it were, but a substantial minority argued that there were always training facilities available if needed, and that people had only to ask.

> If there is a project which requires knowledge of some new technology, they will train me—it's mostly self-study but sometimes it's on client's time. F pays for the time if they endorse it but you pay for your own time if you decide to train yourself.
>
> I want to go on any training course that is available and I have made that clear within F. Consequently, I have been on all sorts of courses. I have a three-day residential course coming up next week and probably another two-day one in a few months' time.

FI panel members are paid for their mileage to attend training sessions plus a retainer of £25 per day. Some of them argued that this hardly makes it worth their while but the company cannot be blamed here; it is an Inland Revenue requirement.

> One gets paid expenses for going on these courses and a small amount on top, but not at the working rate. It is not directly cost-effective since I have to take care of my domestic situation and pay a childminder. Maybe this isn't quite fair, even though the training is useful.

Training was recognised as essential for keeping up to date in such a rapidly moving industry, besides having a secondary role in overcoming isolation. However, training for training's sake is not especially productive and must be followed up by practical application unless the new skill is simply to evaporate. FI's new electronic mail network will require more training if its true potential is to be realised—a fact that the company's management fully recognises. There is also increasing emphasis on training in fourth-generation languages. The sales force, too, is being trained assiduously, with outside consultants teaching sales assertiveness and closing techniques. Future training requirements for the industry in general were expected to enhance the popularity of homeworking.

> There is going to be a continual need to keep training homeworkers and indeed, everyone in the computer industry. Anyone who takes time off to have a child and bring it up is going to be seriously jeopardised. Networking and improved distance learning will help, but even so people will find it very difficult to take a sabbatical of any kind and come back and pick up the threads where they left them. There will therefore be an increasing call for home-based flexible working in future, because otherwise people will just get out of date.

Meanwhile, although the necessity for training in the future is recognised by all concerned, in the past neither organisation has gone without criticism. As a group, ICL is very training conscious, and everyone is expected to do a certain number of days training a year—the same applying pro rata to CPS part-timers. This includes not only technical training but also such aspects as time management, communications and assertiveness skills. On the other hand, some feel this has not been enough, even though others are swift to aver that it was all there to be asked for.

> I think the record is very mixed, and personally I haven't been too pleased about it. CPS is becoming more aware of the problem, however. Originally they thought that people would simply work with them for five years and then go straight back into full-time employment. As it happens, because they like the way of work they are staying on and need considerably more training and retraining as the whole industry changes. Apparently F have had the same experience here and are upgrading their training in consequence, too.

One possible reason for some reluctance on the part of CPS is the financial burden involved. The CPS training budget is on an overall annual basis and geared to business requirements, to which homeworkers' personal training plans have to take precedence.

> People are not as easy to train when they work remotely. It costs more, too, as you have to get them in and pay them while they are training—somehow one doesn't feel this so acutely when people are working on site full time.

CPS had bought into a number of ICL training packages, but also uses outside consultants, and is building up its own special training programmes with internal video and audio libraries. The technical authors' section seemed to be particularly training conscious.

Management training had in the past been stressed more at F International than at CPS, it seemed. Some FI managers particularly mentioned the value of the training sessions they had attended on their introduction to management—some internal and some with outside consultants —which included role-play workshops to simulate difficult conditions with clients or staff. One manager contrasted F's management training with that available to panel members, however.

> Training is very good at managerial level, but I must say I don't necessarily think that F has always lived up to its ideals about training the panel. It has not spent that much on the activity in the past and that may well have been a false economy. There are welcome signs, though, that things are improving here.

At CPS, management training was also on the up and up. All area managers have been on week-long residential courses and regional managers on three-week intensives. The top management team has also undertaken a 'third-phase planning' exercise from which emerged a blueprint of critical success factors and an upgraded Mission Statement.

### Fulfilment and development

Because of the stringent recruitment procedures of both organisations, those who made it through the hoop were clearly of high calibre already. After this, therefore, they seemed able to develop themselves the way they wanted better than most in conventional employment. Some were fulfilled simply by the variety of interesting work—they had as much career development as they were asking for, they did not want any more responsibility, and they had outgrown personal ambition. Others were determinedly constructing their careers, however, money being less essential though a useful extra. These people felt they were keeping up to date with events and with their ambitions.

> I can see myself being developed, but I wasn't looking for a career when I first joined. It just happened. I did not think about careers before and now I find myself growing into this management thing which I enjoy more and more.

One particularly positive aspect at F International concerned the new annual assessments for freelancers, to match the annual appraisals of the employed staff. These have been common practice in CPS for some time, but in FI the novelty of them had brought home for many panelists the fact that they actually did have a career to promote if they wanted to. The process revealed how they could progress either technically or in terms of management.

> These assessments are still at a formative stage. But requests for interviews were much more numerous than expected—something like 90% wanted

> them as opposed to an expectation of around two thirds. Management did not see the workforce as being as ambitious as it clearly is.

In CPS too, there was evidence of career paths opening up. Some workers had been regularly upgraded and many felt that the potential offered was greater than in traditional employment, and more specifically than in ICL as a whole. Choices were available and here also the homeworker could opt for either a technical or a management route. CPS respondents saw no limit to the possibilities as far as the company was concerned, and a new sense of respect within the ICL group for what was happening at CPS had clearly encouraged some of them.

> Yes, there is a career path. I want to do more when the children are in school, but I shan't be forced by the company to leave programming and switch into management if I don't want to. People here have more control over their own careers, which is as it should be because if you are happy about that you work better.

## Manipulation and exploitation

With CPS there was no problem about rates of pay, as its homeworkers had the same salary levels as everyone else within ICL, pro rata according to their grade. Compared to other homeworkers, their situation was extremely favourable—'a dream world', as one put it. There were only two complaints—one saying that for doing the same job she was earning less per hour than when she left employment four years ago; the second lamented that she had no guaranteed minimum when working off-site, even if because of the nature of the contract the hours fell below 20 per week. A few others found it difficult to say no to managers.

> There is such a striving towards group excellence that one is slightly forced into sustaining it at any cost. I have been asked to do things and really put on the line about them in the past, and I would not get that in an office situation. It is good for the soul I suppose, but there is a fine line for managers to tread between manipulation and getting the most out of people.

When it came to FI, one manager also admitted that the company did expect a lot from its staff, while three or four homeworkers also said they were sometimes pressurised into doing work they would rather leave, mostly because of long travelling or other geographical problems. On the other hand, three others felt it was entirely their choice whether or not they took up projects and could always turn them down. They added that since most panel members stayed on with FI for years and years, conditions could hardly be described as exploitatory.

A bigger bugbear at FI was the rate of pay, with half the respondents bringing up the subject. Four were quite adamant that the rates were too low—they claimed they could get £1 to £2 per hour more working freelance, and if the rate slipped any further compared to what was available outside, they were liable to go back to full-time working eventually. But more of those who had reservations about the rate also admitted they had not got the confidence to market themselves as lone freelancers, and that they would find hunting for contracts psychologically difficult. Further, the lone freelancer is solely responsible for the work in its every aspect, whereas at FI worries are resolved through managerial back-up or discussion with colleagues.

Some pointed to the fact that FI workers were paid a fortune compared to other part-timers. Outsiders might possibly feel that F exploited them, said some others (and two or three from CPS thought that it probably did) but they argued that surveys of the rates paid by competitor software houses were carried out regularly, with F fixing its own scale somewhere around the middle of the range. They added that all expenses were allowable, including a generous travel allowance, on which some people ran their cars entirely. In the end there was only one panel member who stated defiantly that she did not accept the various arguments put forward by F in defence of their rate structure, and that they did not spend as much money on the panel as it deserved because the company had lost money on various extraneous projects.

## PAST, PRESENT AND FUTURE

> I have developed my own self-esteem and self-confidence and grown enormously in my attributes as a person. This is reflected in my husband's and my family's eyes. But also in general there is a greater sense of awareness about. People are saying to themselves 'How can I best play my part in helping the company achieve what it's setting out to do?' and 'Hurray, I'm in it and we're going places!'

The survey's few criticisms did more to evince an air of authenticity than to cast doubt on either of these organisations. Most comments, like the one quoted here, represented a ringing endorsement of the pair of them and of the future for homeworking in general. The past may have held its share of problems but the future looked more than encouraging. Hilary Cropper and Diana Hill were leading their respective organisations in a manner which reflected the aspirations of their teams.

> We are now working on projects that involve analysis, problem definition and feasibility study. We are moving further back to the source of why people actually want computers in the first place, and also moving further

forward to take in the implementation and training at the end of the installation process. In future programmers will become senior programmers and systems analysts, who will be capable of doing the more complex user friendly programming that the computers themselves cannot.

Clearer career paths, closer communications and wider intellectual scope were both recorded and anticipated, with the two organisations' controlled expansion and progress. Respondents expected them to grow well up to or greater than the average industry rate, particularly as there would be more publicity for and acceptance of the homeworking method in line with technological advance—meaning bigger sales and a boost to recruitment on the horizon.

> The technology is clearly going our way. There will be more standardisation of equipment and before long everyone will have a common interactive tool. We will thus be able to message each other completely, which will lead to a far deeper integration of the unit.

Equipment changes will make possible not only remote programming for direct input to the clients' mainframes but also remote diagnosis, once more emphasising the total project approach, with the need for more training in special technical skills and an even greater emphasis on team-work. Management information systems will be able to be accessed internally from the network and a more professional use of statistics will also be possible. However, this technological paradise could have its teething troubles, if some experiences to date are anything to go by.

> If one is working at the peak period between 9.00 a.m. and 1.00 p.m. or on a windy night, the telephone is an irritation—it can take 60 minutes to do something instead of 20. One simply gets rubbish on the screen if the wires are being blown about. I also have a black box which removes the errors, but in that case there is just a blank when nothing happens, which is also infuriating.

Tomorrow's more complex world will require higher capabilities. This will entail a greater emphasis on training, but many people in both organisations are already working beneath their full intellectual capacities so that there is a talent residue and an elasticity of potential which will be able to absorb the demands made upon it. Programming will be needed whatever the forecasters say; it may well be upgraded but the need for the skill will endure. Thus both businesses are liable to become more expert as the industry becomes more sophisticated. They will be working on larger projects and with larger teams.

There was some difference of opinion as to whether this would mean more work off-site or on-site. An increase in on-site work was expected within CPS in the shorter term, but ultimately the pendulum ws thought likely to swing back the other way as under the influence of technological change, face-to-face communications become less important in theory. In FI where the implementation of the network is providing a foretaste of this, there is however a clear realisation that people need human contact and will still want to work on site for part of the time, or at least have project meetings, team-building and training together.

> Some on-site work is vital since people must get out. We now have a disabled man who will come into the office and go upstairs backwards on his bottom rather than being cooped up at home the whole time.

Looking further forward to the closing years of the century, the majority of the survey's respondents were not thinking in terms of working after their husbands had retired or once their children had become independent and left home. However, over a third of them felt they were still likely to be homeworking—or telecommuting, as by then it would have truly become—just because they so much enjoyed the variety and flexibility of this working mode. Having once tasted it, they profoundly hoped not to have to change back into traditional employment, at any rate. Some who would be approaching retirement age by that time were looking forward to tailing off their activities gradually, and saw this as another big advantage over a conventional full-time job. But the final stages of their working lives were likely to be very different from the early days.

> There will be further application of the technology towards the wholesale sharing and distribution of intellectual knowledge, piping it in and shunting it from country to country so that we will then become truly International—an international software factory. This ultimate concept is light years beyond the original basis of a few mothers with small children.
> (*Hilary Cropper*)

# 6
# The Manager's Tale

The CPS and F international managers in the survey answered a similar, though somewhat less structured questionnaire than that used with the homeworkers and panel members themselves. It focused more on management aspects, and they were asked, among other things, to comment on the advantages and disadvantages of distributed working to them—as managing a business organised in this way.

## ADVANTAGES AND DISADVANTAGES FOR MANAGEMENT

The chief advantage came though clearly as the commitment of a qualified, experienced, self-motivated and productive group of people. Some managers who were required to work with other extraneous personnel on site found them to be of a lower grade and more difficult to deal with in comparison. Homeworkers are paid for the work they do on an output basis—here just as with Rank Xerox—whereas to these managers it seemed that the others felt they were paid simply to attend work. In the case of F International, a further related advantage lies in the fact that a self-employed workforce involves fewer fixed overheads, so that the company can respond to the fluctuations of the market and act far more flexibly to meet clients' needs. The concept of variable overheads extends to CPS as well:

> The fact that people are only paid for the hours they do means that the head-count is a variable rather than a fixed cost. As such the Group has less control over it, but doesn't need so much control. The whole outfit is therefore freer and more flexible, and can operate in a way which is actually more attractive to the homeworkers than they would otherwise be able to enjoy. Both sides benefit as a result.
> (*Ninian Eadie*)

This is a more exciting and exacting world than traditional employment—the tempo has more peaks in it, every contract has a deadline. Morale is therefore high in both these organisations, but this too can lead to problems of comparison with ordinary on-site workers. Running such a business is no simple matter. With expansion there is a constant search for above-average senior managers who must be specially trained to meet the requirements of the position. Certainly, the experience of having worked remotely themselves was invaluable for managers, but there was more than that to the job. Overall, the demands on management were higher than normal; all the well-tried traditional techniques were needed, but they had also to be applied with particular skill. These managers were constantly aware of the fine balance between consideration and firmness, being sensitive to their homeworkers' situation without letting them get away with it. Much of their work involved a counselling role, and they tended to draw on their own experience for helpful advice.

> Managers must know the staff's environment and any special considerations that may be difficult for them—like having a disabled child—far better than managers do on-site. They must be empathetic, but not maternalistic towards their homeworkers—knowing how far to push them and also how far to let them have their heads.
> (*Diana Hill*)

All this involves higher than usual management overheads—not only better managers but more of them, too. The other major expense common to all distributed businesses is, of course, communications; here overheads are also higher than normal, both as regards time and telephone bills. High-technology networking will ease the problem in future but will not cure it entirely. At a personal level, managerial communication needs to be strong but not overpoweringly so, combining 'ear-stroking' with a high information content.

> Most organisations with ordinary offices don't know they have a communication problem, even though they do. Being distributed, we realise we have an automatic and inherent communication problem, and therefore we tackle it. As a consequence, traditional office communication is frequently not as effective as ours. I have recently supervised two teams in a conventional situation where I could easily see the problems in the interaction between the sub-systems: but the individual office-based managers to whom I was reporting never saw them, even though they were working next door to each other.
> (*Janet Davies, CPS*)

Because the work has to be output-oriented, in order that homeworker and manager can agree objectives between them and gauge precisely how far they are being met, procedures need to be both formalised and simplified, with written reports measured against targets. Paradoxically, in order to create the flexibility both for homeworker and client, the business itself has to be more structured, with more care taken over procedural matters—by fining them down to the bare essentials so that every facet counts, rather than relying on the traditional blanket of bureaucracy.

Another difficulty for managers has been the recruitment of suitable homeworking candidates, especially those prepared to go largely on site. Both organisations demand four or five years' experience from applicants but they also demand that they conform to a certain personal type. This, though a hard row to hoe, is well worth while.

> One doesn't employ anyone who is not experienced and excellently suited—therefore it's possible to produce a fast and completely conceived job. It is much better to have work done by a single brilliant person than by five average people who require a lot more supervision.
> (*Diana Hill*)

Mavis McLean presented a paper 'Negotiating the Boundary Between Work and Family' at the Marriage Research Centre Conference in January 1987. What she found as a consequence of her research was that in homeworking really effective recruitment was a vital constituent of the management package. The investment of the company is so great in terms of training and management and the trust has to be so absolute, that even more stringent requirements are needed by the employer of the employee than when the employee is in conventional employment and constantly under the boss's eye. Domestic complexity makes this all the more difficult, and homeworking is therefore not an easy option for the single parent. The recruiter has to be convinced that the potential recruit is emotionally stable, and McLean suggests that employers tend to avoid the emotional tangles that may be the consequence of a recent divorce. In her view, therefore, women who are working at home tend to be more stable than the average.

Both CPS and F International have attracted a steady flow of new entrants, sufficient to cover needs, but certain areas have proved more difficult, particularly the North, where characteristically middle-class wives do not go out to work as much or entertain the thought of careers that might threaten their husbands' egos. It was thought that recruitment problems could well have deterred other potential employers from setting up similar operations. There was however a sense of hope among respondents that the increased publicity surrounding the success of both companies would encourage more applicants in future—especially since they tended to be triggered more through word of mouth than by advertising.

A further demand on managers is the necessity to read new recruits very quickly and assess their personal and technical capabilities, since unlike in an ordinary office relationship they will probably not meet each other very frequently afterwards. Parallel to this is the difference in training between the traditional and the distributed business. FI and CPS found training more demanding, since in offices there is a constant informal learning process but here, homeworkers have to pick up everything on their own initiative. More formal training is therefore necessary to fill the gaps. But for FI at least, the company cannot be seen to be overemphasising the training aspect for fear of threatening its homeworkers' self-employed status.

The foregoing reflects much of what has been previously gleaned from the answers of the homeworkers themselves, and it is reproduced here for that very reason; to emphasise the unusual oneness and sense of integration to be found in both businesses. Whether manager or managed, it made no difference to the answers, and the claim that there was no us and them in either house was a valid one. This must be highly encouraging to all concerned.

## THE SENIOR MANAGERS' REVIEW

> Why is none of this being replicated by other people? Other people probably only find it possible if the remote workers involved can operate a separate entity. It is very hard just to say, 'Oh, now we're going to disperse our accounts workers.' Senior managers also have to have the commitment to make it work, and when they are not committed it doesn't work.
> (*Frits Janssen*)

In answer to that comment, the six senior managers interviewed —three from each organisation including Janet Davies of CPS—were asked to put all this into a wider context, especially as regards its actual and potential impact on the outside world. Certainly, the two organisations, especially FI which has been around longer and is moving up the City escalator towards a probable quote, are becoming better known for their unique features in informed circles. However, with both of them, the general image has been somewhat woolly until comparatively recently. People know them as 'those businesses run by women', and that they do whatever it is they do rather well. But what exactly *is* it that they do...?

Certainly, few have succeeded anywhere else in emulating their ability to manage large numbers of people remotely, and why this is so was a question that exercised several of their top managers, just as it did Frits Jannsen. They are a remarkable bunch, for a start, having had not only a baptism of fire but a confirmation to boot. Because so few women went on working after marriage in the past and the bars on female managers were so unyielding, British business now has very few senior women managers in their forties and fifties. Those that there are, who have had to survive against prejudice as well as ordinary business strains, are therefore by now remarkably battle-seasoned.

> Nobody in their right mind would start an organisation like this! It needed someone like Steve to do it.
> (*Penny Tutt, F International*)

> Others have tried to do all this and failed—Marconi, the Dataskil department of ICL and so forth—mostly in the early 70s. Why I think it never took off anywhere else is that CPS and FI are both independent enterprises run by people whose own success is tied in with the success of that enterprise. We have either to fly or to crash and there is no third alternative. This forces one to be precise and extremely disciplined as a manager and makes for good quality leadership.
> (*Hilary Cropper*)

It all comes back to the argument that there does not have to be any unusual kind of management or any difference in style or technique to run this kind of organisation—it just has to be extremely good. And, interestingly, the flexibility and the very fact of decentralisation helps this to happen.

> When you go home to work as a manager those left behind in the office grow as a matter of course, since they are forced to act on their own initiative when you aren't there. It requires faultless monitoring procedures but as long as these are effective, this way of working provides an excellent spin-off in the creation of new management talent.
> (*Penny Tutt*)

> Managers must be more organised because they are remote from their workers, and this means more and better systems. But also, a manager who is given extra responsibility responds. She will seize on the opportunity to make decisions and act on her own initiative.
> (*Diana Hill*)

One still asks, though, whether the high proportion of women managers has more to do with it. Commentator Rose Deakin describes FI as illustrating that women do make a special contribution to management skills because the company, founded by a woman who understood the average woman's problems, met them on their own terms. It was thus able to extract contributions from them which they would be unlikely to provide in other circumstances, either because they were reluctant to do so or because they were not given the opportunity.

> There is an unusually high proportion of managers in the company because of its peculiar problems, and the majority of them work part-time and from home as well. This would be unthinkable in a normal company and yet it

> manifestly works, leading one to believe that the major obstacle to this kind of structure is hide-bound thinking. Its 800 workers cannot be so very far from a normal distribution of the professional population even if they are self-selected and following an unusual pattern.
> (*Rose Deakin, Women and Computing: The Golden Opportunity,* 1984)

Hide-bound thinking is indeed probably the most fundamental reason why it has never worked anywhere else. There is a lot of it about.

> What's blocking other people I talk to about it is that they cannot flex their minds. They react by countering, 'Ah, but' or 'yes, but'—not looking for ways of adapting their own thing, just merely defending its status quo.
> (*Steve Shirley*)

Take just one aspect. In both enterprises there is an unusual freedom to make mistakes. Outsiders have criticised this in the past, but it means that people grow remarkably. High standards of quality and productivity are demanded from the top downwards and inefficiency and sloth are jumped upon from a great height. But genuine mistakes are pardoned quickly, and lessons learned from them. The system is allowed to throw up freely admitted mistakes so that it can be improved as a result. With the traditional management method of blame, guilt and punishment, errors are buried six foot down by those who perpetrate them, and the system is never improved. No one dares admit it is imperfect for fear of getting clobbered themselves.

The corollary here is that, particularly in an organisation that has grown like the proverbial mustard seed, there is a need to find safe slots for those who have been outdistanced by the pace of the company's development. In F International they have a splendidly feminine answer to this one.

> There is need for some kind of personal security to allow for re-grouping and structural development. Our way is to play down stereotyped positions on the organisation chart. Status here is signified by having a gold bracelet or a gold watch for ten years service - and this is awarded from the top to the bottom regardless of position or contractual relationship.
> (*Steve Shirley*)

Another feminine feature is found in the team-building processes of both organisations. Women perhaps have a greater tendency to look for people's strengths because many of them suffer from a deep-seated conditioning that they are not good enough themselves. So although the conventional wisdom has it that the strength of the chain is that of its weakest link, the strength of a women's team like either of these, uncluttered by internal rivalries, is its strongest link. The shift in perception from the egocentric I to to the team We produces a great surge in voltage.

> In our team the will, the driving process is noticeably more focused, shared and coherent than in other companies I have been closely involved with.
> (*Steve Shirley*)

There is also something here which stems from the ability to take a broad view and see all sides of a situation at once. It is wrong to stereotype differences between men and women, but, as was emphasised several times in interviews with homeworkers, most women seem to find it easier than most men to perceive the whole and to live with its uncertainties and imperfections. The male approach is, all too frequently, to take it to pieces and try to put it right like clockwork, bit by bit. They may not understand that though some questions need asking, they don't necessarily have an answer, and they are often ill at ease with paradox. Women are happier about this.

> Success in this kind of organisation is something to do with solving the paradox of needing both flexibility and the discipline required to solve that flexibility.
> (*Diana Hill*)

> I quickly realised that if you optimise the parts you will probably be far from optimising the whole. We can only function properly if all the teams can see the whole picture.
> (*Steve Shirley*)

For everyone to see the whole picture adds another dimension to the whole process of communication. The need for it, both technological and personal, has shone through every facet of these case histories. Their very existence is built on the concept that people communicate with rather than commute to an office. When all the members of an organisation have their own nodes linked electronically to each other and to central ganglia, and are able also to interact with the world outside, then the organisation becomes in effect a living brain. But then, the strength of the strongest link truly comes into its own, and the communication of that strong vision is of paramount importance. The inspiration of team leadership at the very top spreads through the whole as the members of each management team at every level individually build up their own teams, and the royal jelly permeates by communication throughout the entire hive.

Again, it is no accident that the metaphor that comes to mind here is an essentially feminine one. In a distributed organisation, people are linked by trust as well as telecommunications. The old-fashioned 'go there' style of leadership is out, and has nowadays to be replaced by 'come here'. People are not prepared to be pushed around any longer, and 'management by laceration' is increasingly at a discount in any form of organisation today, not only a remotely organised one. These two, CPS and FI, are now demonstrating a new way of patterning work and how it can be enhanced by technological means, but they are also demonstrating the essential human flavour of all successful future management. There is nothing actually new about it, however—it is just the very best of the old, adapted to new circumstances.

Men should take heart, therefore. There has been a keen debate among the interviewees as to whether men could comfortably work in such an organisation. Old-fashioned traditionalist men can quite evidently not do so, either as homeworkers or their managers. But if women claim that men do not have it in them to operate in this fashion they are mistaken. It will be a learning process for some men to utilise parts of their nature they have not previously felt relevant to the working environment, and which they may have even felt were dangerously irrelevant to it. It will mean exercising some painfully untried emotional muscles they did not even know they possessed. But possess them they do, sure enough.

> I recently went down a Wakefield coal-mine, and here there was a sense of familiarity which was very interesting. Like ours, it was a process involving output-based remuneration, mutual support and safety and a very strong reliance on teamwork and communication. I'd have felt more at home working there than in a great many other jobs.
> (*Steve Shirley*)

Much stress was laid in the interviews on the fact that managers had experienced for themselves the problems of their subordinates in the difficult task of balancing the demands of the home and working life. However, if there is to be growth in these enterprises, it would soon seem to be necessary to widen the recruitment of managers to take in more outsiders. Bringing in new management blood can be equivalent to taking on board a team of consultants—FI has found that they keep them in touch with all kinds of new things that are going on in the outside world. But at the same time, they have to be trained to work within the organisation's own culture.

> As far as management by empathy is concerned, it did make you understand at the beginning how you had to behave, having done it yourself. However, now people are coming in as full-time managers who have never worked part-time, and this will become a common theme in future. There does, though, have to be a perception of the whole person by managers and this is not yet so usual. It is easier if you have done it yourself, but new managers will just have to learn how to behave in these situations even if they have not themselves experienced them.
> (*Hilary Cropper*)

The sharing aspect is never going to be lost, however, since the networking phenomenon, both technological and personal, strengthens the ability to communicate shared experiences. The FI Freespeaks are very much a manifestation of this, but CPS has its own parallels too.

> By getting people together for a strategy conference, say, the very process commits them to the course adopted because we ensure that people can see how their current role fits into the overall plan.
> (*Diana Hill*)

The shared intensity of early triumphs and near-disasters is an engine that still powers both these enterprises, and provides a vital clue to their continued progress. Common involvement is all. Admittedly, they have a great deal going for them by being largely homogeneous groups—socially, sexually and intellectually. Being, as working women, members of what is a normally somewhat disadvantaged group they do stick together that much more closely in order to prove themselves—this being perhaps another subconscious reason why they are not very competitive internally, but give full rein to their ambitions when competing in the marketplace. Because they feel open and unthreatened by each other, they actually listen to each other—to what is said as well as to what is not said—rather than working out what they can say next when they have a chance to chip in.

Not every commentator is totally approving, though. In *The New Homeworkers*, Ursula Huws sees FI as having developed a particularly demanding method of exercising strict control over its panel members. First, she points to the great emphasis that is placed on the accurate estimating and monitoring of jobs. Secondly, detailed staff performance records are kept, including qualitative comments and quantitative gradings on each panel member going back to the very start of the company. Thirdly, there are very high management ratios; and fourthly, all assignments are broken down into discrete and relatively short time-periods so that staff have fixed targets they must meet at regular intervals, with reassessments being carried out at each break-point.

It clearly works, however, and having established a successful culture, management can only perpetuate its own style by selecting as other managers those who also speak the same language. As such, these two units recruit from outside and grow organically from within those who are not only communicative team-builders with a holistic outlook but who are firmly oriented to change. Naturally it is to be hoped that any change will be positive in nature, in which case these managers will be able to grasp the opportunities it yields. But sometimes change may be negative, when they will also have to be able to overcome its dangers. There is no room in tomorrow's management for the change averse.

All this emphasis on good management is, of course, expensive. There are both more managers and more tiers of management than the pundits might consider appropriate for a professional organisation. But in practice they are worth every penny, in two senses.

> Overheads are not spent on rent and rates, but they are spent on communications—our telephone bills are horrific—and on management. But these expenses are variable—when times are bad one can damp them down and when times are good one can gear them up.
> (*Steve Shirley*)

> The final plus is that an organisation like this is very easy to manage once it is set up efficiently with the right management. I have far fewer problems with this particular unit than with some of my other responsibilities as a main board director.
> (*Ninian Eadie*)

It is easier, after all, to deal with a pool of self-motivated, intelligent, ambitious people, even if the natural process of team-building cannot take place through physical proximity like it generally does. But also, where the overall goal is so clear—enshrined particularly in its Charter in the case of FI and in its Mission Statement in the case of CPS—since physical proximity is not a feature, the constant rearrangement and regrouping of teams is far more feasible, which is why once again flexibility is such a strong characteristic of these project-based organisations. They can be broken up so much more easily into semi-autonomous geographical, sectoral or functional parts, some of the latter being of a non-operational or staff nature, such as legal, planning, technical or whatever—forming and re-forming so that the individual's experience in each is diffused around the whole. It is this stage that is now being entered upon, particularly at FI which is older, larger and more independently able to do this.

One therefore sees leadership in such circumstances as almost not the characteristic of the person so much as that of the entity itself, which if set up on this distributed basis demands and automatically receives the style of leadership that will most suit it. That will ensure its survival, in fact, since the old-fashioned autocratic approach would kill it off in a flash. It is an extraordinarily healthy plant, a system which grows in lusty fashion if allowed to do its own thing and to be its own thing organically—subject to appropriate pruning. But with the introduction of some alien outside substance, some artificial controlling agent, a distributed organisation such as either of these would wither away.

Much of the leadership here has been intuitive in the past, and successfully so. But there have also been attempts to look for technical reasons to back up instinctive personal judgements.

> Personality testing definitely comes into this—we've recently used the Myers-Briggs method, and earlier the Luscher colour testing here. We don't intellectually analyse every problem in the light of the individual

characteristics of team members, but rather, it works by creating a mood, a climate of trust—once everyone has seen everyone else's personal assessments and knows what makes them tick.
(*Steve Shirley*)

These psychological insights into themselves and others accelerated the understanding of each of the team members into everyone else's capabilities and characteristics. Thus when differences of opinion arose after that, people were not regarded as being stupid or obstreperous but just as seeing the problem from a different though tenable point of view. This illuminated it, and made the final team solution better than it would have been if owned by any one individual alone.

At the top of FI, too (CPS, as a unit within a larger group cannot replicate this) there is insistence that common ownership and contractual worker's participation in the company's equity is as important as their participation on the strategic side, in order to ensure that they fully identify with the organisation. Though few of the actual panel members interviewed in fact echoed this sentiment particularly strongly, other and more detailed research certainly bears out the contention.

So, then, there are lessons to be learned. The first is that here are two successful operations, not one. Although CPS was set up a while after FI, it too has made it, and under very different circumstances—as a federalised unit rather than an independent one. This shows clearly that the phenomenon is no mere flash in the pan, and that it can be a plausible model for a variety of organisational structures. It is therefore of general rather than particular significance.

Secondly, now that the phenomenon is becoming more widely known, both organisations are being bombarded with requests for advice on how to set up similar ventures—clients and new contacts from within the UK and all over the world are avid to explore how they can also reorganise themselves on a remote homeworking basis. Homeworking, due to a combination of technological and social change, is just about to start climbing the steep part of the curve, and the awareness of this is in the air. The prosperity of business in the UK and elsewhere will depend in future on a large number of small, extremely efficient organisations, and the discipline required to make these function will be irretrievably bound up with management lessons learned here from the distributed working mode.

As far as the scale of the operation is concerned, on the up side, neither CPS nor FI see any particular restraint on the number of people they can manage in this way or the profits they can deliver.

There is no limit as far as I can see—no problem about having double the number of people, with the same management team, which could take

> our revenue up from £10 to £20 million. Once you have a success you can attract them and spend your short term profits on communicating to them and managing them so they are motivated. The management style would have to develop further of course, but it would be an organic development.
> (*Steve Shirley*)

> I want CPS to grow as fast as it can; at any rate we should be able to get over the 1000 mark. But once you get a lot bigger than that, communications deteriorate and bureaucracy sets in.
> (*Ninian Eadie*)

In principle, scaling down to the dimensions that will be most effective in future implies the corresponding break up and federalisation of large companies into small inter-linked networking units. This, however, is likely to prove a much more difficult process than for small organisations to grow to a viable size. The reason is purely one of power—few of today's senior managers will have the nous deliberately to reduce the size and elaboration of their spheres of influence; that would be tantamount to abdication in the traditional tribal culture.

But returning to our two prime examples, they are both making history and they delight in it, hard grind though it may be. They pay dearly for their uniqueness—pioneering is tough work and there is always the danger that someone will creep up behind them and steal their clothes. The trick here will be for them to keep on opening up new markets and creating new products out of their experience, but the whole team philosophy and the proven effectiveness of their communication gives them enormous advantage. They have far less staff turnover than their competitors, who also have fixed overheads where they have variable ones. They are thus protected against any sharp downturn and can move faster and more determinedly into new markets as soon as they appear. They understand the concept of management by project, where production is not only formulated in terms of output but also in terms of measurable quality. They trust, manage and develop their people well. The odds must be that they will continue to succeed.

## THE FEMININE IN BUSINESS

> A greater feminine influence is excellent for business and I am thankful that women are beginning to play a stronger role. We won't get industry right until there is much more female input, and I don't mean surrogate men. Up till now women have felt they have had to compete on a male basis but this is not so any more. We need all the brain-power we can get from both sorts of brain—from both the masculine and the feminine viewpoints. Business has been much too male-orientated in the past, but there is a vast improvement among the young.
> (*Sir Peter Parker, quoted in Francis Kinsman, The New Agenda,* 1983)

In his book, *Megatrends*, John Naisbitt has described how ten new trends are transforming the whole fabric of society and hence of management also. Two of them together have a major impact that is highly relevant to our study. The first is the emergence of what he calls the new variegated workforce—no longer dominated by the male breadwinner, but younger, better educated and increasingly female. Hand in hand with this is the demographic revolution of working women by which so many more women are continuing to work except for a few months or years when they are fully occupied with raising children. As he tells it, today's women workers are re-inventing both career patterns and motherhood—and etching their new life-styles on corporate policy in the process. Plenty of other distinguished thinkers have made the same point.

On the down side, Kurt Waldheim, as UN Secretary General stated to the UN Commission on the Status of Women that women represented half the global population and one third of the labour force, but still received only one tenth of the world's income and were responsible for two-thirds of all working hours. On the up side, the Harvard Business School graduated its first women in the 1960 MBA programme, and by 1971 women were still less than 4% of graduates. That year Stanford had under 1% and Wharton 2%—but all of these, recognised as being among the top half dozen business schools in the US, now graduate one third female MBAs.

The implication is that the feminine influence on business is here to stay, and since homeworking offers a totally new solution to the old conflict between working and staying at home, intelligent women will accept it avidly as long as they can be assured that their careers are still maintainable.

Homeworking, however, is just one part of the process whereby business will increasingly have to come to terms with the new conditions that technological and social change are combining to create. There is, in fact, a new feel about in the world of management. For a long time to come there will always be numerous men prepared to play the old game of winner and loser, torturer and victim, as it applies to internal business relationships. There are great quantities of people around who have not yet appreciated their own wholeness, let alone the potential for wholeness in business. But like holistic medicine, holistic management that not only combines the best of masculine and feminine characteristics, but also takes account of the whole person—financially, intellectually, emotionally (and dare one say it, spiritually)—will be the mainspring of post-industrial society as it evolves to meet us, a concept that is explored more fully in Chapter 9. CPS and FI have adapted their essential femininity to compete to great effect in a masculine business world—increasingly, male managements will also have to take on board some of these feminine business concepts and combine them with their masculine thrust if they are to survive the waning industrial age.

Charles Kiefer and Peter Senge, contributing to *Transforming Work* observed a new management style, mainly in small organisations and characterised by:

- a strong sense of purpose and a broad vision of the future
- a close alignment of members of the enterprise at all levels, involving commitment to this shared vision
- a shared sense of ownership and a personal responsibility for performance
- a decentralised and flexible organisational structure
- an environment that emphasises the growth and empowerment of the individual as the key to corporate success

Familiar enough to those who have read so far, no doubt, and necessitating as a fundamental management principle the acceptance of the humanness of human beings. But it is not merely confined to a few way-out pioneers, and though in its entirety it is still evidenced very little among the successful businesses we are accustomed to, aspects of the philosophy are popping up all over the place—flexibility in particular.

## THE RESTRUCTURING OF MANAGEMENT

Thus, according to the National Economic Development Office report, *Changing Working Patterns*, based on a survey of literature, representative organisations, and managers and trades unionists in 72 large firms, what comes through is this enormous striving towards flexibility in every form—numerical flexibility which enhances firms' abilities to adjust the level of labour input to meet fluctuations in output; functional flexibility which changes not the number of workers but what they do; distancing strategies involving the adjustment of employment relationships by such means as sub-contracting; and pay flexibility. Tomorrow's flexible firm has begun to gear itself up to achieve all these flexibilities.

Nine out of ten respondents had introduced numerical flexibilities since 1980 by means of temporary workers, part-timers, overtime, new shift patterns and flexible working hours. Nine out of every ten manufacturing respondents had introduced functional flexibilities. Seven out of every ten respondents had increased their use of distancing since 1980, in particular the sub-contracting of ancilliary services, and 22% had increased their use of self-employed workers. Increased distancing was associated with the aims of concentrating corporate resources on areas of comparative advantage, finding cheaper ways of undertaking non-core activities, shifting the burden of risk and uncertainty, and reducing or containing the formal headcount and thus the wage bill.

There is a strong indication in the report, particularly underlined by union respondents, that the traditional corporate demarcation between management, staff and manual workers is already changing to one of core workers (who would be largely at management level but include some staff and manual) plus peripheral groups of all three activities who were further distanced—maybe to their personal disadvantage. It completely endorses the validity of the Charles Handy model in *The Future of Work*, where a central core of permanent workers is surrounded by a contractual fringe of self-employed specialists and an outer-ring of part-time and/or temporary labour for whom work is a paid job rather than a fulfilling career.

Viewed from the traditional Red–Blue, Flatland version of society, this may look threateningly exploitative. But the NEDO report also picks up Catherine Hakim's estimate that in 1981 there may already have been 630,000 true homeworkers in England and Wales—some 2½% of the labour force—besides all those who work partly from home. The number has grown significantly since the early 1970s, and the traditional manufacturing homeworker is now in a minority with most homeworkers being involved in white-collar service and professional activities. As we have seen, this is no cause for dismay; on the contrary, there are now a host of colours in the spectrum other than red and blue. The Flatland version of events is giving way to the perception of third dimension—not only depth or width but height; not only left or right, but up.

Because now, individuals are taking this matter of flexibility into their own hands. Those who have the skills that are in short supply, those who know they are in demand and do not mind mentioning the fact, for them flexibility is a release and not an imposition. In the teeth of the system's innate conservatism, they are beginning to change the whole pattern of their activity to suit themselves. The rise of individualism at work, like the spread of homeworking itself, is much due to the impact of computerisation, but is also spreading to other sunrise industries and the whole service sector. However, there are deserts of incomprehension even in the most promising terrain.

> British business is incredibly conservative—even the parts that seem to be up to date. I know a small, very high-tech company in the North-West which is unbelieveably old-fashioned in its warehouse management, for example. There are simply not enough people around who have the imagination to see how new technology can get things done better in a new way.
> (*Sheila Rothwell*)

Nonetheless, the writing is on the wall—the graffiti of independence are everywhere, the aerosols and magic markers keep reappearing no matter how often they are wiped away.

> For a while, many businesses will remain wary of homeworking as they feel that it loses them a degree of control over their employees. But the psychological retreat from employment forces companies to be more open and flexible towards those who work for them. The old, closed system underlying universal employment cannot last much longer. As for people, we have also to learn to be not like battery chickens any more—no longer the bland consumers of everything that comes their way, but people exercising judgement about things that matter.
> (*Denis Pym*)

> Companies do not like managing people they cannot easily control. Resistance to homeworking revolves round the fact that in most companies people are bad at setting objectives. Management by objectives is admittedly not easy and a lot of managers run away from the problem unless it is a matter of survival. In the computing field as a whole it is easier than in most businesses, but traditional companies with low trust and high control find it extremely difficult. However one must say that now they are finding everything extremely difficult, even managing today's professionals and R and D people. Hiving off an extraneous outworking section of an existing business won't work unless they see things differently.
> (*Sheila Rothwell*)

Admittedly, telework is at present mostly confined to computing organisations because manufacturers obtain their equipment at cost and can afford to spread it around, and, as noted, the computer mind adapts well to the loose-tight characteristics of remote working. So homeworking, as an aspect of this new management revolution, is at first more likely to flourish in an IT context where networking is part of the culture, and where the need for true communication and coordination is accepted.

> The success of homeworking is an indictment of the way we normally work. Normal negative things are absent in the home environment—like lack of trust, bad management and an environment unconducive to reflection because of open planning or other sources of constant interruption. At present, however, this is not recognised and many businesses are a frenetic shambles of people's interactions.
> (*Graham Milborrow*)

Ronnie Lessem in his chapter 'The Enabling Company' in *New Patterns of Work* describes enabling organisations as those which contain both employees and what he calls imployees—the former being conventional managers and workers and the latter consultant networkers, such as at F International and Rank Xerox, who provide an independent service to the company as part of their business activity. He cites progressive managements as performing an enabling function which permits entrepreneurs, craftsmen, innovators, networkers, etc. to fulfil their individual potential, and in the process to realise the company's business potential. Every 'imployee' operates in a way that not only is quite different from conventional employment but differs from every other; and unlike the conventional company the enabling organisation can accommodate this independence and variety.

Judi Marshall (*Women Managers: Travellers in a Male World*) also offers F International as a prototype of this new way of working. She describes it as continually defining and redefining itself, adapting its form by matching members' needs and potential contributions with market requirements. In this matching process there is minimal dependence on a rigid organisation structure; working procedures are more important to effective functioning than are fixed official relationships. The company takes its shape from the workers' and the clients' needs which create it, rather than being a self-sustaining structure into which individuals must fit. Classically speaking, one might perhaps label this as a protean, as opposed to a procrustean management style.

> In the enabling model, the philosophical assumption of the way the future is going to look is that people will increasingly be responsible for organising and indeed financing their own work, partly because the technology to enable them to do so will be getting cheaper and cheaper and they will be able to get the attractive flexibility at manageable cost. Freelance homeworking, though at present it may strike some as isolated and oppressive, can therefore be seen as a more advanced way of working than the alternative of ordinary employment (as can working in voluntary associations, cooperative groups and community businesses). These people are taking back the responsibility for their own lives from the employing institutions to which they had previously abdicated it.
> (*James Robertson, independent writer, lecturer and consultant*)

There are other inherent problems for management here. Organisations will have to accept that as far as belonging is concerned there will be a lessening of one-company loyalty. People in future will also have cross-loyalties to their professions and their various networks. Already, after the City of London's Big Bang, the conglomerates that have been created out of all the different branches of the financial services industry are finding it difficult to retain employees' loyalty. People feel differently from the way they did before, and lack the sense of intimate belonging as things become more monolithic. They express a greater loyalty to their occupations—dealer loyalty, for example—than to their employers. In future it will be more a matter of maintaining control on a day-to-day basis, by setting measured work targets which can be completed in the individual's own way. This is what Charles Handy calls the 'inverted donut theory of management'—the spelling being American rather than English for culinary reasons.

> The American donut, as opposed to the English doughnut, is solid round the outside and has a hole in the middle. Up to date management really consists of building jobs with a solid hole in the middle (that bit which if you don't do it you have clearly failed), and a vaguer outside portion which has a limit to it. Within this outside area management cannot quantify and has to allow

people discretion. Boring jobs have no outside ring, but with executive jobs one has to specify the core and the outer boundary, and then leave the intervening space empty. The workers can then respond to things that you haven't foreseen as a manager, and have the capacity to improve. Having defined what is the overall measure of success, the manager then leaves them to get on with it. He or she details the chunks of work in the core but leaves the rest unspecific. (*Charles Handy*)

Distributed organisations *must* be run this way, but nowadays all organisations *should* be run this way, difficult though it is to do this. With output jobs it is much easier, however, and one cannot get away from the suspicion that far more jobs could be defined as being as least partly output in nature if managers took the trouble to define them. Rank Xerox did so, according to Judkins, West and Drew, distinguishing between two fundamental modes of employment that they labelled the 'continuity mode' and the 'output mode'. The former has geographical location at the root of the contract, and 'being there' is an essential feature of the job, which can be of two kinds:

- *Personal service work,* such as a receptionist, bank cashier or personnel counsellor where face-to-face contact is required.
- *Managerial continuity work,* such as the head of section who gives a total operation its day-to-day backbone of consistent direction and decision making.

Output jobs involve the achievement of defined objectives, and their location is incidental. They are also of two kinds:

- *Output service work,* where the task can be defined as the supply of a specified piece of work within fixed parameters of cost and/or time, such as with computer programming.
- *Nomadic work,* where individuals such as audit or sales staff spend much time either travelling, or engaged in discussions at other offices or sites.

The enabling manager must make these output workers feel that they belong, but at the same time they may well require the freedom to work for others. This brings up the whole data protection security issue and the handling of sensitive business information. Many computer people have an anarchic cast of mind; the hacker and the 'phone-phreak', for example. The criminal mentality is, if not rampant, at least passant regardant, even if only in fun.

This and other other legal issues will constrain managements from going for homeworking like a bull at a gate. Legally, things seem clear but they have not yet been adequately tested. What is the position on legal liability for the freelancer's fraud, say? Are we absolutely certain that the position on contract working will remain unchanged in the case of redundancy or other events where the worker is now unprotected? Here a legal framework is needed that redefines work so that there is no artificial difference between Schedule D and Schedule E, and where some kind of worker protection is built in. But this must not be so restrictive on the employer as to put him off the whole idea. All depends on public policy which, as usual, is miles behind the debate. The danger is that some single scandalous case will set off a flurry of panic legislation which will tie up the development of homeworking for years—the Rachman effect, where stopping one malevolent landlord resulted in the destruction of the whole private rented sector.

## HOMEWORKING MANAGEMENT —SOME FURTHER CASE STUDIES

Meanwhile, like Galileo we must mutter, 'But it does move.' It does require a keen development of new management skills, even of additional tiers of management, but homeworking can be made to work in more cases than might be expected—though not always, it cannot be denied.

> We are an example of a new breed of architects. What makes our business tick is the interaction of different professions and we actively discourage people from working at home—one has to lock them away for a week together to make them work as a team. People can go home and write a report but most of the creative energy comes from further processing it through others. It does help to work at home when you can define tasks and break them down into parts of the whole, but output measurement is very difficult with the creative process. The technology to help all this has to be very slick, too, and at the moment it is very slow.
> (*Bob Pell*)

Another creative member of the expert commentators' panel confirmed from his experience that even the loosest of remote creative teams benefits from occasional social contact.

> There must be a club networking atmosphere. I was *The Times* career editor off-site with something like 18 freelancers working for me. Once a quarter we had a four hour session in a wine bar with a lot of brain-storming, and it was useful for the creative spark that came out of being together. Because they were all home-based workers without an organisation to bring them together to discuss technical difficulties, this was an essential part of the system.
> (*Michel Syrett*)

However, there was one of the survey's commentators who had both experimented in depth with the homeworking method in a consultancy context, and who had successfully persevered when the going got tough.

Dr Robert Reck is managing director of Index Group, the UK office of an American computer consultancy dedicated to introducing its clients to the ways in which information technology can give them a competitive edge. In the UK he has ten professionals and a support staff of four; the American operation has 120 professionals and 30 in back-up.

Originally, the British strategy was to start up a small central London office which would act mainly as their reception and conference room where people came in to meet each other or to meet clients. They would have shared 'hot desks' in the main office but most of them were going to work exclusively from home, with quick networking communication through Easylink, the electronic mail service. One third of the staff lived in London and two-thirds outside, up to a maximum of 60 miles away. They comprised both men and women and covered a total range of the spectrum of familiarity with information technology. Skills profiles were wildly disparate, some being management consultants and others IT specialists. In this aspect, the team was not unlike Bob Pell's variegated one at Conran Roche.

The nature of their work is highly conceptual. The documents they produce are not long, typed reports but more 'presentation notes' which are used with a physical presentation to push their message home. Activating their clients' mental processes and stimulating successful business change is something they regard as more important than the content of the report itself. These people are all high communicators, effusively verbal and articulate and more than averagely intuitive. Besides using the electronic mail to shunt through the actual report writing, they use it for administrative purposes (such as time-sheets, financial projections, etc., which are kept updated on a tactical basis) and also marketing in the shape of brochures, letters to prospects, article writing in the management press, and so forth.

> The original strategy did not work. To use Pascale and Athos terminology, the *systems* part was OK—they had their personal computers and worked at home on consistent formats and so forth—while the *structure* was flat and rankless; and *skills, style and staff* were OK too. What went wrong was *shared values*. Top of these was teamwork, a major aspect of which was openness and the sensitive handling of praise and correction by seniors. There was a great deal of interaction involved here and the need for a sense of interdependent trust, given a style which was loose rather than hierarchical. The staff was new—four came from Cambridge, Mass. and the rest from Europe—and hardly any of them knew each other before they started working together. The skill range was extremely wide. Some were purely business-oriented and some were experienced in information systems but had never had hands-on technology experience. They were aged 23–50 and had a corresponding difference in outlook.
> (*Robert Reck, Managing Director, Index Group*)

What happened was that they moved documents around in perfect fashion but there was no interactive brain-storming. The Pell factor was absent—the high-tech was fine but the high-touch was lacking. Interdependent trust was eventually established by a complete change of plan—having people in the office during their first year so that they could meet up with all their colleagues as they came in. In place of the original small central London office which was to have been a reception and conference room, two years later the office took up five times the intended space and included the hot desks as well. However, after a year of this, people were happily working for about two-thirds of their time outside and one third inside, and the volume of interactive electronic communication shot up. But they had had to get to know each other first.

Reck took himself as an example. He only travels back to the US occasionally but feels quite comfortable with an electronic link to his head office as long as he is communicating to people he knows. However, he finds he cannot overcome the language barrier with new US people, even if he has been electronically introduced to them—and this is regardless of age, sex or any other variable factor.

Once this barrier has been overcome by personal contact, it is in an international context that electronic intercommunication is seen by Reck as so vital—given the different time zones. At Index it has been possible for them to talk to each other on computer between Cambridge, New York, Los Angeles and London, contributing together to plug into the requirements of an Australian client, thus eliminating both time and distance. They have even persuaded a number of clients onto this system too, using BT Gold, and he regularly communicates routinely with them by electronic mail. Again, this is a comfortable way of working with established clients but is likely to fail with somebody new.

> One of the problems with clients is the keyboard; a lot of them are terrified of it. However when forced into using it with two fingers they soon do fine. People get fascinated from creating their own end-products, particularly when their output is measurable. After a while they really enjoy it—they are quite happy to send their messages down electronic mail or come into the office with a disk which they have created at home.
> (*Robert Reck*)

Again, rather like the F International network, Index has defined a prototype electronic mail system for a client which will link them with their executives at home, their sales department and their own customers. And using themselves as a model, Index can see how this can become a very powerful consultancy sales tool. Admittedly, at Index they have had the advantage of being able to recruit a team from scratch, so that there is no conventional wisdom to batter into submission. With an existing team, Reck admits that a lot more give and take is needed to by-pass the traditional and habitual constraints that exist to the detriment of the networking method.

> One of these is the suspicion that people are 'goofing off' rather than doing the work, and the feeling that when one is trying to manage a distributed team there must be an inevitable element of slackness. The answer is to establish an acceptance of mutual interdependence and trust.
> (*Robert Reck*)

There are also moments when a project team simply has to be together for maybe three or four days on the run in the office or in some hideout away from it all, so that they all reinforce what they know about each other and about the common project, and can work even more effectively together. As managing director, Reck is now personally paying more attention to orchestrating events, in order to get people together face-to-face at the right time and in the right way. He has a hidden agenda which involves organising things so that people are together for morale-building sessions and are able to work separately for longer periods as a result. First, he has started a weekly electronic newsletter which gives information about prospects, clients and social chat ('Jim and Annie are off on a ski-ing holiday—don't break anything, we need you'). It is hard to draw the line on office gossip, but there has to be an element of it, he insists; people want to know what their colleagues are doing. The office also gets electronic news from the US parent.

Apart from this electronic news input which is collected from everyone centrally each week and then distributed on Friday afternoons, there are regular staff meetings every three weeks which are totally apart from project meetings. Here Reck acts as impresario for presentations of projects, or brainstorming sessions about some present or future development. The focus is intense between 5 and 8 p.m., at which time the meeting is cut off completely and they all go out to an extremely relaxed and expensive dinner together.

As a consequence of this method of home and group working, the staff become incredibly involved, putting in very long hours and frequently pulling up clients to their own level. There is apparently no difference between men and women, old or young, in the extent to which they are able to conform to this method of working. They are a non-destructive though competitive group and for them work is a game. Some prefer to work at home or with clients on site, while others prefer to be in the office more and rely on direct rather than electronic contact. There is no rhyme or reason, except for the rule that everyone can play the way they want.

It is by now becoming established that organisations that introduce telecommuting need to create procedures to ensure that these essential face-to-face meetings do occur and to offset the isolation that many may feel. Attention also needs to be paid to the communication of general information via memoranda and employee newspapers, both direct and over the terminal. With a large company, employees of several divisions who live in the same area may advantageously be organised together to form peer support groups. Personnel staff may have to visit employees in their homes, and training, performance assessment, quality control, general supervision, benefits and compensation all require close attention. These are some of the ground rules for management of the new working style.

Meanwhile, Reck, albeit with a small team, has taken on all these complexities of the telecommuting mode, and won. He accepts the difficulties found by Bob Pell and invests them with the camaraderie of Michael Syrett and the main transforming principle of Steve Shirley, Diana Hill and Phillip Judkins. He too epitomises the fact that, in the nicest possible way, at the centre of every network there has to be a spider.

## BIBLIOGRAPHY AND REFERENCES

Deakin, Rose, *Women and Computing: The Golden Opportunity*, Macmillan 1984

Hakim, Catherine, 'Homeworking in Britain', *Employment Gazette*, February 1987

Handy, Charles, *The Future of Work*, Basil Blackwell, 1984

Huws, Ursula, *The New Homeworkers*, Low Pay Unit Pamphlet no. 28, 1984

Institute of Manpower Studies, *Changing Working Patterns*, NEDO, 1986

Judkins, Phillip, West, David and Drew, John, *Networking in Organisations*, Gower, 1985

Kiefer, Charles and Senge, Peter, 'Metanoic organisations'. In *Transforming Work*, ed. John Adams, Miles River Press, 1984

Kinsman Francis, *The New Agenda*, Spencer Stuart and Associates, 1983

Lessem, Ronnie, 'The enabling company'. In *New Patterns of Work*, ed. David Clutterbuck, Gower, 1985

Marshall, Judi, *Women Managers: Travellers in a Male World*, John Wiley & Sons, 1984

McLean, Mavis, *Negotiating the Boundary Between Work and Family*, Marriage Research Centre, January 1987

Naisbitt, John, *Megatrends*, MacDonald, 1984

Naisbitt, John and Aburdene, Patricia, *Reinventing the Corporation*, Warner Brookes, 1985

Pascale, Richard and Athos, Anthony, *The Art of Japenese Management*, Simon & Schuster, 1981

# 7
# Telecommuting in the World at Large

We have seen something of the UK experience of telecommuting, but to maintain a sense of proportion, this must be appreciated in a world context. The short message is that more is going on in Britain than anywhere else. There may be a great many sole homeworkers or small networkers in other places, but the lessons of distributed management are largely British-made.

## THE BONN CONFERENCE

The first major international conference on telework took place in Bonn in March 1987. First impressions suggested that telecommuting was becoming a product surrounded by a certain amount of hype—one consultancy's brochure offered a special report '...on how you can achieve increased productivity of 20% – 40%, dramatic cuts in personnel costs and office space expenses and sharp reductions in employee turnover ....read on to discover how you can obtain the secret to these and other important benefits FREE for 15 days!'

The homeworking conference attracted over 120 delegates from fourteen different countries. Only ten were British, and only four—all British—had actually ever been homeworkers. The rest were academics, researchers, theorists, sociologists, psychologists, consultants, bandwagon manipulators and ergonometricians. This led to a German delegate remarking that for every genuine telecommuter in the world there must be two people studying the subject. The conference displayed little optimism. There was great emphasis on risk, possible exploitation, downside potential, the lonely housewife and the inadequacy of existing data—but little on the realities of telecommuting.

> I felt rather like an early aviator, to whom people were continually saying, 'It'll never fly!' I am flying it, though, like the bumble bee who can't understand why the experts say it's impossible.
> (*Diana Hill*)

In this atmosphere of professional interchange and academic cynicism, the problem was that the majority pessimistic faction was concentrating on the poor and unskilled whom they regarded through nineteenth-century eyes. The abstract of the conference complained that in the absence of reliable information it was easier to identify questions than answers. Empirica GmbH, the conference organisers, reported that other European countries are less enthusiastic about electronic home-based work than the UK, though out of a total workforce of 90 million, 13 million would accept telework. In the survey concerned, which polled over 10,000 people in Germany, France, Italy and the United Kingdom, the overall UK interest was top at 23%, that in Germany being only 9%; 60% of British employees who have home computers are interested in the concept—and Britain has more home computers per head of the population than any other country in the world.

> My impression of Bonn was that there is an explosion of interest both in Europe and the US. Practical experience is however low, and there is very little understood about its management anywhere else except in Britain. (*Frits Janssen*)

Bonn evinced the feeling that what would determine the immediate future of homeworking would be attitudinal negativism rather than technological positivism. No account was taken of the fact that the ECC PTTs are genuinely working towards the standardisation of equipment, and, for example, have already done so successfully in the field of cellular radio-telephones. Furthermore, the conference did not seem to accept that technology is now enabling people to do jobs of higher skills as simpler ones are being taken over electronically, and that therefore, in this respect, exploitation will be avoided. Finally, moreover, there were suspicions that potential EEC regulations were in train which would tighten up contractual employment laws to the disadvantage of the homeworking movement and its spread.

## FEDERAL REPUBLIC OF GERMANY

Much of the interest in West Germany is being fostered by consultants Empirica, organisers of the Bonn conference and initiators of regular workshops and reports on the subject. However, according to Clutterbuck and Hill, the spread of German telecommuting is likely to be stifled by strict laws governing homeworking, where it is difficult for employers to obtain permission to use homeworkers in industries in which there is no tradition of the practice. The West German authorities are concerned because they have passed elaborate legislation to improve the standard and quality of the workplace and cannot monitor this in homes. Added to this is the fear that telecommuting lends itself to sophisticated forms of moonlighting, and in aggregate the official attitude is therefore negative.

Empirica produced a report on decentralised electronic working in the German banking, insurance and software industries for the European Foundation for the Improvement of Living and Working Conditions in October 1986. This was based on a workshop which attracted a wide range of participants in these industries and drew attention to the fact that not only the authorities but also the German trade unions were antagonistic to the concept of electronic homeworking. Furthermore, the German PTT was seen as a hindrance and an obstruction to such development, and there was general dissatisfaction at both the quality and cost of the telecommunications infrastructure. The workshop also demonstrated that decentralisation of work in the financial sector was often rejected because of fears surrounding data security and protection, and that the reaction of customers to the use of portable terminals in the insurance industry 'varies between amazement and dislike'. Nonetheless, the Wüstenrot Building Society had 800 representatives equipped with portable terminals and acoustic couplers operating from 18 satellite offices, and had experienced this as optimising the advice given to the customer.

Lastly, a Bonn delegate complained that female teleworkers in Germany found their menfolk expected even more housework out of them because they were at home all day, which contrasts vividly with the generally enlightened attitude of British husbands according to the FI and CPS respondents, and puts yet another damper on the potential for homeworking in the Federal Republic.

> The reaction I met in Germany was that 'it'll never happen here'. 45% of their workforce is still in manufacturing compared to 21% in this country. The concept of the entrepreneurial/contractual fringe is not yet in their nature.
> (*Charles Handy*)

## FRANCE

> France is like Japan in that it is smart to be in an organisation. People from the *Grandes Ecoles* always go into organisations and are not such individualists as Oxbridge graduates here. They have all the technology they need to allow them to work from home. That is not the block to homeworking, rather it is in the need to be a member of a prestigious organisation.
> (*Charles Handy*)

France has already jumped one attitudinal hurdle, however—it has a growing population totally used to electronic networking. Minitel, a videotext computer terminal connected to the telephone, was installed to replace the ramshackle directory enquiry system in 1982. All subscribers who wanted were supplied with a free set, of which the essential characteristics were that it was a complete package, compatible nationwide, and available on the nod without the hassle of coming to any detailed decision about it. But then much to the surprise of the PTT everybody started using it—not only for the host of information banks from news headlines to astrological predictions, and agony aunts to dating services—but also for personal interchange between strangers on matters of common interest, much of it erotic.

Five years after the network was installed there were 2½ million Minitels in operation. In the summer of 1986 it broke down for a while because its enormous popularity seriously overloaded the system. There is a legend about a man who clocked up 80,000 francs worth of calls in six months, but it is not all sex and games—politicians also make themselves available to answer questions from their constituents. However, there are anarchic elements about it too—a journalist wrote an article adversely commenting on a group of people who then set out to get him by systematically raiding his data and then publicising it.

Apart from familiarising people with the delights of networking in general, the French PTT takes the widespread development of cabling extremely seriously, and is particularly active in pushing the concept of electronic remote working. The few examples of it there derive from this source. *Tele-travail* largely involves groups of individuals working in neighbourhood work-centres distant from urban business agglomerations. The most extensive project has been at Marne-la-Vallée, where it was planned for 100 employees from 15 different organisations to share the same office building and communicate with their own headquarters via terminals, fax and telephone.

It was hoped that employees of the various companies would grow together as a sort of corporate community based on the neighbourhood centre. However, several employers dropped out of the scheme, mainly because of the organisational problems involved in the necessity for co-operation between the building's various occupiers. Other problems arose from arguments about the aid given by the telecommunications authority, an unattractive site, and management problems of supervision and control. Only 50 workers were established there in the end, compared to the projected figure of 100, mainly employed in the telecommunications industry itself. It is from the PTT that the main thrust from employers has come altogether. For example, several of the telephone authority's secretaries due to be made redundant in Corsica were offered and took up the chance to work for the company in Nice on a telecommuting basis, since good secretarial help there was in short supply.

The official attitude is that to accommodate telecommuting, at the very least new ergonomic regulations will be necessary. Another problem is the time people spend at the terminal and the difficulty of regulating working periods at home. There is also the problem of inspection, since an inspector of labour has the right to enter any factory or office but not to enter homes.

According to Clutterbuck and Hill, Lionel Stoleru, sometime French Secretary of State for Works and Participation, predicted that 400,000 would be working at remote terminals in France by the middle 1980s. They are not. Now officials at the French Ministry of Labour cautiously predict that home-based telecommuting won't be big until the mid-1990s. They estimate that it will take until then for companies to feel sufficiently comfortable with electronic mail and other equipment to think of progressing in this direction.

But there are two final bull points for the French telecommuting potential when it finally begins to be realised. First, as a Catholic nation to which the concept of the family is highly important, the people are geographically extremely well rooted in the sense of being attached to their local base. There is an emotional and spiritual affinity to the place they come from and where their roots are. Working there could be seen as a bonus. And secondly, every secondary school-leaver of either sex can type.

## SCANDINAVIA

According to Rosalyn Moran and Jean Tansey, in Denmark it is estimated that there are 220–500 women working at home using IT, with approximately twenty work-centres employing a total of 200 women offering IT services. The practice is obviously current, though note should be taken of F International's reservations about the Danish teleworking scene, as described in Chapter 3. In Norway, Norsk Hydro also have a scheme, described by British commentators as fairly primitive. However, the main Scandinavian initiative has come from Sweden.

Here particular interest has been shown in neighbourhood work-centres; though on a smaller scale than in France. The best known is at Nykvarn, a suburb 50 km from Stockholm, set up by Nordplan, the Nordic Institute for Studies in Urban and Regional Planning. The landscaped office takes up an area of only 180 square metres, with eleven people working more or less permanently there and five or six others also using the centre for short periods. Participants divided their working hours between their ordinary place and the neighbourhood centre itself. They were furnished with the equipment they needed to communicate with their employers' offices and other common office equipment was also installed. Work in the centre created a wider range of personal relations, according to most participants, because of meeting new people from other enterprises as well as colleagues at their old place of work. People co-operated together in technical matters relating to their knowledge of the equipment at the centre, but also in situations where their capabilities complemented one another.

The project was sponsored by the Swedish Department of Telecommunications and the Swedish Building Research Council. The breakdown of jobs was six from the computing industry (keying, programming and training), three drug product planners and one each from banking, telephone sales, self-employed consultancy and the local municipality. The research programme lasted 18 months and the results were:

- Employers were relatively neutral in their response, neither actively promoting the working methods for other employees, nor withdrawing from the scheme.
- Employees all wanted to continue to participate.
- Unions' fears about isolation and the creation of boring, low-paid jobs were unfounded.

Another interesting Swedish remote-working innovation is the office train. Employees of the electrical engineering company ASEA who commute the 120 km between Stockholm and Västerås now have their own travelling office, a custom-built passenger coach adapted at a cost of £400,000. It can seat some 40 passengers and has about 20 work-places, a conference room and saloon. The work-places are provided with telephones connected to a conventional exchange, which in turn is coupled to a mobile telephone system. There are also a number of typewriters, as well as personal computers allowing passengers needing special information for their work to obtain this from different databases.

Employees who live in the capital and use the train's facilities can claim half the journey-time as work-time and the company pays one third of their rail fare. Inaugurated in November 1986, the carriage removes the need to drive to work on Sweden's dark and icy winter roads, and precludes the necessity for employees to live in company flats during the week. It represents another and imaginative adaptation of the remote-working concept.

## THE UNITED STATES OF AMERICA

In its weird and wonderful way, the USA has produced yet another and even more imaginative adaptation of the remote-working concept—the peripatetic freelance author and journalist, Steven K. Roberts, and his eight-foot-long, 36-speed, recumbent bicycle, carrying no less than five solar-powered computers which store over a megabyte of memory on board. Roberts reckons he has cranked out some four million pedal strokes and about the same number of key strokes in the four years since 1983, the latter being shunted off to publishers or to his Ohio office though electronic networks and packet satellite links via whatever payphone he happens to be near at the time. He has covered virtually every state in the union on his electronic musemobile.

This splendid individuality characterises the American approach to homeworking. A large number of computer-literate individuals have experimented with the concept in a host of different ways to help their working output and enjoy life more in the process. But most of these are also individuals in the working sense; few are employed by anyone else.

Take as an example the story of one of the survey's expert commentators, Professor Tom Stonier, an American by birth and author of *The Wealth of Information*, but currently directing the School of Science and Society at the University of Bradford.

> My personal experience of electronic homeworking involves myself, my wife and my son. I happen to like writing in bed, and the computer is ideal for this, from a word-processing and a data retrieval point of view. This is a trend that's on the increase—having creative ideas in electronic form in a home environment.
>
> Now, my son is about to go to Paris for six months. He is a computer programmer working in a consultancy co-operative in New York. Sometimes he spends weeks or months on site and sometimes weeks or months at home. For the six months to come he has decided to have Paris as his home, taking his computer with him and just working from there.
>
> Finally my wife is a handloom weaver who designs textiles and sells them through agencies in the United States. Before, the process involved a lot of pencils and graph paper and the design was finally transferred to a little thing called a dobby, like a piano-roll on top of the loom. Now, she sits in the house creating the design on her Apple computer, and then transfers the disks to another Apple hitched up to a Victorian floorloom in the garage. The computer is showing itself to be a marvellous tool for converting a vision in one's head into a reality. What would have taken her six hours using the traditional method now takes fifteen minutes.
>
> (*Tom Stonier*)

In the US, all graduates, because they have to submit a typewritten thesis, have a qwerty skill, which explains the keyboard familiarity of most bright Americans. They like to experiment with computers to help them accomplish what they are interested in doing. Three of the survey commentators had picked up straws in the wind related to this, which also sharpens the trend towards electronic homeworking, since so much information processing no longer needs to be done in the office.

> In the US, particularly California, they have houses with 'communications rooms'. The thing here is the definition of personal space. There are shared media and intensely private media—the latter demonstrating the need for different room arrangements and for more room to communicate in private.
>
> (*Rex Malik*)

> There appears to be some US evidence of two phenomena, mainly from the high-tech environments of both the West Coast and Boston, which may provide pointers for the future. First, the computer sophisticate who hires out his skills to the most attractive bidder and can therefore dictate his working

terms, which may well include some working from home. Secondly, women refusing to sacrifice their careers and demanding from their husbands that the responsibility for staying at home to keep an eye on the children is split between them. Both will come to ration their working lives so that approximately half the time can be spent doing their work at home with some electronic aid or other.
(*Jim Cowie*)

In the US people are beginning to put things together—little scraps of information from a vast variety of sources—in a consultancy mode, making incredible use of data banks and creating whole new industries in the process. They are getting totally different holistic visions of a given subject. It is the epitome of the scanning and monitoring system that is the essential part of any intelligence network—and it can all be done from home.
(*Christine MacNulty*)

The guiding ethos in the US is that of the small business or entrepreneur, whereas in the UK it is more the ethos of the professional. Tom Peters, author of *In Search of Excellence* described American business as 'overmanned, overlayered and under-led'. In the continuing shakeout of the American economy, the leadership there is not leadership in the truest sense—the attitude is more, 'We pay you; we kick you'. Hence the preference of many Americans for their own small businesses. Meanwhile there is also impetus in the fact that the whole electronic networking concept is given leverage because of the vast distances people have to travel.

The US Chamber of Commerce reports that ten million businesses list home addresses as their place of business. The National Association for Cottage Industry, of Chicago, Illinois has listed over 300 jobs that are currently being done from home. There is a significant growth of cottage industry buildings and communities where people both live and work. Neighbourhood work-centres (or 'half-way houses', to give the American terminology) near residential areas have also cropped up across the country, people's work locations being divided between home, office and electronic half-way house.

On the downside, labour safety, insurance and zoning laws make homeworking difficult, while as in Germany government officials also harbour the fear that many home businesses do not pay their share of taxes. In 1983, the AFL–CIO passed a retrograde resolution that called for a ban on computer home work except for the handicapped. However, the State of Oregon with its declining industries of fishing and timber concluded that cottage industries were the most promising area for its economic redevelopment, and is consequently assisting residents in starting home businesses by offering courses in marketing their products and services.

According to a 1985 report from the Office of Technology Assessment of the Congress of the United States, it was estimated that 10–11 million Americans earned part of their income by working at home in a wide variety of craft, production and service occupations. The 1980 Census counted about 1.2 million people in the labour force whose primary place of work was in their residence. About 16% of American households had a computer in 1985 and this was expected to double by 1990.

Estimates of the population of telecommuters in the USA have often been wildly exaggerated and one report commissioned by AT & T predicted that all American executives would be homeworkers by 1990. Other guesses from such authorities as futurist Alvin Toffler, Professor Jack Nilles of the University of Southern California and the Stanford Research Institute have varied from 5 million to 26 million people, the latter being 50% of all white-collar workers. By now the usual guesstimate for the early 1990s is 10 million, who will do at least part of their work at home or at satellite centres.

According to Steve Shirley, the very first example of teleworking was a company called Computations Inc. which as long ago as 1957 offered the services of a small group of home-based computer experts to the scientific communitiy around Boston. It prospered for many years under its founder Elsie Shutt, but apparently did not endure as researchers can find no trace of it today, though interestingly, the first steps towards telecommuting were thus taken within the computing industry and by a woman.

By 1981 there were only a handful of homeworker programmes for white-collar workers though by the following year there were 35 involving perhaps 600 employees. Estimates of the number of home-based office workers at present using electronic equipment in the US range from 10,000 to 30,000, the most frequently used estimate being 15,000 from 350 organisations.

> There are large numbers here and it sounds impressive, but though the UK scene is smaller and has less high technology it is far more creative. And above all there is the British management of it which is unique.
> (*Hilary Cropper*)
>
> The impression I have is that in the US there are a lot of one-man bands, but culturally people still need the office and the mutual support it provides. They are more outer-directed and herd-orientated. When MIT came over to see what was going on in this country they were astonished.
> (*Ninian Eadie*)

Let us then take a few examples of how corporations in the US are already using the homeworking technique electronically.

*Control Data Corporation*

Initially the company recruited 50 physically disabled people and trained them to become home-based computer programmers. The 'home workstation' scheme involved three components—training the employee to write software; finding the employee a suitable job in the company; and training the manager to deal with the unfamiliar situation. There are strong echoes of the British DTI scheme here. The company calculated it would cost $30,000 to keep an injured or sick employee on medical leave for six months. In contrast, the same employee cost only $13,000 to train as a programmer, after which he could make a contribution to the company rather than being a drain on its resources. In 1980 the concept was extended to 27 able-bodied people. Each of these telecommuters had two workplaces—the home or a desk in a satellite office nearby, and a shared desk at one of the company's main urban offices which they visited regularly once or twice a week. Most workers noted productivity increases ranging from 12% to 20%, but some found they needed the proximity of co-workers and the stimulus of an office environment to produce. Some managers equated a loss of visible employees with a loss of power and had to be persuaded that their reponsibilities would be enhanced under a system with remote workers, since over the long term they would be able to supervise people more efficiently.

*Blue Cross/Blue Shield*

This South Carolina health insurance company experimented with four data-entry operators using portable terminals to enter health claims, with a resulting increase in productivity and lower error rating. When the experiment was extended, management also reported a staff turnover reduction from 33% per annum to almost zero.

*Blodgett Computer Information Systems*

This Salt Lake City data entry service bureau started with home-based key punch operators in 1968 and gradually increased their numbers to around 100.

*Continental Illinois*

The bank's trust department started putting out word-processing work to remote terminals in 1978, and a gradually increasing proportion of the department's typing is being done this way, with small branches benefiting by replacing half-occupied, full-time typists with shared homeworkers through a local work-station.

*American Express*

'Project Home-bound' successfully converted ten disabled people's New York homes into fully automated word-processing work-stations in 1983, leading to a general endorsement of the fact that computer technology was going to focus the corporation's strategy more on this mode of working in future.

*Best Western Hotels*

The company, based in Phoenix, Arizona, had problems in meeting the need for reservation clerks in its 1,900 hotels during peak seasons. Its solution was to hire between 20 and 50 women, depending on requirements, who worked from terminals at the Arizona women's prison. They learned marketable skills, and indeed several graduates of the prison programme are now working on the regular staff at Best Western headquarters.

*US Army*

Some 200 army programmers worked from home in an interactive computer based office support system started in 1980.

*Mountain Bell*

This Denver telephone company recruited eight managers to participate in a six-month trial of technical manual writing on a home-based system, which showed a 40% increase in overall productivity. But three of the eight managers who enrolled in the programme eventually dropped out. A female manager was desperate to get back to the office after gaining 20lb in two months because she was always running to the refrigerator for nibbles. A male executive plagued with marital problems claimed that being in the house all the time contributed to his divorce. The third drop-out missed social contacts with his working friends and could not discipline himself at home.

*Freight Data Systems*

This small California company with a workforce of twelve let people work at home when they were not needed in the office, but encouraged them to work on or ahead of time by means of a bonus system. They increased productivity so much that it paid for the $1,700 capital cost of each terminal inside five months, and the rapid growth of the company did not result in office space problems and the need to move to more expensive accommodation.

*Index Group*

This computer consultancy, based in Cambridge, Mass. (and featured in Chapter 6) uses a software package called 'Participate' for its largely home-based executives, in order to keep the interactive creative spark alight.

> This lets you lay out a series of electronic mail 'forum tracks'. One can thus create a systems development decision-tree, where people interact electronically and there is a chronicle of what everyone has said. Someone can come in

> half-way along after a week away for example, and read what everyone has been saying about the particular subject. They may create a new branch on, say, fourth-generation languages which takes the debate off at a tangent. There is a menu to guide participants through the forest of trees and one can read what has gone on, or leave a message or whatever. It is a splendid way to share information on a particular subject in an organised fashion.
> (*Robert Reck*)

Alvin Toffler in *The Third Wave* quotes a number of eminent US company presidents who affirm that between 25% and 75% of what they do could be done at or from home once the necessary communications are provided. In the United States more and more businesses are building electronic links to their customers, transmitting concepts, ideas, accounts, cadcam, information and service. Information technology as a major element of comparative advantage is getting to become a blindingly obvious strategic factor there. And with this, the corporate searchlight is bound to be swivelled ever more frequently onto telecommuting on the other side of the Atlantic.

## OFFSHORE

In this connection, there is one word that should send a shiver down the spine of the thoughtful onlooker: Barbados.

> Barbados is preparing itself to be the absolute offshore information centre of the future, just as the Cayman Islands were the absolute offshore financial centre. They are wiring themselves up and equipping people to handle business such as American Airlines' ticketing operation. One question is, is there a European equivalent for us here? By the end of the century when telephone charges have dropped dramatically, multi-nationals could well be manipulating jobs over a global chessboard with information technology work being carried out at very great distances in countries like Taiwan or Hong Kong. Whole countries could lose much of their vital skills base.
> (*Frits Janssen*)

American Airlines is not the only one. The data entry company Satellite Data Corporation relays printed matter via satellite from its New York headquarters to St Michael's, Barbados where entry clerks type the information into a computer for transmission back to the mainland by satellite again. The chairman of the company claims that they can do the work in Barbados for less than it costs in New York to pay for the floor space. And from California, Saztec Inc. flies paper copy to Singapore for keying in, and then beams the finished work by satellite to an office in Sydney, daily updating the database files of its Australian clients.

Pessimists dub the next century as the era of the telescab. The US Congress's Office of Technology Assessment has bent its collective mind to the problem of high domestic labour costs leading to an international division of labour in information technology. It warns that data-entry clerks in Barbados and other Caribbean countries earn weekly wages that range between $15 and $60, while their counterparts in the United States earn at least six times the latter figure. Even the women prisoners at Phoenix, Arizona notched up about $150. So it is not surprising that several data-entry facilities are currently operating in the Caribbean region and their number is expected to increase markedly. Labour costs are low, the region is easily accessible and close to the United States. Transportation and communication networks are reasonably well developed, literacy rates are high and there are favourable tax provisions for foreign investors. There are already at least twelve US firms who have read the message and set up data processing operations in the Caribbean, Barbados having seven of them, but with Jamaica, St Kitts, Nevis and Haiti all coming up behind. Altogether 2,300 workers are directly employed in Caribbean offshore offices, though three of them in St. Vincent, Haiti and Grenada recently closed down due to managerial and transportation problems.

Other countries including Mexico, India, Singapore, Eire and the Peoples Republic of China also host at least one data-entry firm each, China citing a wage of two dollars per week (let us repeat that—US$2 per week) for clerical workers, while in India the labour cost for keyers is as little as 1/10 to 1/15 of the US rate. All signs indicate that off-shore data entry could become pandemic over the next 10 – 15 years and the vendors who provide these services are optimistic about the future of the industry and its development into more sophisticated channels. Several other US companies are studying the possibility of setting up their keying operations in the Caribbean, with the likelihood of at least 2,000 additional jobs being created over there before long.

There may be inherent limitations on the growth of offshore keying, when the use of facsimile transmitters and optical character readers makes human intervention in data entry unnecessary. However, with the linkages established and a degree of additional training it is quite probable that other competitive work will be found for such people. So meanwhile any existing software house planning for the future is going to have to upgrade its skills to defuse the Barbados effect before it has a chance to make an impact. With fourth-generation languages, who will need packages? (Let alone with fifth—whatever they may be). Training and retraining is going to be the means of survival for tomorrow's electronic sophisticates; and possibly even acting in a consultancy role helping other industries relocate their own workforces to a home base with the installation and training involved in those systems.

Representatives of US labour unions are naturally beginning to feel nervous about the movement of data-entry operations offshore. But these foreign countries are immensely enthusiastic about the introduction of offshore office work—labour-intensive, requiring only a moderate capital outlay, rapid in employment generation, and a clean industry. The US Congress OTA has decided in its wisdom that 'at the moment offshore office work does not have a significant influence on the US economy, but that growth could be quite rapid in the short to medium term.' Possibly it never said a truer word.

## JAPAN

'We're going to win and there's nothing you can do about it.' Thus spake not Zarathustra, but Mr Konosuke Matsushita, founder of what was Matsushita Industries and is now NEC. He was addressing the Universe at the time.

An inordinate amount of printer's ink has been spilt on the Japanese phenomenon. But a short journey round the sociology of Japanese business and the anatomy of the 'salaryman' is essential to understand the relevance of telecommuting to the future of Japanese industry. Here, there can be no better pilot than Michael Houser, of the School of Oriental and African Studies in London.

Houser explains that there is a distinction between the four levels of Japanese employment—family firms, small firms, medium firms and large firms—for which there are four different words. Japanese industrial and commercial society is divided into these four tiers, structured like a wedding cake, one on top of the other. Most large companies depend upon a raft of smaller ones—Toyota, for example, has 37,000 suppliers. There is no particular distinction between blue and white collar within this framework, since people can slide easily from blue to white. For example, someone can be a union negotiator one moment and a company negotiator with the unions the next. There is in fact no word for 'manager' in Japanese, a somewhat disorienting fact, if that is the right adjective. The four tiers are as follows:

### *Tier 1*

The permanent employed who are mostly men and represent about 25% of the 69 million working population. They are normally employed from the age of 22 to 55/60 at which stage they get the 'tap on the shoulder' which means that it is time to submit their resignation. (You don't fire people in Japan.) After that they may be asked back as consultants, but on the other hand they may not. Directors of large businesses are however never tapped on the shoulder, and for them there is no retirement age. None the less the permanent employed are employed for the whole of their working lives, and that is what every Japanese wants as a matter of prestige.

*Tier 2*

The temporarily employed; they are also often employed for the whole of their lives but there is no guarantee of that. (There is nothing like our contracts of employment in Japan.) They are also often women and may well find themselves being laid off. They exist mostly in the large and medium companies but do not have the academic degree that is needed for permanent employment in them.

*Tier 3*

Doing piecework at home and semi-skilled, working on a cottage industry basis. Many of them are self-employed and in the small and family-size sector.

*Tier 4*

part-time workers, students, etc. with no security of job tenure at all.

It must be re-emphasised that there is a wider distinction between these four groups of workers than there is between blue- or white-collar status within the grouping and, in many respects, a Tier 1 blue-collar worker is regarded as superior to a Tier 4 student-worker who may be about to be taken on permanently with a potentially bright future by a large international house. This is the puzzling structure of Japanese work and employment. It means that there is no way that the real decision-makers could work at home, though many in Tiers 2 and 3 could certainly do so. Tier 4 people are temporary, so there might not be that much point in their homeworking anyway. There could be a few junior people in Tier 1 who could work like this, but not for long because they would then get totally out of touch with the essential culture of their company.

However, there are various other positive factors that have to be taken into consideration in the possible development of Japanese telecommuting. The first is that land costs are so huge in Tokyo that there is an enormous pressure on office space. This, however, also imposes stresses on the size and location of the home. The reason that the Japanese are so brilliant at miniaturisation is that they have been forced into it because there is no space for anything large in their homes. Hence it is possible that the homeworking phenomenon may be containable in Japan even though there seems to be no space there at all—partly because they are so good at putting everything into a nutshell whatever it may be (compact discs are a manifestation)—but also because they are culturally able to change the 'reason' for the room between different hours of the day; in other words they can roll up their futons and make the bedroom into an office. A major problem here, however—the children, like western children, would still get in the way.

Having made the point, the Japanese desire to live in a house is enormous and in their dislike for flats they have something in common with the British as opposed to the Continentals. But the desire cannot be satisfied because people's salaries cannot keep pace with land inflation. The alternatives are therefore twofold. Either they have to move further and further out and endure the agonies of Japanese commuting travel, or the wife must earn an income. In this way the family could live closer to the centre, but even if not the wife's income could still be earned on a remote basis. Meanwhile, the savings in travel cost and concomitant hassle are both very desirable goals, and could be attained either or in combination by the wife working from home.

However, there are substantial cultural difficulties with the technology, too. The Japanese PTT, NTT, has introduced a pilot plant model of its INS (Information Network System) in Mitaka-Musashino, a Tokyo suburb. INS skips the ISDN stage that is planned for introduction in Europe, and creates a highly advanced wide-band system capable of all manner of tricks, but at a vast cost. However,the pilot provision of the various services, which commenced in September 1984, was not by any means a total success, even according to NTT. Under a section in their brochure entitled 'Realisation of System for Our Happiness', they admitted that 'while the information-intensive society has a possibility of developing bright future, it has some social problems.'

The system integrates diversified services such as telephone, cable, telex, fax, data communications, and video into a single digital network. However, where examples of its business application are given in the NTT brochure communications systems, broadband teleconferencing and satellite offices are mentioned where 'work can be done as if from a centrally located office'. But there is no mention of the application for home telecommuting even though home shopping, home banking, home study and a home medical system are highlighted.

There is a simple video telephone, the Scopephone, which the brochure admits is of limited image quality, and a 1986 report found subscribers complaining that its operations were too complicated or that it was impolite to use the machine anyway. Users also felt uncomfortable with the video-conferencing facility because of important cultural inhibitions about where to look and who should speak first. Japanese mores, impenetrable to the outsider, were befogged by the medium of advanced electronics. Though home shopping was recognised as partially effective, delivery and payment systems and the range of items offered were criticised. And the survey also revealed a large number of social concerns such as the invasion of privacy, the security of the system and adverse comparison with conventional services.

As may have been suspected, Japan is a neurotic society, bedevilled by the stress of the pace of work. Now that so many Japanese have acquired the physical comforts brought by prosperity, they are obtaining less and less satisfaction from their efforts. Japanese companies seethe with jealously and competition, and most major corporations now have resident psychologists to counsel employees with serious mental problems. Rapid advances in technology and changing family values have compounded the difficulties, most of which are affecting men in their forties and fifties who have devoted themselves slavishly to the post-war industrial surge. The number of male suicides aged 35 to 59 more than doubled between 1975 and 1984.

NTT, clearly never one to pass up a commercial opportunity, has begun offering an unusual outlet for all this stress—for 30p a minute Toyko residents can gain solace from its 'Dial-an-Apology-Service' whereby the caller shouts all his complaints into the telephone and hears a recorded voice cringing in reply 'I'm sorry it's all my fault, yes, you're right, oh please forgive me.' Meanwhile the culture gap between middle-aged managers and younger workers is adding to friction at work, with so many of the latter beginning to suspect that the only way to personal happiness lies in breaking out of the corporate straightjacket and pursuing new life-styles. And the electronic calendar is clicking on towards the year 2002, when because of the country's demographic profile and the immutable system of the corporate ladder, there is going to be an army of general managers with absolutely nothing to do, unless somebody comes up with an alternative solution.

Is there a place for homeworking in and among all this? Well, possibly. Certainly it is a topic in which they are profoundly interested. The Japanese Electronics Industry Council led by a senior representative from Mitsubishi sent a team to the UK to investigate it in 1986, and were so impressed they came back again three months later. They talked little but listened very hard to CPS and F International, even though they were women, which must have cost them something in cultural terms.

> Fujitsu were also much involved in this tour and gathered a great deal of data from us and others. They didn't admit much, but let slip that they were considering a homeworking network of 7000 people. The company is however a little unusual by British standards. In Japan, companies have to pay union dues and Fujitsu negotiated a union deal so that its robots would count as union members as far as the payment of dues were concerned... all those in favour, raise your antennae, you might say.
> (*Phillip Judkins*)

Joking apart, however, something is going on behind the inscrutability. But what the devil is it? In Tier 1 of the business society privilege lies within the organisation and there is no space for homeworking. In Tiers 2 and 3, where there is a tradition of outworking, it is possible, perhaps; but with the complete separation between home and office, the idea of wives working from home could be sociologically disturbing, for example. On the other hand, the JDIDA mission made it clear that they too had low-cost competition in the shape of the Koreans and Taiwanese, and high overheads in central Tokyo. In a sense the philosophy of the central business core plus a satellite raft of homeworking suppliers is appropriate to the Japanese culture, and for that reason homeworking could take on. According to all who met them, they did seem extremely receptive about the ideas they found here, but on the other hand were unprepared to share their own thoughts.

> If you're looking for free information handouts you can wait for ever. You have to say to the Japanese—I won't talk to you if you don't talk to me. (*Michael Josephs*)

But there is always the problem not only of status, but of the fact that so little in Japanese business is done by individuals, and so much by the group. Since homeworking is by and large a very individual process, it is hard to see how the group mentality can be maintained by this means. Where does this finish us up in the labyrinth? Probably with the conclusion that the Japanese will try the telecommuting concept at home with limited success. But having done so, they will then take the lessons they have learned and transplant them brilliantly into Taiwan, Hong Kong, Mainland China, Singapore and the Philippines. They will take the Barbados factor and grind our noses into the Pacific Basin extension of the principle.

Unless we react to the danger in time, that is. The development of the electronic homeworking service will depend on the political and economic environment of each country and the extent to which it is regarded as an imperative.

> Here in the UK we have a relatively high labour and a low electronic content in our work so far, and if things stay this way the motivation for the introduction of IT in the home will be less strong. On the other hand, homeworking IT is a key to the possibility of galvanising ourselves to tackle the next century. (*Ken Edwards, Consultant, Strategic Information Technology, Imperial Chemical Industries*)

We need to remember that.

## BIBLIOGRAPHY AND REFERENCES

Board on Telecommunications and Computer Applications, *Office Work-stations in the Home*, US National Research Council, National Academy Press, 1985

Clutterbuck, David (ed.), *New Patterns of Work*, Gower, 1985

Clutterbuck, David and Hill, Roy, *The Re-making of Work*, Grant McIntyre, 1981

Congress of the United States, *Automation of America's Offices 1985/2000*, Office of Technology Assessment, 1985

Electronics Services Unlimited, *The National Work-at-Home Survey*, 1986
Empirica GmbH, *Decentralised Electronic Working in the Banking, Insurance and Software Industries—Experiences, Potential and Future Developments*, 1986
Empirica GmbH, 'Telework—Present situation and future development of a new form of work organisation', *Conference Abstracts*, 1987
Eosys Ltd, *Opportunities to Promote Remote Working in the Highlands and Islands*, 1984
European Foundation for the Improvement of Living and Working Conditions, *Telework—Impact on Living and Working Conditions*, 1985
Huws, Ursula, *The New Homeworkers*, Low Pay Unit Pamphlet no. 28, 1984
Kuwabara, Moriji, 'Basic plan for INS', *JTR Magazine*, January 1986
McConnell, Patricia, *The Woman's Work at Home Handbook*, Bantam, 1986
Moran, Rosalyn and Tansey, Jean, *Telework: Women in Environments*, Irish Foundation for Human Development, 1986
Murakami, Tadasu, 'Inception of INS experience', *JTR Magazine*, January 1985
Pascale, Richard and Athos, Anthony, *The Art of Japanese Management*, Simon & Schuster, 1981
Peters, Tom, *In Search of Excellence*, Harper and Row, 1983
Roberts, Steven, K., 'Electronic cottage on wheels', *Whole Earth Review*, Spring 1987
Sahlberg, Bengt, *Remote Work in the Ecotronic Society*, Scandinavian Housing and Planning Research, April 1987
Toffler, Alvin, *The Third Wave*, Collins, 1980
Wolf, Tamara, 'Working at home: the growth of cottage industry', *The Futurist*, June 1984

# 8

# Ten Years On—Constraints and Releases

We should indeed take Ken Edwards very much to heart and remember that 'homeworking IT is a key to the possibility of galvanising ourselves to tackle the next century'. But the auguries are that we will collectively not do so, at least until the next century has dawned and is thinking about breakfast. Panelists in the survey were asked what they thought was likely to be the status of telecommuting in 10 and in 33 years' time. As far as the former period was concerned, though there were encouraging factors that could lead to a great release of homeworking activity, the constraints likely to prevent this happening to the full were more apparent to them. Their aggregate opinion is endorsed by written forecasts in the literature on the subject, though all are agreed that there will undoubtedly be a solid advance during the 1990s.

## A RANGE OF ALTERNATIVES

What they thought probable was for there to have been a gradual increase in the practice, but rather in the sense that more people will work at or from a home base for part of the time, than a straight black-and-white division between homeworkers and office workers. There will be more discrimination over what is suitable to be done where, more alternative ideas tried out to suit different circumstances, and more practical research into how best to manage the split.

> Trends in information technology will make it easier and economic for more work to be carried out remotely, including people working at home, but few organisational decision makers are ready yet to explore the implications for their companies. The 'pioneers' of new working lifestyles will come from: a) People like authors who are homebased anyway; b) People who are tied to their home for a period of their career, i.e. with young children; c) People who

> reach a period in their career where they are ready to shift direction, perhaps with the assistance of their existing company; d) People who start earlier in this mode as a deliberately preferred lifestyle.
> *(Jim Cowie)*

Jim Cowie envisages that this will come about in a whole range of alternative ways, following the James Martin line in Chapter 1 and reflecting the 'and/and' mode of thought rather than the inherently more daunting 'either/or' one. For him, many of the isolation problems of the home-based and mobile worker can be mitigated by the growth of neighbourhood work-centres, either shared between local freelancers and the employees of different organisations, or dedicated to one employer as a satellite office. There are already precedents for neighbourhood small businesses giving each other intellectual spin-off, professional support and practical counselling—such as the Briarpatch Network of the San Francisco Bay area; the Boston/Cambridge interaction of like high-tech minds, echoed very much by the Science Park movement in the UK; and the Commonbox Club of small businessmen in Whitby, North Yorkshire. The undedicated work-centre of the future is an extension of this natural business development. The cement of a number of small businesses sharing a friendly cohesiveness will be reinforced by the sharing of technological equipment, methodology and practical support.

As evidenced by the French and Swedish experiences of Chapter 7, managements are suspicious of shared work-centres, but as will be suggested in Chapter 10 there are reasons for thinking that this will not always be the case. Nonetheless, the large organisation's preference until the end of the century will be for the dedicated work-centre, in all probability—the Haywards Heath portacabin for the 30 employees of the Cosmos Insurance Company who live in the area.

> The organisation may be able to network the branches on a regional and on an area basis. The individual who now trundles up to head office from Haywards Heath will then be able to plug in from home, or from an area office five miles away, or from a regional office fifteen miles away. This fits in between either working from home or working at headquarters, and the thing to remember is that it is not necessary for people to get stuck in any one of these modes. All are possible and all should be experimented with to meet whatever is the individual and organisational requirement.
> *(Jim Cowie)*

The flavour of the technique will be the recognition and acceptance that everyone can have choices—a very fundamental 21st century concept. On the other hand, from the organisational point of view, it is somewhat more demanding as it involves a whole new set of different ground-rules. The manager of the Haywards Heath portacabin will need, for example, to manage it in a way to which he is unaccustomed. People may not be able to pop in and out as and when they want. They may have to give him notice so that he can set up the technological requirements through which they can interface with whomever they need. This may be a temporary feature, however, and once the system begins to catch on and it is obvious that organisations are moving in this direction, the technology will be developed to answer market requirements and the individual will be able to plug in his/her personal work-station wherever it is most convenient to do so.

The shift towards an alternative range of job patterns was also expected to continue by the panel, with more job sharing and more flexitime, for example. In the intermediate term, this would have two paradoxically opposite effects. On the one hand, it would open up thinking to accept different kinds of working practice of which homeworking could be one. The old-fashioned hidebound 9 – 5 existence will be gradually broken down even in a ten-year timescale. On the other hand, because of more job sharing (inevitable because of an increase in white-collar unemployment) and a generally more flexible approach to full-time work (with provision for mothers by various means from crêches to career-breaks) the urge to embrace a more radical form of working practice such as telecommuting might be dampened down. Much of the future endorsement of the homeworking principle will depend on the socio-economic and political climate at the time, and will relate closely to both the level and the type of unemployment that is being experienced. Governments will tend to encourage the uptake of unemployed men at times of high unemployment and discourage women from working part-time at home, whereas when unemployment falls they will use fiscal means to encourage women homeworkers to continue their economic activity, particularly if they are trained in scarce skills.

Furthermore, an economic downturn would probably entail a retrenchment and a retention of existing systems, whereas in a period of expansion with booming markets and healthy competition, more experiments of this nature will take place. However, another macro-economic factor to be considered is the possibility of restraint on fossil fuel consumption and thence of increased petrol costs. The price of oil is liable to undergo cyclical fluctuations, so that at any one moment it may be considerably over or under what it should be according to the rate of inflation; but on the whole, while petrol costs are low the impact of travelling costs as an encouragement to homeworking will be diminished, while any time that the oil price is significantly increased, people will once again begin to think of homeworking as an alternative mode of work-style.

Whatever happens, however, some jobs are never going to be done in this way—indeed some boring repetitive ones will probably be overtaken by computerisation before they can even be adapted to a home-based system. Many professional, administrative and clerical jobs of all kinds could be so adapted, but as emphasised, not those aspects of them that require a face-to-face element. This period will therefore mark the beginning of the movement to break down work into its component parts, and to decide which of them may be more advantageously done at home and which in an office where human contact is more important. The trend will become visible as inter-office and intra-office communication becomes more automated and technologically-based. Such innovations as electronic mail and more effective video-conferencing, used between different offices within the same organisation and between offices of organisations doing business with each other, will highlight the fact that such forms of communication are feasible, possible, acceptable and adaptable to office/home usage.

It is likely though, that for the time being, the computing industry will still be leading the way in the application of distance working, due to its familiarity with the technology, the pressing need to retain and improve skills, and the fact that there are such strong precedents for its activities to be carried out in this distributed manner. Having said that, the computing industry will probably be beginning to look a very different and greatly expanded animal to what it does now. The skills will have been upgraded to embrace both a more rounded business knowledge and the means of enhancing products and services of all types through the application of microprocessors. There will also be a need for greater people-skills as the industry takes off its metaphorical white coat and comes into closer touch with the realities of the man and woman in the street. It will probably not be until the next century, however, that these characteristics will also have been massively taken up by the industry's own customers and clients.

## THE NEW TECHNOLOGY

Telecommuters by definition use computer technology to communicate with a remote office, but many now also use telephone, telex, fax (increasingly), cellular radio (increasingly) courier or postal services. Nonetheless, it is the opening up of the UK telecommunications market, by separating data transmission networks from the public telephone service and ushering in the potentially widespread use of cable systems, that can pave the way for a dramatic drop in charges for this type of service—necessary before the telecommuting concept really takes off.

According to the panelists, most of the reason why telecommuting has not yet evolved to any general extent can be laid at the door of the inadequacies of the present telephone system, which at the moment is hardly even able to handle text particularly well and therefore serves as a brilliant excuse for the unimaginative and the lazy to do nothing. Nonetheless, criticism is well founded.

JANET (the academic telecom network to which all university computers are linked) has an incredibly slow messaging system. There are also frequent pauses and garbled passages. The BT engineer said to me when I complained—'Yes of course, living in the country, it's the farmers, you see; they shoot the pigeons on the wires and particularly in the rain it tends to short circuit.' Roll on fibre-optic cables!
(*Professor Jonathan Gershuny, Professor of Sociology, University of Bath*)

Electronic mail was a disaster for us. The speed of access was very slow, bits got lost and competition for the use of computer time was also very tiresome. One would be told, 'We are in the middle of doing the accounts so you can't have your message.'
(*Bob Pell*)

There is some difference of opinion as to just how soon and just how cheaply British Telecom will be able to provide the necessary technology to avoid these accusations. There will clearly be a progressive enhancement of the portfolio of products available; and in five to ten years' time one would expect to see supporting facilities for extending the use of home micros, for example, which will by then begin to be able to replicate mainframe programs.

One of the main facilitators for telecommuting will be better quality broadband communications with high-resolution screens, and in ten years' time it must be hoped that this will be available due to the incidence of both fibre-optic cable and ISDN (Integrated Services Digital Network). As far as the former is concerned, though resolution is now as good as on a TV screen, the problem is that to date, BT has no competition there. People are reluctant to pay the monopolistic connection charges, and without this it is impossible to demonstrate the benefits and sell the services to them. Consequently, there is a little home shopping and home banking here and there, but nothing much else outside mere entertainment. It is felt by some that competitive voice transmission services at local level and run by entrepreneurial figureheads may be needed for the industry to thrive, but the necessary legislation may well not be enacted in order to bring this about within the ten-year timeframe.

The secret of ISDN is digital coding; the very life-blood of computers themselves. Computers' digital signals are now incompatible with the analog signals that normally pass through telephone wires. Thus to send computer data over the telephone today requires not only a line but an intervening modem which translates digital to analog, and back again at the other end. With ISDN, everything in telecommunications will be standardised universally and internationally, and everyone will have the necessary tools for electronic communication with each other, not only as regards voice and text, but visually, too.

Within ten years, ISDN networks will have spread very widely across the country, giving ample scope for products and services to develop and fulfil most

of the imaginative ideas that one can postulate, except for those services which need quality moving video. There is considerable scope for improvement using the technology that will be available. I think that the most significant constraint that will inhibit progress in a ten year timescale is inadequate progressiveness, understanding and ambition on the part of individuals, of society, and above all of organisations.
(*Jim Cowie*)

At present, we are way behind all that, however. A photophone is about to become available, which will give screened images of a chart or a plan, but moving video-phones are many years away. Moreover, some claim that even with ISDN there is likely to be a problem with the bandwidth of the image; and that the resolution obtainable is nothing like as good as would be available on an ordinary TV screen. If so, the man in the street is unlikely to be impressed with its suitability. Though ISDN will create an enriched environment, and the video element will open up the idea that remote working of all kinds is a viable possibility, it will not really be until the next wave of broadband improvements that bells will really start to ring (in a manner of speaking) and the use of telecommuting will be seen to depend merely on personal and managerial preference.

One could well spend a higher proportion of time working at home, as long as it doesn't involve anything that requires persuading, cajoling, debating or negotiating. Videophones will be a help for this sort of face-to-face contact though, and in ten years they will undoubtedly be available. However, this may then still be only on a slow scan basis and not conducive to full communication - also for quite a few years to come pure cost factors will restrict their distribution to homes, too. But in ten years, access to text and data of every sort will be as easy remote from the office as in the office.
(*Ken Edwards*)

But for homeworking to be natural and obviously appropriate even to the occasional user, one needs cheap flat screen technology and a video-linked interaction, not feasible in the early days of ISDN. One needs the next increase in bandwidth for anything other than information on a predetermined topic. Till then, personal idiosyncracies will be misunderstood, whereas if one could see somebody absolutely clearly on the screen, a couple of shrugs and a nod of the head would put the message over without any words, as in a face-to-face situation.
(*Michael Josephs*)

People are experimenting even now, but always coming up against the ceiling of technological capability when it comes to visual human interaction. The consensus of opinion is that this will continue to be a restriction for some time to come.

At the moment there is no video-conferencing network across all government departments but there are several pairs of conference centres within

> departments. These are between London and Brussels; London – Cardiff within ECGD; London – Sheffield within Manpower Services Commission, etc. Costs of such services are high due to dedicated accommodation, high transmission bandwidth and low utilisation. Futhermore there is a psychological block about going to a studio on a formal basis so now the new deal is to examine the possibility of using video terminals on selected desks. The studio conferences have to be very formally structured and almost take place under a 'producer'—in any event they must be very strongly chaired to be successful. This new scheme is to try and get away from the rather awe-inspiring formal structure.
> (*Roy Dibble, Head of Advanced Technology and Telecommunications, Central Computer Telecommunications Agency*)

In the field of voice rather than vision, there is more optimism, however. The imaginative uses of cellular radio will proliferate the incidence of remote working, just as the imaginative use of fax is doing already, with round-robin letters, for example. Furthermore, the possibilities of voice recognition are only just over the horizon. This will relieve the present problems of keyboard anxiety that restrict the usage of electronic potential for many business people. Many manufacturers are near to marketing general voice recognition machines which will give displayed text from the spoken word. In a matter of years it will be possible to buy a portable telephone with a high-quality video adaptor built into it and an international account number. When travelling you will thus be able to take it along and on arrival in a foreign city, plug the 'electronic slate' into the nearest wall-jack. It will then give you the messages waiting for you, either when you key in the code or simply ask for them verbally. This development should be available five years from now in Japan and the USA, and in ten years here.

The cost of all this is going to be as much a problem as the availability, however, given the timescale we are considering.

> In the mid-term future, line costs are going to be critical to the development of all kinds of remote working. The general trend in telecommunications costs is down in real terms and prices are more closely related to costs of provision of service. The improvement for the business customer is more marked but in a time frame of ten years from now, it seems unlikely that businesses will be drawn into homeworking due to dramatic savings in costs. The viability and attraction of the concept will still be 'in the eye of the beholder' and will be determined by the imagination and drive of those who see benefits for themselves and their organisations in moving in this direction. I am cautiously optimistic that there will be a trend towards more remote activity but not a stampede inspired by dramatic savings in costs.
> (*Jim Cowie*)

There are reasons for this, many of which are technical, but others of which are attitudinal within BT, as the following opinion—by no means a lone voice—demonstrates.

> With ISDN the cost of moving information will fall rapidly, but switching capabilities and connection costs will stay expensive. It is a function of the logarithm of the number of subscribers involved, i.e. the cost for two people should be multiplied by three when there are eight of them, by seven when there are 128 etc. With new technology, one can maybe fix a cable with as much as five hundred miles between repeaters, and with fibre-optics one can have 120,000 circuits in a cable. The individual circuit cost makes up a smaller and smaller part of the total. There are many other costs—not only switching, but administration and database access—and these will remain at a high level, especially the former.
>
> With regard to database access, taking the Stock Exchange as a typical example, this subscription is about the same as when the service started, but now there is more and better information. Though some productivity increases can be anticipated, administration costs will always remain at an extremely high level in an organisation like BT, which is technologically driven rather than customer driven. It may well take ten years to break down the monopoly-bureaucratic attitude which ensures that the organisation is more concerned with the viewpoints of people inside it than with that of the world outside.
> (*Michael Josephs*)

To counter this with a more optimistic assessment one should turn to Ian Mackintosh, who, however, is admittedly looking at the question from a European rather than a British viewpoint. Nonetheless, with the efforts of the European PTTs to struggle towards integration and compatibility, some of the resolve may rub off onto BT. In *Sunrise Europe—the Dynamics of Information Technology*, he sees new imaging techniques and videophones, high-capacity information storage systems, and a proliferation of intelligent work-stations as ushering in the transition to the integrated office. Integration is the key word. By the late 1990s, one must expect all computerised office equipment to be integrated into an entirely new class of system. This will incorporate the functions of today's mainframes, minis, superminis, personal computers, word processors, PABXs, photocopiers and facsimile—all in one machine. Much of this work-station equipment will attain very high levels of intelligence, while voice and pattern recognition techniques will become well established. However, the essential force of technological change at work will be based on efficient methods of interconnecting all these work-stations so that they can communicate effectively with each other, with whatever mainframe computers they need to, and with the rapidly expanding number of databases. In Mackintosh's vision, all these pieces of equipment will be united through local area networks, cables and satellite links by enormously sophisticated software which will allow any machine to communicate absolutely with any other part of the system.

But bearing in mind the panel's reservations about the cost, availability and reliability of all this ten years on, we may well have to wait for longer until it has its impact on homeworking. Meanwhile, things will have been moving somewhat. Till now, modern technology has been seen as highly complicated, requiring a trained specialist elite to operate it and based mainly on the provision of centralised services. As a result ordinary men and women have felt themselves deprived of the ability they previously had to control their own environment. However, in ten years so much will be available in and from the home that has in the past been developed outside it, that people are going to begin to ask—why not work, too?

In *The Wired Society*, as long ago as 1978, James Martin had already listed no less than 99 services which advanced telecommunications could provide in the home by the late 1990s—through passive entertainment, people-to-people communication, interactive television, still-picture interaction, monitoring, home printing and computer terminals. Ranging from the customised news service to home banking, from medical diagnosis to computer dating, from public opinion polling to the remote control of heating and air conditioning, the basic motivation of this technological explosion will be the need for manufacturers and the providers of services to sell to the home-based. Here is Christine MacNulty, who co-operated with NEDO in *IT Futures...It Can Work*.

> In ten years, a computer-literate generation now in their teens will be able to assimilate anything there is available. Furthermore, things will be so much friendlier that even our generation will catch on. Home banking is now thought of as impossible, and it is, so long as a customer is tied to one bank or one building society, but a computerised nationwide system giving one access to any financial institution and any kind of financial product would make it vastly popular. The same can be said for teleshopping which will be far more sophisticated than anything we have now. It will be an electronic yellow pages and an interactive Exchange and Mart, besides a means of being able to buy one's soap powder on it.
>
> Think of services like travel agents too—we'll be able to call up travelogue films and brochures, or textual details of where we can slot in for a late booking. Selling domestic services over the screen is another aspect. Window cleaners won't have to knock on the door, they can just leave a message as to when they are available and key it in to their potential customers Self-employeds and small companies are going to be doing all kinds of things like this. New businesses and new services will be able to advertise their facilities and the result will be both a proliferation of brand new types of home-business and the movement of existing businesses into a home base.
> (*Christine MacNulty*)

## THE CONSTRAINTS OF MANAGEMENT

The next step is not only to sell goods and services to those at home, but to buy their labour there. The travel agent in the above example does not have to operate from the high street any more, the insurance clerk can work from home, and the shop assistant can assist from home too, while the goods are in the warehouse but displayed on the customer's screen—all as long as the technology makes it convenient and/or human and/or fun and/or advantageous enough for everyone. Have you ever seen a queue of people at a cash-point outside a bank while the tellers inside are hanging about with nothing to do? Well then, technology is sometimes preferable to human interaction, even now.

Tell that to most of today's managers, though. In the minds of the panel of F International and CPS managers and homeworkers, who must be judged to know the form pretty well, probably the most restrictive of all constraints on the development of telecommuting is the lack of vision, imagination and dedication of average British management. At present, the older managers—many whom, after all, are still going to have an effect on how their organisations are being run even ten years from now—are badly disposed towards computers. They are not acquainted with them or educated in their use, and having no experience of them, are averse to the change involved, particularly where they feel they may lose control through lack of knowledge. Frightened and reluctant, they are also suspicious about working at home because they do not trust their workforce and are convinced that unless they monitor people's hours they will not be producing as they should.

> Particularly in cases where security is important, they are always going to want control over people's clerical, administrative and professional roles. There is a cultural bias towards smoke-filled rooms where managements are concerned, even though cost pressures on offices will be immense. Where it is necessary to get together as a team to exchange issues and to feel and explore ways of tackling them, there is also going to be a need for people to work in one place for some time. On the other hand a more universal flexitime will come when it is much easier to take off time to work at home and there will be plenty of machinery available to do this. The brake on such progress will be management, however.
> (*Ninian Eadie*)

Of course, as we have seen, the management of homeworking must be output-based, and present-day seniors regard the discipline needed to gauge output accurately as extraordinarily irksome. They will hold back from initiating it in case they get it wrong. There is no point in going over all the old ground again to prove how beneficial the remote working concept can be, how productive, how flexible and how actually conducive to improved management. Only the most farsighted managers will begin to move towards this position, the vast majority claiming that the technology is not advanced or cheap enough, the workforce is not controllable or enthusiastic enough, and they didn't get where they are today by adopting radical solutions.

Another stated concern among employers is that of security. Certainly, fraud is more theoretically feasible given a homeworking environment, and there will undoubtedly be fears of industrial espionage, malicious wrecking and all kinds of similar horrors, made more possible in an uncontrolled electronic context. This is going to be another reason given by reluctant and idle employers who do not wish to get involved in the development of telecommuting. Manufacturers will catch on to the demand here, however. One can imagine equipment with integrity and security features for legal, financial or advertising work, say—what could be called bonded work-stations. Moreover, taking the financial sector it is interesting to see how very rapidly—within a year—after the Big Bang, the floor of the Stock Exchange has emptied and the Market is now being conducted almost totally electronically on a remote basis. It is nowadays not a matter of 'my word is my bond' as much as 'my word is my byte'.

> If the content of the work is financial, employers will be incredibly careful of the possibilities of fraud and will want to keep key people very tightly controlled. They will also be frightened about industrial espionage, which could be a growing problem. We have to sign confidentiality agreements but they are still nervous of us going into their mainframe until they recognise how totally ethical we are.
> (*F International manager*)

Granted, these are reasons for caution. But unfortunately they will be much used as reasons for doing nothing, and as they have so often done before this generation of managers will ask 'Why?' instead of 'Why not!' According to David Gleicher (referred to in *Organisational Transitions: Managing Complex Change* by Richard Beckhard and Reuben Harris of MIT), the likelihood of the success of any change is a function of the current pain of the status quo, the clarity of the first step and the demonstrability of its advantages. If these three together come to more than the cost (in every sense) of the change then movement will take place. If not, not.

> Traditionalism is the enemy. People stick to tried-and-tested formulae unless they can see a big pay-off as a result of changing—either because it cuts short a hopeless situation or enormously improves an adequate one.
> (*Ninian Eadie*)

Deliberate change and growth generally require the spur of pain in the human experience, creatures of habit as we are, and where there is no impetus for businesses to change they struggle on in the same direction. If they can get people to work in offices only a certain amount less conveniently and only a certain amount more expensively, managers will do so.

> At the moment there is more pressure towards homeworking on the supply side (i.e. to fill skills shortages) than the demand side (i.e. to reduce office overheads). The demand side comes into prominence where big companies are pressed for office space, but not for those that are shrinking or hold

> unmarketable property. On the other hand, the cost of rent and rates is continually increasing that aspect.
> (*Michel Syrett*)

> The biggest constraint will be the failure of traditional companies to recognise the opportunities offered through this means and then to go for them. It is much easier for a green-field company to introduce. Office accommodation is relatively cheap and abundant outside large cities so existing businesses may well ask, why get rid of it? As far as ICI is concerned, it has already sold off some of its offices outside the factory sites as its needs have reduced. The remaining large office spaces, inside secure factory sites, are therefore not particularly marketable to anybody else, and there is no great push for ICI to divest itself of them and create a homeworking force instead.
> (*Ken Edwards*)

However, managers seldom object nowadays if their conventional employees occasionally work at home for the odd day, in the recognition that report writing and much other work is easier and more productively undertaken there without interruption. What may happen, therefore, is that the method of working from home gradually creeps up on people as a possible more permanent alternative, where the individual is skilled and psychologically adjusted to the concept, where the appropriate technology is available, and where it is also quite obviously advantageous to the employer. It will be a case of suck it and see.

## THE TRADE UNION MOVEMENT

Managers may be out of touch with the realities of telecommuting, but the poor trade unions are on a different planet. They have the strongest reservations about homeworking because in the past it has always involved people being exploited. However, the teleworking phenomenon now largely embraces women, freelancers and high technology—all areas where unions have found it most difficult to make an appeal because they fail to understand them. The experience of GMBTU, EETPU and TASS must have been disheartening; when they went out to try and recruit homeworkers they got a very dusty answer.

> Not a single union is actually thinking along proper lines about this. They have about as much idea of how to do it as my left boot. All those involved are activists, rather than nice people with a different set of problems, like the homeworkers themselves. Unions say that they cannot have branch meetings if people are working at home because it cuts across the democratic process. This is ridiculous since normally only eight to ten people turn up to any branch meeting anyway and the democratic process is a dead duck. On the other hand something may happen, when homeworkers suddenly recognise they are a force to be reckoned with and should band together for their own protection.

> Although the current exponents are all scrupulous, some people who are far from it will try and get onto the bandwagon. When this happens there will be total panic and the whole thing will lurch violently into change. The tragedy is that at the moment no one is yet looking at it sensibly and constructively.
> (*Barrie Sherman, freelance consultant*)

This is salutary talk from the ex-head of research at ASTMS, co-author with Clive Jenkins of *The Collapse of Work*. His point of view has support from other quarters, too.

> The unions can't do anything very much to stop the spread of telecommuting, but it must be admitted that these outworking people will need to belong to some kind of professional association or guild so as not to be exploited in future. The unions could and should fulfil this role, but looking at them right now they probably won't.
> (*Charles Handy*)

The ASTMS Winter 1986 *Electronics Bulletin* concentrated on the high-tech homeworker. It featured the fact that IT World was managing the DTI project for disabled remote workers, and promised to make employers aware of the possibilities and impress and encourage them to employ more disabled men and women. So far so good. But the leading article featured Ursula Huws' book, *The New Homeworkers*, which has already often been both quoted and cited here, stressing the fact that her survey showed that self-employed high-tech homeworkers fared worse (with 24% lower salaries) than those with employee status. ASTMS then went on to admit that these people were not exploited to the same degree as traditional sweated labour, but nonetheless claimed that they had a disadvantaged position as regards isolation, lack of career development, pensions, health and safety hazards. But it then ventured onto even shakier ground, claiming that within CPS, there were problems of pensions, payment for heating and lighting at home, lack of knowledge of and access to relevant training courses, lack of information on new products, lack of annual counselling and appraisal, and too many visits on site. CPS most obligingly agreed to circulate its workforce with an invitation to an ASTMS meeting, at which these theoretical grievances were to be aired. In the event, the homeworkers obviously started from another dimension as compared to their would-be representatives.

> Five people turned up to their recruitment meeting. The Union representatives were totally out of touch. They started from the assumption that homeworkers were mistreated and quickly found that this didn't go down very well. They also appealed to the homeworkers way below their intellectual calibre, and went rambling on about pensions when they didn't realise that there was already a pension scheme in operation. All in all, from the Union point of view it was a disaster.
> (*CPS homeworker*)

A TUC statement, *Homeworking*, of March 1985, describes developments in computer technology which affect homeworking, and cites a number of examples from the USA, as listed already here and focusing on American Airlines' closure of its data entry operation in Tulsa, Okalahoma, and the transference of that work to Barbados using a satellite link to connect data entry in Barbados with data processing which remained in Tulsa. In the UK, mention is also given to F International, ICL and Rank Xerox, while once again there was stress on Ursula Huws' survey of 78 homeworkers earning on average £3,981 per annum compared to the £5,208 they would have earned on site. Disadvantages apart from low wages (and these, of course, were unrealistically compared to contract freelancing rather than hourly rates for software employment) were listed as: extra lighting and heating costs at home, loss of promotion and training prospects, loss of side-benefits such as subsidised meals or social activities, possible health risk to all the family from VDUs and machinery, the effect of deadline stress on the family structure, loss of contract work, absence of trade unionism for protection, and loss of employment rights and protections for those who were self-employed. Homeworkers have signally failed to respond.

There is thus an attitude of union confrontation, though an ineffectual one at present. The danger is that since neither side is talking to the other, there will have to be the most unholy row before they ever do. By then it will be shouting not talking, and our commentators might be proved right—that ultimately trade union attitudes may well inhibit telecommuting growth due to the mistaken generalisation of some particular incident.

## THE INLAND REVENUE AND THE DHSS

> Labour law and tax regulations are not conducive to people who want to transfer from employment to self-employment and maybe back again. The need is for a legal and tax framework that clarifies the grey areas, since at the moment the position is unsure and is disinclining companies and individuals to make experiments. We want a framework without bureaucracy, because the will towards this homeworking thing is beginning to be visible on the part of both some workers and some managements.
> (*Michel Syrett*)

In 1983 a parliamentary question was raised as to the number of people who had claimed to be self-employed and had been reclassified as employed by the Inland Revenue. The answer was 107,000 in that year. It included part-time exam-markers, scriptwriters, museum attendants and teachers, some of whom are indeed part-employed but some definitely self-employed, revealing a totally indiscriminate reclassification process. As a result of this, the National Federation of Self-Employed and Small Businesses mounted a parliamentary campaign to ask the Inland Revenue for criteria and tests for self-employment and bring the whole argument into the open.

The NFSE were by no means in the business of helping people evade tax where they should pay it, but they felt strongly that people who were totally innocent should be left alone, and that a climate should be created in which one-client self-employment was recognised as a genuine mode of work. As a result of this and other representations, leaflet IR56 *Tax: Employed or Self-Employed*, was issued by the Inland Revenue in May 1985 (and revised a year later), setting out their guidelines to help people decide whether they should be assessed as employed or self-employed, but emphasising that the taxpayer had to look at his or her job as a whole and all its conditions in the process.

If you can answer 'yes' to the following questions, you are probably an **employee**:

- Do you have to do the work that you have agreed to undertake yourself (that is, you are not allowed to send a substitute or hire other people to do it)?
- Can someone tell you what to do, and when and how to do it?
- Does someone provide you with holiday time, sick pay or a pension? (Though a lot of employees don't get any of these)
- Are you paid so much an hour, a week or a month? Can you get overtime pay? (Though many employees are paid by commission or on a piece-work basis.)
- Are you expected to work set hours, or a given number of hours a week or month?
- Do you work wholly or mainly for one business? (But remember that many employees work for more than one employer.)
- Are you expected to work at the premises of the person you are working for, or at a place or places they decide? (But remember that a self-employed person, such as a plumber, may, by the nature of the job have to work at the premises of the person who engages him.)

If you can answer 'yes' to the following questions, it will usually mean that you are **self-employed**

- Are you ultimately responsible for how the business is run? Do you risk your own capital in the business? Are you responsible for bearing losses as well as taking profits?
- Do you yourself control what you do, whether you do it, how you do it, and when and where you do it? (Though many employees have considerable independence.)
- Do you provide the major items of equipment you need to do your job (not just the small tools which many employees provide for themselves)?

- Are you free to hire other people, on terms of your own choice, to do the work that you have agreed to undertake? (But remember that an employee may also be authorised to delegate work or to engage others on behalf of his employer.)
- Do you have to correct unsatisfactory work in you own time and at your own expense?

(*Tax: Employed or Self-Employed?* Inland Revenue, 1986)

No fault of the Revenue's, but all those qualifying clauses in brackets do show that the law needs a thorough overhaul. The Policy Division of the Revenue, in a letter to the writer in April 1987 enclosing this leaflet, hoped it would be helpful but pointed out that:

> Whether a person is an employee or self-employed depends upon the precise terms on which he is engaged and works. There are no general statutory definitions of employment status. The Inland Revenue role is to establish the facts and apply them to the case law established in this area.

It would seem that registration for VAT and/or limited company status, as with the Rank Xerox networkers, are the only definite criteria here. This is at most a holding position, and more likely to turn negative rather than positive towards the idea of experimentation with new forms of working mode. For example,

> There is already trouble with the Inland Revenue in the freelance film and TV industry. Cameramen are freelance, but they insist on having an assistant cameraman who is actually employed by them. Therefore, even if he goes from job to job he is technically an employee and this causes untold trouble. As these kinds of problems multiply, if legislation does not move fast enough to keep up with the times it will constrain the development of the remote working freelance habit.
> (*Barrie Sherman*)

Rank Xerox networkers are totally at arm's length and CPS homeworkers are fully employed, but as mentioned in Chapter 3, at one stage F International had considerable difficulty over the tax status of its panel members. Now, a precedent has been set, which can be relied upon by any of its panel who have difficulty with their local Inspector. However, FI has to be careful not to get involved with their tax problems, pensions, or the many of the normal personnel functions of an employer, so that the panel's freelance status is not jeopardised. Panel members must be working on projects that have a clear beginning and a clear end—and furthermore they have to be able to say 'yes' or 'no' to the next contract that is offered them, and to an invitation to undergo training. Moreover, the Revenue insists that some roles have to be salaried—anyone who hires and fires, anyone who has to do with administration and anyone in marketing or sales.

Ironically, a fortnight after this deal was sorted out by F with the Revenue, the DHSS sent someone round to argue the toss, and the whole nightmare of justification began all over again. At that time, the two departments did not work in conjunction with each other at all on this, but on 19 March 1987, the Inland Revenue issued a press release *Tax Help for Small Firms and the Self-Employed*, co-ordinating the efforts of the Revenue and the DHSS from 6 April of that year, so that they now each have one local nominated officer with combined responsibility for all enquiries and decisions about employment status.

We should be grateful for small mercies, but the outlook over the coming decade remains grey in this respect. Thin slices of technical assistance are not enough and the whole presupposition that people's homes are not places of production and work must change. At present the homeworker has to pay capital gains tax on a proportion of his/her house if it contains a room exclusively for work purposes, the overheads concerned with which are deducted from income for tax purposes. Furthermore, nannies or childminders and their cost are not tax-deductible. The Equal Opportunities Commission has frequently urged for changes here but to no avail. So as it is, the secretary who serves the boss counts as a business expense, but the nanny who enables the boss to start the business and employ the secretary does not. Perhaps this is only a minor cavil affecting few people at present, but the problem is that until things are sorted out in a more distinct and favourable light, at any time in the future a clampdown could occur, should the government in its infinite wisdom consider that homeworkers were in some way 'getting away with it' in tax terms, or deserved a pounding for political reasons. It would be tragic if, to smoke out a few miscreants, the whole telecommuting movement was rocked back on its heels by blunderbuss legisilation. But until the matter is thoroughly considered and codified, this is always going to be possible.

## OTHER LEGAL CONSTRAINTS

The first question here is whether homeworking affects residential status, and whether there are constraints about carrying on a business in or from a house. Nowadays local authorities generally turn a blind eye to technical infringement of the regulations governing commercial use of residential areas, since these were historically drawn up with the intent of controlling offensive manufacturing practices. Nonetheless, problems can arise. At F International once again, in the early days Steve Shirley herself had a problem when neighbours complained that there were too many cars blocking entrances and too many people coming and going. They took her to court even though she had by then anyway changed the whole system, which just meant one additional difficulty she could do without.

In *Home-Based Economic Activity: The Legal and Town Planning Implications,* Peter Walsh, Keith Thomas and John Porter consider the legal aspects of home-based economic activity, or what they term HEA. They suggest that development control agencies have proved inconsistent in the past and misapplied legal principles, to the extent that official guidance should be given to them to be more tolerant in dealing with HEA. According to Bob Pell of Conran Roche, one of our own study's panelists, the Department of the Environment is now much more relaxed in principle about this kind of multiple usage, but permission in detail still depends on the local planning authority. In future there seems no logical reason why white-collar work should not be carried on from home unless it becomes intrusive, but one cannot be sure. Local taxation, however, is a horse of a very different colour, and it is fervently to be hoped that when the whole restructuring of the rating system is finally enacted, legislation will prove to be supportive rather than restrictive towards working from home. If not, this could be a time-bomb ticking away under the whole concept.

Walsh, Thomas and Porter contrast the UK position with that now pertaining in Eugene, Oregon, where planning permission is not necessary for HEA as long as certain specified standards are met—in practice, not only reasonable but informally enforced without recourse to the courts should there be complaint from neighbours. It may be remembered from Chapter 7 that Oregon is one state in the USA that is encouraging homeworking to replace its dying primary industries. The UK too could benefit from an understanding of Walsh, Thomas and Porter's three 'Oregon principles'—first, that with new work opportunities, starting small businesses in the home can help alleviate the problem of unemployment; secondly, that the growing hi-tech service industry can be readily fitted into the home; thirdly, that this industry is less objectionable than those of the past and can be carried on in residential areas without any particularly adverse environmental effects.

In terms of restrictive covenants on house purchase, mortgage terms, and insurance wordings, actual or potential telecommuters will have to keep their eyes skinned, too. Walsh, Thomas and Porter are also critical of the way many of these are framed to restrict homeworking. Only 24% of Britain's homes are owned outright; and the 35% mortgaged, 12% leased from private landlords and 29% council owned may well be saddled with restrictive clauses on their use. As for insurance, according to the Consumers' Association booklet *Earning Money at Home,* anyone who sets up business in their home on however small a scale is technically invalidating their normal householders' comprehensive policy. Insurers always require to be informed if any part of the building is to be used for any purpose other than mere residence. With innocuous activities and professions carried on at home insurers are generally willing, possibly with some exclusions and a small additional premium, to continue covering the premises as though they were no more than a private dwelling. However, numbers of people visiting the house on business affects insurance cover for theft and for liability to third parties. Furthermore, car insurance also requires consideration when business use is involved with more than one person driving.

These things are not exactly restrictive, they are simply matters which homeworkers have to take into consideration, deal with and if necessary make a fuss about.

> It isn't only things like rating, insurance and mortgages but the very way everyone is treated by the Post Office or BT. The self-employed resident of a house does not have the pull if things go wrong. These organisations go out of their way to favour conventional business and industry. They don't recognise that there is a growing army of people who are actually very much in business and highly industrious from a home base.
> (*James Robertson*)

The telecommuters must be prepared to fight their corner here but also, if it comes to the crunch, in the even more exacting corridors of Whitehall and Westminster, where grants and legislation are up for grabs, where the large and the organised carry the weight and God is indeed on the side of the big batallions. It may well be that within the next ten years the potential increase in homeworking will madden some dying institutional dinosaur into a final paroxysm of counter-activity. Let us not be insensitive enough to conjecture which of them it might be, but one can imagine that though mortally wounded it will still be enormously strong and influential in its death throes.

At present the Department of Employment is sympathetic to homeworking as long as it does not exploit the low paid. But there are plenty of areas, such as health and safety regulations, where if marshalled to implement an overall doctrinaire decision of government, it could flatten the telecommuting movement. Further, if local authorities find they are losing revenue as businesses in their areas dwindle or decentralise, what will be their reactions? What of the possible growth of neighbourhood work-centres on the fringes of big towns and the requirements for change in the restrictions for suburban office development? What, since this growth will exactly coincide with a crisis for the cities and their mammoth office developments of the past? By 33 years out, these problems will probably have been overcome, but in the ten-year time-scale, the temporary threat to remote working could possibly be at its peak, and one may well expect adverse legal and fiscal reaction as a result.

## THE RELUCTANCE AND UNSUITABILITY OF EMPLOYEES

It was probably significant that the panelists surveyed came up with many more answers about employers' reluctance than about that of employees. Nonetheless, what we have seen already will be preparation for the fact that within the next decade there will still be many workers who resist the idea of this method of work. Much of this ground has been covered already and it is probably sufficient merely to summarise the points made.

- *Social change* of any kind is a slow process—ten years may not be enough to make a significant dent in the status quo: the David Gleicher principle holds as well for employees as for employers; and people tend not to realise how much they hate doing something until they stop it, especially if the burden of it increases by infinitely small stages rather than with a sudden unbearable imposition. Unconscious, they would rather embrace habit than change, and pretend they are happy enough with the way things are.
- *Fear of technology* is the second most vital factor. Most office people are still not used to communicating through computers anyway, unless they are already in the computer business. Hence they will have to be familiarised with computers first, before they begin to think that networking with them from home could be an attractive proposition. After all, they have not yet embraced home shopping, although that technology has been around for the last ten years. Furthermore, some are sensitive to the fact that technology may be imposing itself on them, and demand more human interaction at work, not less.
- *Inadequacy of technology* as we have seen, is probable in the ten-year time scale, and many people will disappointedly refuse to believe that any advance is possible at all. At present, technology is quite inadequate to supersede the human interactive role—there is no likelihood of teleconferencing taking over the functions of the shared coffee break, the business lunch, the mutual intuitive spark of actual human contact. To some degree enhanced video is bound to answer these criticisms, but maybe not enough within ten years, during which face-to-face dialogue will be required in those fields which have already been described and listed here.

  Many important social and motivational needs, flowing from human contact and required to make business actually work, may also be missed by those who try to operate from home. For example, as stated, one cannot compare notes with a friend at the next desk, one cannot easily get help when stuck, one cannot bounce ideas creatively between colleagues. Programmers and computer people in general are claimed to be more introverted and less in need of so much human contact, however.
- *Psychological types*. In contrast, many assert that the average office worker of today is more gregarious, dislikes and even fears isolation, and actually prefers to go out to work at whatever cost for the purpose of social contact. New young job-seekers in particular go to work in order to meet people,

possibly in the hope of finding a mate. Work to them is a new adventure and a means of getting away from home rather than staying there, so while this new mode of work may appeal to the older generation, it will not do so to the young. There are three other aspects of many people's psychological makeup—the need to belong, the lack of self-discipline and the fear that being at home somehow offends against the Protestant work ethic—that may well also make them less suitable as telecommuters.

- *Women and homeworking*. Without the above psychological restraints, telecommuting is often proved to be ideal for many working mothers with small children, but two other factors may mitigate against this. Many women try to conform to the old out-of-date stereotypes beloved in advertisements, soap operas and TV sitcoms, and identify themselves as home-based consumers rather than home-based producers. Secondly, as mentioned, employers are in any case organising more and more facilities for mothers to work full-time, (career-break mechanisms such as crêches and nurseries) and these position homeworking as only one of a number of options.
- *Men and homeworking*. In contrast to women, for whom home is anyway a place of work, for men home is now largely a place from which to leave for work—males, it is argued, need to go out to prove themselves among their peers. They also need the security of a full-time job to pay the mortgage and support a family. This male stereotype, too, is not as adept at communicating as the female, and homeworking to be effective requires a high level of communication in all directions. Result—as we know, homeworking is unsuitable for many of today's men.
- *Impact on the home and family*. There are two main constraints here. First, there is need for other members of the family, both spouse and children, to accept and support the fact that one of them is working from home; this requires a basic emotional stability but also a good deal of organisation and adjustment. Second is the fact that rising prices mean that houses are getting smaller and thus destroying conditions in which one could reasonably work at home; there being now all too frequently a lack of space for homeworkers to shut themselves away.
- *Education and training* is another serious constraint identified by many panelists and which needs to be treated in somewhat more detail.

> Within the context of ILEA I am appalled about how teaching is done. The name of the game is mediocrity not excellence, and everyone is pulled down to the level of the least able. The children are not motivated even to compete against themselves because no value is placed on excellence. The requirements of homeworking like confidence, self-responsibility and self-motivation are simply not being taught.
> (*Christine MacNulty*)

In the UK we have to go a long way down the post-imperial path for the next many years. Certainly during this century we will be ten or fifteen years behind the future—partly due to the failure of the educational system, which tends to produce under-educated working class people and change-averse ruling class people. The US is producing more graduate degrees than we are undergraduate degrees by a long chalk, and although undergraduate standards are lower in the US this comparison is weighted miles in favour of them and shows a very murky picture for us.
*(Jonathan Gershuny)*

The main problem now facing our society is therefore that of educating people to match the growth in technology, since the manual jobs for which they might be suitable are now rapidly disappearing. There are, again, a number of threads that contribute to this one important restriction. First, computers are still being taught as a separate subject rather than as tools to be used in other subjects, so that at the moment people are not as familiar with them as they should be. Secondly, as we have already seen, girls in particular tend to hold back from computers, being programmed to think that this is a no-go, male area. Thirdly, attitudes among the teaching profession are simply not conducive to the spread of computer literacy. One panel respondent had a lawyer friend who recruits sixty graduates a year, of whom he says only ten on average are computer-literate. However, others had a somewhat more optimistic view of the future, given the fact that technology will be moving in friendly fashion to meet tomorrow's users.

There are likely to be serious shortcomings in the educational system, and in particular in the extent to which people will be able to relate to computers. But there will be far greater keyboard familiarisation in the next generation of users. At the same time manufacturers are trying to reduce the use of keyboards with friendlier equipment. Even now it is possible to annotate a draft on a flat screen display using a light pen, by creating a space between two lines and typing in an insertion with standard symbols by pointing at the letters. Soon it will be possible to do this annotation by inserting something in handwriting.
*(Roy Dibble)*

However, it is not only pure training in the right skills that is now said to be lacking, it is education in the broadest sense.

Training is about narrowing and fining down, and education is about widening and adaptation. The emphasis on training in the educational process will improve the ability to be trained, but mitigate against people being able to cope with change. The GCSE is designed to activate the basic training stage and allow people to cope with everyday life. However it does not educate people on how to learn or how to prepare for the unusual. This is profoundly lacking just when it needs to be pre-eminent.
*(Barrie Sherman)*

This sense of balance should certainly be in the 1987 Thatcher government's mind when it tackles the problem of technological weakness in its educational proposals. Much is heralded—one can only hope that the principles guiding not only the city technical colleges but the system as a whole are both practical and rounded.

This has possibly been a somewhat gloomy prognosis for the next decade, but the period also holds the germinating seeds of a number of far more positive factors. Many of these have already been mentioned and they are also summarised at the start of Chapter 10. It should not be felt that they weigh less in the aggregate than the constraints that have been detailed above. The increasing influence of telecommuting is inevitable as from now—not least because society and its values are undergoing a barely detected but enormous change.

## BIBLIOGRAPHY AND REFERENCES

ASTMS, 'The hightech homeworker', *Electronics Bulletin*, Winter 1986

Beckhard, Richard and Harris, Reuben, *Organisational Transitions: Managing Complex Change*, Addison-Wesley, 1977

Consumers' Association, *Earning Money at Home*, revised edn, 1986

Huws, Ursula, *The New Homeworkers*, Low Pay Unit Pamphlet no. 28, 1984

Inland Revenue, *Tax: Employed or Self-employed*, Leaflet IR56, May 1986

Inland Revenue, *Tax Help for Small Firms and the Self-employed*, Press Release 3X, 19 March 1987

Jenkins, Clive and Sherman, Barrie, *The Collapse of Work*, Eyre-Methuen, 1979

Mackintosh, Ian, *Sunrise Europe—the Dynamics of Information Technology*, Basil Blackwell, 1986

Martin, James, *Future Developments in Tele-Communications*, Prentice-Hall, 1977

Martin, James, *The Wired Society* Prentice-Hall, 1978

TUC, *Homeworking*, March 1985

Walsh, Peter, Thomas, Keith and Porter, John, 'Home-based economic activity: the legal and town planning implications'. Working Paper No. 94, Oxford Polytechnic Dept of Town Planning, 1986

# 9
# Three Glimpses of Future Society

According to the Holy Koran, anyone who foretells the future is a liar even if he turns out to be right in the end. In this matter the average person does not go quite as far as the average ayatollah, but nonetheless reserves a healthy scepticism for those who claim to be able to forecast what is going to happen with any degree of accuracy. Even racing certainties come unstuck. When examining the future and its possibilities a more respectable approach is therefore to assess the current situation and its trends as closely as possible; and then to try and gauge the impact of these trends (both patent and latent) upon each other, in the form of a range of alternative scenarios.

For long enough, economists and technologists have insisted that the most important of these trends, the prime movers of the future, were bound to be facets of their respective interests of economics and technology. The effective counter to this is that we have for too long been obsessed with figures and measurements and they have been found wanting. Quantity is after all only one of the qualities, and the expert in the white coat is all too frequently confounded by pure human cussedness—not least, as we have seen, in much of the human response to the theoretical attractions of telecommuting. Our very society is undergoing a period of unprecedented change, and it is this social change that may well turn out to be more influential than economic, political or even technological factors in the long run.

For example, the prestigious Stanford Research Institute (SRI) of California was successfully involved in technological forecasting for the American Defense Department and its suppliers during much of the Vietnam War. Their technological forecasts for bigger, shinier and ever more sophisticated weaponry were duly met as a combination of bellicose generals and bottomless budgets ensured the self-fulfilment of their prophecies. At the end of the war, however, the companies concerned had somehow to switch their production from military into consumer goods, and were dismayed to find that the uptake of technological wonder was very different in civilian life. Their anticipations remained unsubstantiated because some hidden social force, antipathetic to technological development, seemed to be at work there. They therefore turned once more to SRI to interpret these harsh realities. In response, SRI examined 19 different psychological working models to see if these theories of individual motivation were in any way mirrored in overall societal behaviour. Their chief researchers, Arnold Mitchell and Christine MacNulty, found that one developmental model based on a hypothesis of the psychologist Abraham Maslow answered the problem particularly neatly.

## THE HIERARCHY OF NEEDS

Maslow, a follower of C. G. Jung and a bastion of the humanistic psychology movement, postulated what he termed the Hierarchy of Needs. Analysing human psychological development, he suggested that once the basic requirements of food, clothes, warmth, shelter and sex are satisfied, an individual will switch his aim to belonging to a group of other like-minded souls for mutual comfort and protection. When this urge is satisfied in turn, he concentrates on staking out his position in that group by means of material display and achievement. However, there is a limit to the charms of materialism, and the individual may then find himself asking disquieting questions like, if he has four television sets already does he actually need a fifth in the loo? And furthermore, how can it be that, in spite of all these trappings of success, he is still not particularly satisfied with life? What he now finds that he wants above all is to explore and develop himself internally; to be taken seriously as a human being; and to have his personal opinions accepted as mattering to the rest of the world.

The individual has thus moved from focusing on survival as his most important consideration, to the world of group belonging, then on to material success as a touchstone, and finally to what Maslow called self-actualisation. Maslow argued that the earthier needs lower down at the bottom end of the scale had first to be satisfied to an optimum degree before the restless human spirit began searching for some other form of satisfaction. However, he also suggested that some immature individuals become stuck in a relatively primitive stage of personal development, like Mexican axolotls, unable to move further up the ladder because they suffer from a psychological block that inclines them to *maximise* rather than to *optimise* the physicalities of security, or belonging, or material success, depending on the particular stage they have reached.

By extension, the history of mankind shows a similar spectrum of collective needs according to whatever stage of civilisation has been reached. The primitive hunter-gatherer's most urgent need was for survival as he roamed the country for his food. However, by Neolithic times the planting of crops and the husbandry of animals had made it possible for human beings to settle in one place. In order to protect themselves against outsiders who might make off with their stores of food, people banded together into tribal villages of a size sufficient to deter external attack. The members of a nomadic or an agricultural society were therefore sustenance-driven in nature—motivated by the need to survive, and then also to belong to a supportive group. In this simple state of life (and it still exists in many societies today) there is little if any social mobility.

However, with the industrial revolution, everything changed. By diligence and skill a man could rise rapidly in the social pecking order; but equally as rapidly fall down to the bottom through misfortune or mistake. There therefore grew up a society where it was of crucial importance to demonstrate where you stood in comparison with your peer group. Ostentatious show not only to keep up with but to outstrip the Joneses became the order of the day. The industrial age then, is that of materialism, of conspicuous consumption, of the worship of achievement and success. This is the period when the Protestant work ethic holds sway, when competition is the keynote and 'win/lose' games head the programme; though their negative effects are mitigated by the fact that because competition generates economic growth, the scramble for slices of the pie is made somewhat less painful—since for a while at least, the pie itself keeps expanding.

The industrial is now beginning to give way to what is sometimes called the post-industrial, whatever that may foreshadow. Much of our traditional industry is withering and falling, but as yet we are unclear about quite what is going to take its place. However, with the transfer of old-style technology from the developed western world to the newly developing countries of the Pacific rim, in our more lucid moments we do perceive that we have to generate new activities in substitution for the now threadbare panels of our industrial fabric. This may involve us in the tertiary sunrise industry sector—the world of electronics, lasers, holography and bio-genetics; or in the quaternary service sector—information, education, knowledge and health-based. Probably the ultimate cocktail will be a mixture of both with more than a dash of leisure thrown in for good measure.

However, what is evident is that a new breed of person is now in the process of carving out the philosophy of the post-industrial age even before it has arrived in material form. Just as thinkers and scientists such as Luther, Calvin, Newton and Descartes unconsciously designed the foundations of what was to become the industrial age, so the new pioneers are already working on the blueprint for the post-industrial without even knowing it. But the movement embraces not only those who are the accepted opinion leaders of the new, but also a growing number of everyday people who are experiencing an inexorable discomfort with old values and a thirst for different ones. Many of these are in the sunrise and service industry sectors and not only technically suited to homeworking jobs but psychologically suited also, as we shall see.

The situation is complicated, though, by the phenomenon of social faulting. Just as the impact of time on geology creates geological faults, so social faults arise because the physical and self-evident facts of society are out of phase with many of the leaders of thought on the one hand, and the laggards of thought on the other. Today, we can find in the same bus queue the representatives of all three of the major psychological categories represented by the pre-industrial, industrial and post-industrial eras, even though the first has now passed and the third is yet to come. The ebb and flow of general public opinion between these bundles of values, the mind-sets of these three major social categories, have already begun as each struggles for dominance. The immediate future therefore promises to be a period of temporary but intense turbulence at all levels from the nation-state down to the individual family; although ultimately post-industrial values must predominate as the influences of the industrial age gradually become less intense.

## THREE PSYCHOLOGICAL TYPES

SRI, developing its theory along the lines described, named the three Social Value Groups 'sustenance-driven', 'outer-directed' and 'inner-indirected'. they argued that the populations of western industrial societies divide themselves into these three broad groups, whose attitudes are sufficiently at variance with each other for them to be regarded as having three quite different approaches to life. The groups are characterised by their attitudes, rather than by any social or economic status—indeed, members of each are found at every social and economic level and among every age and gender.

The SRI theory is backed up by market research that is conducted regularly by its partners in 19 different countries, based on an annual survey of a national stratified random sample of their populations. The survey contains questions which relate to the attitudes, concerns and choices of respondents; subsequent factor analysis of the data examines the motivations and values of the population in terms of 42 social trends which have been identified by the researchers. The three major groups have to be broken down into different national subsets—in the UK there are seven of them—but the main thrust of the argument holds equally well for every developed country in the world. The dynamic of the model has reached different stages among different nationalities, but the incidence and characteristics of these three groups are universal.

### Sustenance-driven

The motivation for sustenance-driven people is the need for security. Their concern is with just getting by from day to day and with belonging cosily to a supportive group of their peers. Although they are frequently economically disadvantaged—in which case they are, not surprisingly, concerned about physical survival—this is by no means always the case. Many of them are comfortably well off and for these, 'survival' means holding on tenaciously to their existing positions in life. They tend to be conservative, clannish, set in their ways and resistant to change. Even when they are economically able to do otherwise they are inclined to live narrow, confined and class-conscious lives. They are the left-over philosophical products of the feudal agricultural era, strongly represented in peasant and industrial folk societies.

### Outer-directed

The outer directeds are the flower of the mature industrial society, whose motivation is the search for esteem and status. The criteria by which they measure their success are outside themselves. They want to marry the right person, to be seen to live in the right part of town, to drive the right car, and to send their children to the right schools. They are concerned about appearance and behaviour, and particularly that their children should be a 'credit to the family'. It goes without saying that most of these people are materialistic—except in those circles where anti-materialism confers status—and they constantly seek to improve their position in financial and social terms through conspicuous achievement and conspicuous consumption. Outer-directeds are often well, though conventionally, educated, and frequently intelligent, with a reasonably broad intellectual and cultural horizon. They are supporters and maintainers of the status quo, though they will eventually change if they perceive an advantage in so doing. They are strongly represented in Japan, West Germany and Middle America—the locomotives of the present world economy.

### Inner-directed

Inner directeds are the children of the dawning post-industrial age, and their motivation is self-actualisation. They are largely unconcerned about the opinion of them held by the world at large, since the criteria for their success and the norms for their behaviour are inside themselves. This does not imply withdrawn or reclusive behaviour, however. Indeed, the inner-directed individual usually has a wide range of interests and a high tolerance of other people's activities. In general, these people tend to be less materialistic and more concerned with ethics than the other two types. Emotional and spiritual satisfaction means more to them than material achievement. Their values, opinions and belief systems are based on personal growth, self-fulfilment, freedom of individual self-expression, sensibility, and the quality of life and of the environment. The Netherlands, Scandinavia, West Coast USA and the UK are where this phenomenon is at its most advanced.

The core values of the three major psychological categories reflect where each of them is looking for fulfilment. The sustenance-driven looks nervously beneath himself to ensure that the fragile support that is all he can rely on from the world is still there. The outer-directed is looking all around, though sometimes out of the corner of his eye, to gauge the signals that denote the esteem in which he is held by his fellows. The inner-directed, though courteously tolerant of the rest of the world, is looking within for the fruits of self-actualisation, balance and wholeness.

Of course, one objection frequently set against this analysis is the protest that people are not clones and cannot be slotted tidily into a mere three pigeon-holes. Maslow himself, upon whose theory the whole concept is based, fully appreciated that people slip from one mode to the other in their lives as they are dealing with different aspects of them. Even the most rarefied self-actualised man will think along strictly 'belonger' lines when considering the provision of life assurance for his family, and even the hardest-nosed materialist occasionally lapses into higher and kindlier thoughts.

Nevertheless one, or very occasionally two, of the three philosophical modes tend to be uppermost in any one person's mind and characterise his or her normal behaviour patterns. So society as a whole, or any particular subdivision of it, exhibits a preponderance of one or the other, but in gradually changing proportions over the passage of time. In broad terms, this progression shows a gradual and universal shift from the sustenance-driven to the outer-directed, and from the outer-directed to the inner-directed, as individual after individual painfully climbs the steps of Maslow's hierarchical ladder; and as those who are stuck on a particular rung die and fall off, giving place to the more upwardly mobile, younger generation that follows.

So much then, for the broad rationale behind the theory; but how shall we gauge the impact of these three psychological categories on the way that the country conducts itself from day to day? We can fairly easily imagine the requirements of the sustenance-driven group—the maintenance of the status quo and a favourable outcome to the age-old battle between rich and poor, according to which side of the fence the social position of the individual happens to put them. And, apart from that, they seek the cosy feeling of involvement and equivalence with an immediate circle of their own. But because the majority of them—in particular one sub-group, the 'survivors'—are working-class, overall the sustenance-driven are aiming for a greater emphasis on welfare provision and state control, fuelled by a left-wing philosophy and a siege mentality.

The outer-directed alternative is based individually on personal esteem and show, but at a broader level on a floating off of all our inherent political and social differences via the successful application of economic and commercial growth—through the concomitant answers of high technology, science and a stiff dose of more-of-the-same, industrialist, Protestant work ethic. Economic cycles there may be, but the outer-directeds' aim is to mitigate them by dependence on contra-cyclical remedies and the ever more crafty manipulation of economic and fiscal laws. In contrast, the inner-directed philosophy suggests a sense of flowing with natural forces such as the laws of economics, rather than of attempting a Canute-style confrontation with them. As we have seen, the revolution it is engendering has a number of strands to it which relate to the various imperatives that inner-directeds feel as members of this social entity.

The first element is that unlike the group-minded sustenance-driven and the competitive outer-directeds, they are strongly autonomous, freedom-loving and individualistic—and that they wish the same corresponding freedom for others. They resent and avoid situations where they feel boxed in by outside events, and particularly by outside people. They demand to be accepted with dignity by society and by those in it with whom they come into close contact—to be taken as individuals whose values and opinions are important and should be given due weight. They abhor bureaucracies and hierarchies. They resent being pushed around and treated impersonally by big organisations in any capacity, and in their turn they have no wish to push or bulldozer anyone else.

Smallness, informality and flexibility are their watchwords. Small is beautiful for them, and any experience—whether it be work, leisure or personal maintenance—has ideally to be relaxed, laid-back and fun. They do not conform to rigid patterns in their daily lives, preferring instead to react as the mood takes them. Inner-directeds are more concerned with their own self-development than with working towards the benefit of an amorphous organisation. They regard education, in the fullest sense, as a lifelong process. They are concerned with the quality of life rather than the quantity of livelihood—this applying not only personally, but also across the board as it relates to society and the planet as a whole. This is one of the chief derivatives of the growing concern about ecology and the environment, not only locally but on a global basis, and of the increased awareness of humanity's collective responsibility for it.

Within the inner-directeds' life-style there is already much evident blurring of work and leisure—for them leisure is important and should be worked at, and correspondingly work is fun and should be enjoyed. People of this cast of mind are now moving into the position of enjoying a portfolio of occupations, some of which can hardly be defined as either work or leisure in the strictest sense.

The story is told by Charles Handy of his meeting a young woman at a cocktail party and asking her what she did. 'I'm a freelance television scriptwriter,' she said, thus gaining his immediate admiration and respect. But she went on to admit that only one of her scripts had actually been accepted so far and that she had only been paid a pittance for it anyway. 'What do you do for money, then?' asked Handy. 'Oh, for *money* I pack eggs on Sundays,' she replied. Note that she did not consider herself as a Sunday egg-packer which allowed her to eat, but as a freelance television scriptwriter which allowed her to fulfil herself.

With the increasing strains on traditional employment due to international competition and hi-tech alternatives, there is also a melting-down of the historical barrier between work and leisure. So often what have in the past been mere part-time occupations or hobbies have perforce become major sources of income to people, as redundancies have sliced into the heartland of traditional work.

Early retirements, sabbaticals, part-time working, out-working, job sharing, and all the other fashionable variants of the general drive towards cutting down the time spent in a traditional 9–5 framework, have combined in this process, of which homeworking will increasingly become another aspect. As Handy puts it in *The Future of Work*, the old working lifetime of 48 hours a week × 48 weeks a year × 48 years is being diminished to a formula whose factors are going to look more like 33 × 42 × 40. 110,000 hours in a working life will be halved to 55,000 by the merciless application of the Cube Law.

Inner-directeds take this on board much better than the rest—less formal work leaves them with time to do more interesting, even more financially rewarding things. At work they are also quite prepared, and indeed eager, to accept the necessarily complex structures and interrelationships, less specifically defined than in the past, that today and tomorrow demand. In their own private lives too, there is a network of human interaction and extended friendships which overlap according to a complexity of mutual interests, rather than the old dependence on work, family and neighbourhood-based relationships only.

Similarly, the hierarchical, bureaucratic, military pattern of business organisation is anathema to these people. They prefer instead a heterarchical, cybernetic, or circular pattern of command, based on a network or lattice of overlapping cells with variable leadership on a project basis, rather than an organisational structure that is specific and traditionalist. Does this sound familiar? It is of course exactly the mode exemplified by the networking organisations we have been examining as harbingers of the eventual future. Power is the *diktat* of the outer-directeds; but influence is that of the inner-directeds—what they yearn for is a footnote in history, however small and however localised.

Fading are the days of the organisational tree with the chairman at the top and 10,000 worker ants struggling away at the bottom layer. That was a characteristic of the industrial era, built as it was on comparative status. Now we are beginning to see the evolution of the organisational sponge, a structure where individual units work semi-autonomously together, almost like consultancies or intrapreneurships within the whole. These are linked by a central matrix of information and support services which holds them up structurally, and which in turn they nourish by their individual profits in the marketplace, as they work within electronically-defined financial and operational parameters. The sponge with its softer and more feminine outline is appropriate to the post-industrial age just as the shape of the organisational Christmas tree was appropriate to the thrusting masculine industrial one, now past its maturity and into its decline, however.

At work the inner-directed employee will therefore start to make increasing and bewildering new demands. Within the organisation one will begin to see these changes in structure and in the priority of objectives, as the sponge replaces the tree as the ruling organisational pattern. New methods of operation and new personnel policies will bubble up, with a greater regard for personal growth and fulfilment through work and a greater variety of incentive. These new modes of business operation will embrace a whole new relationship between the employer, the employee and the pattern of work, to meet the inherent demand for more open information and more working flexibility.

Attitudes to work itself are changing too, and once again they vary significantly as between the members of our three major categories. The sustenance-driven demand security of job tenure above all, as characterised by the trade union movement's knee-jerk responses that unemployment and redundancy are disasters rather than possible opportunities. And on top, the insistence that higher incomes today are the only means of ensuring against a hole suddenly appearing in the floorboards of worker security tomorrow. Meanwhile, the achiever, or outer-directed employee, also aims for high income but not so much for reasons of security as for the possibilities it provides of splashing out, material advancement and personal success.

In contrast, the inner-directed employee demands a sense of accomplishment and fulfilment in his or her work. These people are certainly interested in money, in as much as it provides them with the ability to develop themselves and engage in the multifaceted range of interests outside work with which they are involved. Apart from requiring work to be nourishing and satisfying—not only to the mind, but also to the body, the emotions and the spirit—the inner-directed employee also tends to prefer short hours to a long purse because of the demands of all those outside interests. Money is needed to engage in extramural activities but so also is time; hence the very personal time/money equation by which each individual solves the conundrum of work versus leisure according to preference.

## THREE ALTERNATIVE SCENARIOS

Taylor Nelson Applied Futures, the British partner of SRI in this work on social change, recently submitted a paper, 'Implications of Social Change for IT Demand and Development' to the information technology EDC of the National Economic Development Office Long-Term Perspectives Group. The contribution was made in October 1985 and was one of the prime sources of the NEDO report *IT Futures ..... It Can Work* published in April 1987, and subtitled *An Optimistic View of the Long-Term Potential of Information Technology for Britain'*.

Taylor Nelson has adopted the alternative scenario approach outlined at the beginning of this chapter, creating three distinct models of the future, 'Autonomy', 'Aggressive Materialism' and 'Retrenchment', in each of which one of the three foregoing philosophies predominates. However, the likelihood is that reality will unfold as a mixture of all three, oscillating between them instead of extrapolating in a straight line in any given direction. The scenarios must therefore be regarded as artificially pure, but they do reveal a vivid picture of what various aspects of life could be like in part.

It is suggested by them that during the remainder of the century both the inner-and outer-directed groups will probably grow at the expense of the sustenance-driven. This will produce a period of turbulence as the latter group feels increasingly threatened and one of the others takes off to become the predominant force in society, ushering in either the autonomy or the aggressive materialism scenario. It is less likely, though possible, that in a period of retrenchment sustenance-driven values will reassert themselves more than very temporarily. The main determinant here will be the political and economic climate that the world, and in particular the UK, finds itself in for the time being.

However, by the year 2020, as outlined in the final chapter, inner-directed values are likely to have predominated to a greater or lesser degree, while outer-directeds will be seeking esteem by exhibiting these values and positively vying with each other as to the extent of their fashionable inner-directedness. The reasoning behind this view relies much on the fact that not only is there in any case a recognisable social shift in this direction, but that information technology is going to make possible much of the autonomy and individualism that the inner-directed wishes to express regardless of outside economic forces.

Table 7 shows the 1985 and forecast percentages of the three major groups in the UK as reflecting the foregoing arguments, given the three alternative scenarios. It signifies that whatever the circumstances, by the year 2020 the inner-directeds will be the country's largest group; and it is worth adding that the trend towards inner-directedness is currently moving more firmly in the UK than anywhere in the world outside the Netherlands and the West coast of the USA.

Table 7 Social value groups, by alternative scenarios (percentages)

| | | | | |
|---|---|---|---|---|
| 1985 (*actual*) | Inner-directed | | 36 | |
| | Outer-directed | | 33 | |
| | Sustenance-driven | | 31 | |
| | | Autonomy scenario | Aggressive materialism scenario | Retrenchment scenario |
| 1995 (*TN forecast*) | Inner-directed | 44 | 39 | 35 |
| | Outer-directed | 35 | 40 | 27 |
| | Sustenance-driven | 21 | 21 | 38 |
| 2020 (*FK forecast*) | Inner-directed | | 55–40 | |
| | Outer-directed | | 30–35 | |
| | Sustenance-driven | | 15–25 | |

From the NEDO report, *IT Futures—It Can Work,* it is clear that the pace and direction of this social change will have a great deal of influence on the uptake of information technology, and thus also on the incidence of telecommuting. The following scenarios illustrate this, with alternative descriptions of their impact on the economic and organisational environment; work, employment and unemployment; leisure; the home and the family; and information technology.

## The autonomy scenario

### *Economics and business*

This scenario is more likely to pertain if the UK economy is neither in a severe recessionary nor a broad expansionary phase, and possibly somewhat less buoyant than the rest of the world. With a large number of individuals who tend towards the inner-directed philosophy, the economic emphasis will be on 'good growth' and 'sustainable development', rather than a hectic boom that carries with it the seeds of a subsequent bust. Organisations will reflect the predisposition of inner-directeds towards small-scale structures and activities in which they can do things their own way. Consultancies and open networks will flourish rather than hierarchies, and large institutions will show a tendency to split down into 'federalised' and project-based units. Human factors in business will be emphasised, and openness and trust will be demanded. Staff functions, planning, creative IT application and research and development will be enhanced.

### *Work and employment*

To the inner-directed, work has to be informal, flexible, diverse and meaningful, both personally fulfilling and useful to society. Income will be of secondary importance and time for increased leisure, education or other self-development will be highly valued. Unemployment will be not so much of a stigma among the majority, who will be less susceptible to feelings of rejection and better able to find or create new and innovative opportunities for themselves. Technological unemployment will therefore bite less sharply for them, in addition to which there will be a sense of active concern for the plight of the sustenance-driven who do suffer from it. By the year 2050 it may not be too fanciful to suggest, with James Robertson, that the main problem will be what to do about that low-status and unfortunate section of the population, the full-time employees.

### *Leisure*

Inner-directeds' leisure activities are as diverse as their attitudes towards work—indeed there will tend to be a blurring of the line between work and leisure, particularly for the inner-directed who has a rewarding job. There will be a fashion for active (not necessarily physically active) and participatory leisure pursuits of all kinds—from squash to *haute cuisine*, and chess to birdwatching—with each following his own taste. Leisure will be taken seriously and less passively than at present. Even television will be interactive and considerably more varied.

### *Home and family*

Since inner-directed people are concerned with realising their own potential and relatively unaffected by outside opinion it is hardly possible to generalise about home and family life in an autonomy scenario. The home will tend to be a reflection of the activities of the people within it, and variety will be the keyword. The home of an intellectual who finds fulfilment in academic research may look like a library and he may spend most of his time there. To a couple keen on sailing, home may be a bed-sit from which they work and travel to their boat, or possibly the boat itself may be their home. The home of an inner-directed woman who pursues a career as an interior designer might look in the latest sumptuous taste, but it is important to note that the size and appearance of autonomous homes are likely to have little correlation with income. There will be a predeliction for useful gadgetry.

Family life is also likely to be individualistic. Loners will live alone and gregarious people will share accommodation, but the sharing may well be on the basis of common activities, interests or even religious beliefs rather than as a result of economic convenience or family ties. These enclaves of common interest are likely to be located in quite heterogeneous neighbourhoods. Relationships based on commonality of interests and goals will in many cases be stronger than traditional family relationships. Parental discipline and authoritarianism is least strong among inner-directeds, so that more parents will prefer to guide their children by reason and example.

*Information technology*

This scenario is the most IT-oriented of all three. Information and education are of enormous concern to inner-directeds, who have voracious appetites for information of all kinds via every sort of medium. They seek knowledge and regard learning (and not merely in intellectual subjects) as part of a lifelong quest. They see education as an individual process requiring different teaching methods and with differences in pace, so will want access to both people and computers as providers of information, education and training.

Information will be universally available from terminals—in the home, in the office and in the pocket. There will be free and flexible access to databanks, libraries, research facilities, business organisations and news services. However, people, particularly customers, will also want to discuss this information with those who are knowledgeable about it and obtain amplification through personal interaction with others. Video-phones and teleconferencing, while useful, are thus not likely to provide people with the sense of atmosphere they need or convey the non-verbal signals involved in personal interaction for another twenty years.

There will be a substantial growth in IT traffic, with systems ranging from large installations owned by organisations to the very smallest personalised packages. There will be a growing use of industrial and domestic robots. Extensive networking facilities and interactive access will be demanded via public switched networks and leased lines. Although an open attitude will be required towards data privacy at government and corporate levels, individuals will be highly concerned about the privacy of personal information.

## The aggressive materialism scenario

*Economics and business*

An aggressively materialistic stance will be the flavour of the month if Britain and the world now happen to be on the threshold of a prolonged period of economic growth, underpinned by the view that science and technology have finally delivered all the answers. In James Robertson's words, this will be a HE (Hyper-Expansionary) economy rather than the SHE (Sane, Humane, Ecological) alternative depicted in the autonomy scenario.

Organisations will grow to even greater size than now, organically but more often by merger, until a very small number of them dominate the planet. The outer-directeds who call the shots will be the organisation-men who seek the status and rewards which these large prestigious enterprises can provide. They will tend to favour mammoth, privately-owned economic enterprises, but many will also have a burning wish to start their own businesses. However, their motivation will be to make money and to show they have made it, unlike the inner-directed entrepreneur whose motivation is to create something valuable and fulfil a vision. The outer-directed woman will act as the power behind the throne, supporting her man in every activity to boost his success, and basking as the eye-catching status symbol on whom he showers his material achievement. Within organisations the marketing, sales and financial functions will become even more influential.

*Work and employment*

Here, work will have two purposes: to enhance position as an indication of status, and to produce income to support the outer-directed life-style. People will want the 'right sort of job' at a good salary. For example, an outer-directed computer programmer would be disgruntled at the notion that programming might have more of the characteristics of a craft than of a profession. Employees may stay in unrewarding jobs if the pay is good enough, but more commonly will want to see advancement for themselves as regards both. There will be a close relationship between contribution and responsibility on the one hand, and salary on the other, so people will be prepared to work exceptionally hard to enhance their own qualifications in order to get ahead.

Unemployment will be reduced by the high level of economic activity, but for those with the wrong skills or in the wrong geographical region, it will be a matter of the devil take the hindmost, though opportunities for retraining will be stressed. Union opposition to the prevailing business philosophy can be expected to intensify.

*Leisure*

Leisure activities will be status-oriented. People will entertain ostentatiously, take exotic holidays, and patronise sophisticated functions. They will enjoy participating in leisure but, as one might expect, there will be an emphasis on fads and crazes. Exclusivity in fashionable sports such as skiing, polo, tennis, golf, etc. will be at a high premium.

*Home and family*

Home and family life will be more predictable because the outer-directed individual strives to succeed within the context of the conventional pattern. The location, design and contents of the home will be as 'nice' as the family's income can support. The children will be educated as 'well' as possible and will be expected to behave so as to be 'a credit to the family'. They will dress and behave as 'one should'. The family unit may or may not be cohesive, but will be a very significant basis for status in either case ('my son, the brain-surgeon').

*Information technology*

In this scenario information will mean power. Outer-directeds will want the appropriate information with which to run their organisations, and will aim to exercise considerable control over its access, with emphasis focused on the central concentration of data storage. Traffic levels will be significantly lower and in general IT demand can be expected to grow relatively slowly because of union opposition. A primarily institutional use of information technology is to be expected with small growth in personal systems. Use of communication networks will be predominantly on a master/slave basis. Library facilities will be limited to data for commercial and government purposes. A high requirement for data secrecy will be experienced, information representing power and monetary value. Demand for interface will be less common, but greater for standardised software.

The prime purpose of education will be seen as training, to produce useful and productive citizens. Standardisation will be important and programmed instruction and teaching machines will be popular. The level of education in the real sense of the word (i.e. to draw out what is already inside) will be lower; it will be primarily status-oriented, exacerbating the differences between the outer-directeds and sustenance-driven groups. The stated aim of training will be to classify people by the degree of their knowledge or skill.

## The retrenchment scenario

### *Economics and business*

In the event of a savage economic downturn due, say, to a collapse of the international monetary system or an all-out protectionist war, the economic and social climate would take on the characteristics of the sustenance-driven philosophy, as more and more of the outer-directeds gave up the competitive struggle and joined their ranks—both these groups being considerably more influenced in their behaviour by outside economic circumstances than are the inner-directeds.

In this scenario, as with the previous one, there will be greater reliance on large organisations which project an image of stability and security, but here the collectivist approach will be favoured, particularly in the shape of state-owned or nationalised enterprises. The majority aim will be to keep one's head down until the trouble blows over while the powers that be sort out the mess. Both the establishment at the top and the masses at the bottom will be averse to change, and traditional remedies will be at a premium over new and imaginative solutions. Threatening messages of any kind will incite sudden and violent unrest; proposals for change will fall into this category.

### *Work and employment*

For the sustenance-driven, work is a means of earning money which he is forced by circumstances to do. He does not expect to enjoy it however, or to find it rewarding in other than monetary terms. At best he considers it a 'duty' to work, and because work is seen as an unpleasant activity, there is accomplishment felt at enduring it, which develops strong ties with colleagues. This will be the prevailing attitude in circumstances of economic retrenchment, and will lead to a considerable increase in trade union influence.

Unemployment will be widespread. Because the majority will still aspire to material consumption, they will be highly susceptible to the feeling of rejection if unemployed, but a tight commitment to the *status quo* and the family/community ethos will make it difficult for them to flush out alternative employment opportunities. There will be a strong belief in the 'right to work' which it is up to society or the state to fulfil.

### *Leisure*

For many, leisure time will be forced upon them by lack of work. Due to economic stringency there will be a far narrower range of leisure activities than in other scenarios. In general the leisure of the sustenance-driven is passive and non-participative. Much of it will also be escapist in nature—reading, the cinema, TV and video, exemplified by programmes such as soap operas, quiz shows, chat shows, spaghetti westerns, etc. The use of alcohol, tobacco and drugs will increase, as will gambling and partisan spectator sports.

*Home and family*

The traditional family roles will predominate here. There will be a backlash against feminism and especially against women 'stealing men's jobs' by working themselves. The greater imposition of parental authority, particularly paternal authority, will strengthen the clan/community spirit as expressed in the form of defensive attitudes to change. The home itself will be the castle within which the family will withdraw from an unfriendly world. Its maintenance and contents will reflect the generally reduced circumstances in which people find themselves, but they will try to keep up appearances as far as possible.

*Information technology*

To the sustenance-driven who will mainly provide the ambience to this scenario, information technology will be seen as a threat—a threat to their jobs, and a threat to their traditional world. There will therefore be substantial resistance, much but not all of it trade union-based, to using information technology and also to being used by it, especially in the increase of productivity by replacing people. The application of IT will therefore be more reactive to specific circumstances which people feel they cannot control and to which IT provides a solution, than one of planned, proactive involvement and development.

## THE IMPACT ON TELECOMMUTING

The extent to which telecommuting becomes prevalent will therefore depend on technological factors, but also very much on social ones, in which these listed characteristics of the business background, attitudes towards work and employment, leisure, the home and family, and towards IT itself will of course all play their parts.

It must be emphasised again that within each of the three scenarios there will still exist people who belong to groups other than its prime mover, so in every case there will be pockets of behaviour very different from the mainstream. But it should also be remembered that however society evolves over the next ten years, for reasons already given the strong probability remains that inner-directed values will finally pertain by the year 2020, as this group becomes the largest and therefore the most influential, representing between

40% of the population in the case of a previous retrenchment scenario, to 55% in the case of a previous autonomy one.

> Assuming that inner-directed values ultimately take the lead it may become something of a cachet for the outer-directeds to work at home. It will be fashionable to communicate with the office from one's home—the move will be parallel to when outer-directed conspicuous consumers began to prefer longer holidays to a bigger pay increase because it was 'the thing to do'. (*Christine MacNulty*)

We shall examine the outlook for 2020 in the next chapter, bearing this sort of social development very much in mind. But to gauge probabilities in the intervening period, let us summarise the findings of this and previous chapters. We know that in ten years from now, most of the technology needed for effective homeworking will be available, though at a cost that may still deter some of the fainter-hearted. The exception will be the lack of high-quality videophone and teleconferencing facilities, which will mean that homeworking will not by this stage be able to provide the full sense of human contact that is so much a requirement of the organisation world. However,

> Inner-directeds get their satisfaction from a variety of different things, and the problems of reduced social contact in working at home are lessened for them since they will get these elsewhere. In contrast, outer-directeds will still need to be seen visibly to perform in order to feel fulfilled by their work. The sustenance-driven are even more of a problem, because they don't get satisfaction from anything very much, except their homes and families. (*Christine MacNulty*)

All social value groups indicate a desire for contact with other human beings, but for different reasons, then. The outer-directed does so to display his achievements and status, the sustenance-driven for reasons of group solidarity and survival, the inner-directed for socialisation. There is therefore every reason to think that until remote vision facilities are so advanced as to fulfil this need to an acceptable extent, full-time telecommuting will be confined to those whose circumstances make it either the only way in which they can work, or a markedly attractive alternative to the traditional office base. Having said this, however, as more jobs are characterised by a higher information content, more will be capable of being done wholly or partly at home, and this alternative will thus be available to more people.

Some types of work will never be able to be carried out at or from home, but the combination of advanced networking facilities, instant access to vast volumes of information, new types of work, changing patterns of existing work, and changing attitudes to all work combine in pointing to an inexorable increase in homeworking over the long term. In particular, parts

Table 8 Positive (+) and negative (−) influences on the prevalence of telecommuting under different scenarios

| | | |
|---|---|---|
| Autonomy (*inner-directed*) | + | The prevailing working mode of open networking, intrapreneurship, consultancy and creative innovation will be most suitable to the homeworking method. |
| | + | The informality and flexibility required by inner-directeds will be answered by it. |
| | + | It will save on travel time which can then be utilised for leisure, education or self-development, allowing people to plan activities to match individual requirements. |
| | + | The applications of IT will make it attractive to inner-directeds, many of whom are computer-oriented, and/or involved in information-based occupations which lend themselves well to telecommuting. |
| | + | Under this scenario there will be more such occupations, anyway. |
| | − | People will miss the socialisation and camaraderie of office life, but will experiment in finding substitutes elsewhere. |
| Aggressive materialism (*outer-directed*) | + | The likely emphasis on productivity may mean that low-grade, piecework clerical jobs could best be organised on a homeworking basis. |
| | + | The mechanical nature and achievement orientation of education and training will be suitable for remote learning systems. |
| | − | There will be an emphasis on large centralised organisations with centralised databanks: the use of IT will be institutionalised, with only small growth in personal systems. |
| | − | Home will be regarded for traditional and well-defined purposes, and work is not thought of as a traditional home activity. |
| | − | Strong union opposition to telecommuting is likely. |
| | − | High requirements for data secrecy. |
| | − | Outer-directeds may want to work from home occasionally, but are far more likely to want to be where the competitive action is, since at home they will be less able to display their working achievements and status. |
| Retrenchment (*sustenance-driven*) | − | Strong aversion to change. |
| | − | Increase in union influence and high unemployment will combine to create resistance to homeworking, regarded as increasing productivity by costing jobs. |
| | − | General suspicion of IT as a threat, in any event. |
| | − | Powerful need for escapism and release at home; homeworking is traditionally envisaged as the very opposite. |
| | − | Resistance to married women with children working from home and 'stealing men's jobs'. |
| | − | Loss of solidarity with and support from working colleagues. |

of a given job will become self-evidently more appropriate for home-based work, and the new skill will be that of breaking it down into chunks which are best performed either at home or away. Finally, the ultimate increase in home banking, home shopping and home education will familiarise people with the idea of doing all manner of things from home, and the concept will be easily extendable to work. Meanwhile, however, the extent to which the phenomenon takes hold will vary substantially with both positive and negative factors dependent on the social climate, as summarised in Table 8.

Clearly the inner-directed autonomy scenario, which is likely to come to fruition by 2020 in any event, is therefore by far the most favourable to telecommuting. That is good news for the imaginative and the innovative, is it not?

## BIBLIOGRAPHY AND REFERENCES

Handy, Charles, *The Future of Work*, Basil Blackwell, 1984

MacNulty, Christine, 'Scenario development for corporate planning, *Futures*, April 1977

MacNulty, W. Kirk, 'UK social change through a wide-angle lens', *Futures*, August 1985

Maslow, Abraham, *Management and Motivation*, Prentice-Hall,1952

NEDO, *IT Futures ... It Can Work*, 1987

Robertson, J., *The Sane Alternative: A Choice of Futures*, revised edn, 1983

Taylor Nelson Group, *Implications of Social Change for IT Demand and Development*, 1985

# 10
# The New Generations

## AND NOW FOR THE GOOD NEWS

Whatever the doubts about the development of telecommuting during the latter stages of this century, by the year 2020 its incidence will thus be vastly greater. The thing will have happened. Two new generations will be responsible for this—a brand new generation of computers and computer languages; and a brand new generation of people. But it will have been a gradual process, with a number of other positive features also contributing to its development—features that will have been making their impact felt from now onwards.

*A hot topic*

First and foremost, telecommuting is an idea whose time has come. The media interest, the consultancy and research thrust, the evidence of statistics, the case histories of success, all of these point to the fact that with increasing publicity the phenomenon will flourish and accelerate, as more and more people become aware if its advantages. At present it is a vast flywheel with a mountain of inertia to be overcome before it really moves. But the signs are that the inertia is beginning to be converted into a momentum which can, once harnessed, enable it to empower and transform the whole economy.

*The pain of the status quo*

Meanwhile, the elements of working life that remain unchanged will increasingly be seen as detrimental: A problem is said to be merely a change that has got stuck, and this is very much the size of it. Thus, managements will grow impatient with, and wish to change, outmoded financial restrictions on their organisations' development. Take the secretary's desk in the City of London, which even now because she has abandoned it to work at home, releases the space for a highly qualified young lawyer who can generate an additional £40,000 per annum in revenue. Or take Bracken House, the headquarters of the *Financial Times*, sold to Japanese interests at a price that will only see them a reasonable return if they ultimately let it at £70 per square foot. These figures, these examples, totally endorse the overall rectitude of the Rank Xerox principle.

As for personal change, the same applies. Commuting can only become both more horrible and more expensive. In the end its costs of stress and strain, as well as its costs in money terms, though endured by the employee, are all passed on to the employer and thence to the consumer. In this connection it must be remembered that the more that commuting time increases as a proportion of the inevitably reducing work-time, the more will be the pressure for its abolition. Once a feasible alternative is seen to exist there will be a rush to endorse it, given the possibility of releasing dead commuting time either for more financially rewarding work, or for additional leisure. Furthermore, whatever the disadvantages some may see in working from home, with the growing incidence of building sickness syndrome other damaging features of working from an office are becoming more obvious.

### *New management awareness*

As the pain of the status quo becomes more intense, the release of the new alternative will seem more beguiling. Managers will therefore become acutely aware of new technology and its promise, and will begin to examine and explore ways in which they can gain access to the benefits of telecommuting:

- the reduction of fixed costs and the control of flexible costs,
- the increased productivity because of lack of interruption, improved concentration, higher dedication and morale,
- the attraction and retention of scarce skills, and
- the fact that the greater management discipline it requires will permeate the whole organisation and improve overall performance as a result.

### *New management capability*

Thus, managers will perforce learn how to manage so that high-tech is balanced with high-touch, and both vertical and horizontal human contact among the workforce is maintained and improved—the resultant balance between flexibility and belonging providing an even greater advantage for the business as a whole. They will also become more adept at subdividing work according to its preferred location, whether at home or in the office, making contracts to cover each chunk of the job and subjecting them to output measurement wherever possible, though maintaining the means of face-to-face personal interaction when appropriate. Management in any event is becoming more relaxed about permitting staff to stay at home to fulfil specific tasks—and this is just an extension of the trend towards the recognition of people's aspirations for working independence.

### *The small business sector*

It is generally acknowledged that it is easier to start telecommuting from scratch in a new business than to impose it on all the framework of an existing organisation. The fact that the freelance/consultancy mode of Charles Handy's contractual fringe is so clearly one of the strongest threads of the emerging pattern of work is therefore encouraging to the homeworking trend. More part-time work, more merging of male and female roles in a working context, and more acceptance by younger people of this evolution of the working process will all combine to reinforce its strength—by the spread of 'office centres' which provide administrative support to the small business, enabling its manager to contain the core of the work within his or her home base.

### *More kinds of remote employee*

A list for starters of some of the potential types of telecommuter was given in Chapter 5, not only the obvious growing number of qualified mothers with small children, would-be entrepreneurs and the disabled, but also:

- the early-retired and retired
- those with time-consuming hobby interests
- those with non-conflicting, part-time, self-employed interests
- mature students and researchers
- carers of elderly parents or disabled spouses
- couples sharing work and/or parenting.

*The home as universe*

More things will be being done from home anyway. There will, in spite of it all, be a greater incidence of home shopping, home banking, home computing and home learning. The greater use of high-tech in the home in order to impart an element of flexibility and individual control into a variety of functions will mean that people will learn to focus their imaginations on ways in which they can work from home too—not necessarily all the time, but part of it in any case.

*The needs of the inner-directeds*

It cannot be denied that for a great mass of people now working, and who will still be working in ten years' time, all this may be wholly alien. Nonetheless, there is a growing number of employees for whom it is already very much not so—the inner-directeds. As technology improves, their predeliction for flexibility and independence will be triggered by the possibility of:

- less time, money and effort spent on commuting
- less money spent on office clothing and office lunching
- more independence of thought and responsibility, with the freedom to work at one's own pace, in one's own time, in one's own way
- holism, balance, self-responsibility and being one's own person
- more and better family and neighbourhood contacts.

For those who say that this cannot happen soon—the 'you can't change human nature' brigade—one can point out the fact that in the early 1900s very few accepted that women above a certain class should go out to work at all. It took a world war to change that; our present status quo will be amended by less dramatic but no less inexorable means, as the previous chapter has indicated.

Inner-directeds will have the imagination to unbundle their whole experience of work and obtain from other sources the side-products they used to get from it before—personal status, companionship, time-structuring, exercise, contribution to a team, and so forth. Yesterday's employees are programmed to think that work is the only source of these benefits, but

> After all, Carthusian monks and nineteenth-century gentlemen did not have jobs as we know them, and were perfectly able to function in a manner where they got their satisfaction from different sources. What we have to

do now is to reinvent this particular wheel—to regain what we lose from work when shifting from 9–5 into a homeworking mode. Working with Ian Miles of SPRU, we found that unemployed people's diaries were very empty, except for mothers whose diaries were extremely full. These were focused round the children and therefore they had less need to get this kind of satisfaction from work itself. Another thing that helps the homeworker is if the nature of the work is a game or an art—or can be considered as such in a creative way, the reward being what other people think of their final efforts. In this sense, computer programming is a game *par excellence.*
*(Jonathan Gershuny)*

It seems to me that there are many conservatives with 101 reasons why new approaches would not suit them, who go on to assume that they would not suit anyone else either. They may be reinforced in this by their friends all having the same view. What they forget is that there are others, such as 'Dinkies' (double income couples with no kids) who may find it convenient to do part of their shopping and banking from home, and investigate how new alternatives fit into their experimentalist lifestyles. Traditionalists cannot speak for them, and so the key question for any new concept is whether there is enough incentive for it to be offered and enough support for it to be economically viable.
*(Jim Cowie)*

## THE NEW TECHNOLOGY

Meanwhile, however delayed the advent of the fifth-generation computer, it will certainly be around by the year 2020 (presumably with its own fifth-generation languages) and might even have been overtaken by a sixth, whatever astonishing shape or form this may adopt. The fifth-generation computer will itself program other computers. It will be capable of knowledge processing rather than mere data processing, and be able to communicate in languages that are much closer to natural languages than the programming languages of today. This will not deskill programmers and make them redundant, however. It will be more a case of rethinking and redefining their roles and then retraining them. They will have to have far greater business acumen than now, for instance, in order to keep that vital step ahead of the process whereby ordinary workers will be able to do much of their own programming, or get other computers to do it for them. The development will involve significant advances in artificial intelligence and the performance of logical operations many times faster than at present. There will be extensive developments in networking, distributed computing and modularity, with the complete merging of telecommunications and computer technologies.

By then one is talking about the nineteen-year-old equivalent of the computer HAL in the film '2001', which is totally voice-oriented. It may even be biologically-based, where the circuitry is not on a silicon chip or on gallium arsenide, but on a DNA molecule ('the year of the clever carrot', as Barrie Sherman put it). There will be the removal of any technological or organisational restraint whatever—the technology will be able to do anything, anywhere, at any time. Both hardware and software will be unimaginably fast, smart, accurate, cheap, compact, portable and powerful. Rex Malik calls this 'the exponential cascade', and as long ago as 1969 perceived it as eroding what were then the foundations of our moral and economic framework.

How do we know? James Martin, in *Future Developments in Telecommunications*, looks at the science of technological forecasting in relation to this. Or rather, perhaps, at the *art* of technological forecasting, since a mere intellectual extrapolation of ideas on a mechanistic rather than a systemic basis is generally wrong. He cites several examples of this muddled thinking, such as the former Astronomer Royal, Dr Woolley, who informed the press that 'Space travel is utter bilge', less than a year before the Russians launched Sputnik 1, but then went on to become a leading member of the committee advising the British government on space.

In his book, Martin starts with two reasons for failures in forecasting as previously defined by Arthur C. Clarke; and then goes on to add another five of his own.

### *Failures of nerve*

These occur when, given all the relevant facts, the forecaster cannot see that they point to an inescapable conclusion and refuses to believe that anything fundamentally new can happen, because emotionally he cannot shed himself of his preconceived ideas. Dr Woolley is the perfect example.

### *Failures of imagination*

This has consistently applied to the communication and electronics industries.

> The story may be apocryphal but it is said that in the early years of the century, ICI installed a telephone link between an explosives factory and the manager's house, for use in case of emergencies. It was used for other business reasons, however—with such success that an internal memo was circulated suggesting that in tne remote future it might be found advantageous to extend the number of sets to a maximum of six.
> (*Ken Edwards*)

Martin mentioned the parallel fact that when the computer came into existence in the late 1940s forecasters reckoned on a commercial market of maybe twelve machines in the US, and IBM made an historic decision *not* to market the computer because it would never be profitable. People simply lacked the imagination to see how it would be used, and what could be suitable applications for it.

*Technological surprises*

Recently, for example, several laws that used to be regarded as fundamental to the whole of physics have been proved wrong. With a constant increase in the rate of new knowledge and new technology, the number and extent of future surprises will also increase.

*Underestimating development time*

But on the other hand, the appearance of a surprise invention does not make obsolete the existing equipment that it will replace. The pause between invention and innovation, though constantly lessening, is still substantial. There are reasons for the delay—reasons of technological refinement, investment requirement and the value of existing technology—but on top of this, is the problem of consumer acceptance before invention can be translated into innovation in its full glory.

*Underestimating the complexity*

The gee-whiz of forecasting is in no way held back by the foregoing constraints, but instead neglects the fact that intelligent human functions are enormously more complex than we generally recognise, precisely because they are human and therefore familiar. We totally underestimate how complex they actually are, once we have grasped the pure concept that they can be replaced or enhanced artificially somehow, sometime in the future.

*Legal and political problems*

In relation to homeworking and telecommuting, a number of these have already been mentioned in Chapter 8. Their impact may well inhibit progress in the early years.

*Failure to forecast market constraints*

There are two sides of any market, buyers and sellers, and Martin rightly takes both into account in his analysis of future consumer trends in telecommunications. With homeworking the two sides are the buyers and sellers of labour, and the social reservations of both must be considered.

So where does all this leave us? Simply in the position that by 2020 the first three 'unimaginative errors' and the last four 'over-imaginative errors' will have been evaporated by the heat of change, leaving a pure distillate of technological and social reality, as far as this particular question is concerned. This book is not a treatise on the precise nature of all future technology, so it must suffice to say that the panels of expert commentators, of managers and of homeworkers, plus those who are prepared to put their heads on the block in written form, all agree that by the year 2020 all the technology necessary for effective teleworking will be totally at hand. It is a valuable exercise here to hark back to the year 1954—33 years ago at the time of writing, just as 2020 is 33 years ahead. The transistor was not available commercially, there was no colour TV, xerography was in its infancy, and the mammoth computers of the time were just about capable of matching today's solar pocket calculator. Chapter 8 has given some idea of what might be available ten years out from here. Quite a lot, perhaps; but 33 years away none of the technological constraints listed by Martin are liable to pertain any more.

In fact, 2020 technology would boggle our poor pre-millennial minds. So rather than rambling on endlessly about telecommuting in a business information context, let us instead imagine for a moment the remote-working, distributed GP of that ilk. Dr Alan Finlay of Tannochbrae is sitting in a boat in the middle of the loch one June morning, after three fat trout for himself, Dr Cameron and their housekeeper, Janet. His concentration is disturbed by a buzz on his wrist-computer, which relays to him an urgent satellite message about one of his patients. Iain Dunbar, on holiday in Malagasy, has collapsed on the beach there after emerging from a deep dive to explore the offshore decorative fish farm. He appears to have an inherent heart condition. What, asks the local doctor who has answered the emergency, is the case history? Dr Finlay rows to the side of the loch, unlocks his car, and calls up the case file from his surgery. Half the car's twin information screen displays the details, which he immediately transmits to Dr Ramphal in Diego Suarez. The screen's other half is used for a video-conversation and for the display of the patient's simultaneous cardiogram, which is then compared with one taken six weeks before in Scotland, and with examples of the same condition accessed from the Zurich Heart Foundation. The two doctors agree he should be moved to the local hospital, so Dr Finlay shunts the whole updated case file to the heart specialist in the Malagash capital, Tananarive, and then returns to his loch trout.

## HOMEWORKERS 2020

The NEDO report, *IT Futures...It Can Work* estimated that 20% of the workforce would be working from home by 2010, so maybe we can estimate between a quarter and a third by 2020.

> The NEDO survey's respondents forecast that by 1995, between 10% and 15% of the skillforce would be engaged in telework. By 2010 the mean had shifted to between 15% and 20% with the mode at 20% representing one quarter of all respondents. (It will appeal) as an option to a high proportion of the workforce for part of their work time, but the form this teleworking may take could involve local offices/communication centres for hire or rent as much as working from home.
> (*IT Futures... It Can Work, NEDO, 1987*)

The report goes on to suggest that after 1995 there will be a discontinuity with past occupational patterns. With the deployment of fifth-generation computing and of program and application generators, IT will become far more user-friendly and move from the rarefied atmosphere of specialist departments and firms into straightforward application by user organisations. IT application will become a necessary skill for every job, and the multi-skilled generalist will use IT with no more thought than today's salesman drives his car.

This is the NEDO projection for 1995. Let us cautiously bear Martin in mind and agree that maybe it might just be in its incipient stage during Chapter 8. But by now in Chapter 10 the new generation will be universal, without a shadow of doubt. This has two important implications. The first is that, as indicated, the new super-programmer will be required to upgrade his/her skills to contribute far more to the design and function of the consumer good or service than at present, and to create new products rather than to solve problems. No tears need to be shed for this kind of homeworker, then, who will be in a much more influential position than at present, having been continuously trained to take on even greater responsibilities as every organisation relies increasingly on automatic and ubiquitous software.

> Furthermore, one may well by that time have electronic scribes (like those of old who would write letters for you professionally if you didn't know the language). A lot of people are not going to know the electronic language by then, and there may well be a gap in the market where somebody will write a home program for you on a bespoke basis.
> (*Barrie Sherman*)

However, neither need the other kind of homeworker—relatively unskilled and trembled for by the trade unions and some of the more pessimistic among the movement's trend-watchers—worry us directly from the point of view of possible tele-exploitation as such. She or he will have taken up some other more appropriate local occupation, having been replaced by infinitely cheaper offshore labour—a feature of the landscape that is bound to take up much government time at international level by then.

We will be concerned with the import and export of data processing and clerical work and printing. Satellites will have leapfrogged cable and with a switching system adequate enough to deliver to individual homes, one will be talking about homeworking in Singapore or China. Printing is now set in London and then carried outside to the cheapest and most efficient areas. 33 years ahead you can translate this into international terms and the UK will probably lose out badly in that respect. It may be that the ultimate function of the English in the year 2020 will be to teach other people English. (*Barrie Sherman*)

The prospect of an ever-greater divergence of skills and training is a chilling one. But once again, we can fall into the trap of lacking the imagination to envisage the whole new spectrum of jobs that could emerge to greet us in place of what must be shed. It is really up to us to create the conditions we want—the choice is all there.

The silicon chip, to use shorthand, is a discontinuity that will totally upset society. Thirty-three years on we will be in a very different world. War on a global basis is probably out, but war on a controlled, maybe economic basis may be in. It could be a 'Roller-ball' society—organised, lethal and involving a considerable degree of violence. At the same time there may well be federalisation of everything so that millions of different choices will blossom and everybody will win prizes of some kind. Everybody has to be a part of the system in some sense. What was it Andy Warhol said? Everybody will be famous for five minutes. In that kind of world good homeworking jobs will certainly have an influence on the running of affairs. (*Rex Malik*)

By this time, though we shall still have a competitive manufacturing industry, instead of employing 21% of the working population the figure will be closer to the 4% now employed in agriculture. Most people will be in computing without even knowing it, and an increasing number will be working in a distributed mode.

Everyone will be computer-literate and recognise computers as a range of facilities only. Computers will be invisible and thus easier to accept, like the housewife today who never stops to think that she has six or seven electric motors in her house—in the hoover, the blender, the waste disposer, the washing machine... (*David Firnberg*)

Companies who don't play this game won't be here by 2020. This is not simply the work-at-home electronic mail bit, it is information technology as a heading—using it for competitive advantage, pervasive throughout the whole organisation. Everyone will have to know the precepts of how to innovate and adapt existing technology to sharpen up the organisation's competitive edge to razor point. Paper will still be around 33 years ahead, though. The office will still be needed as a core place where the shared values are celebrated and developed by face-to-face contact. However, it will be more comfortable to be out of the office than in it—the dominant social pattern will diminish and since high-tech and high-touch have to go together, we will find technological ways of exchanging concepts better at a distance.

One thing here is that people tend to respond either to oral, or visual or tactile/kinesthetic stimuli, and people who respond very strongly to one at the moment find it difficult to understand the responses of another. With new technology it may be possible to have greater recognition through customised technologies, so that anyone will be able to inter-communicate with anyone else because the technology will translate his or her method of communicating into a mode more acceptable to the other person.
(*Robert Reck*)

## THE CONSEQUENCES FOR ECONOMIC LIFE

Economics is misguided in that it has this notion of a rational individual optimising the amount of time he spends on various activities. This is a baroque theory which actually holds no water. Change really only happens at the margins—habit/continuity/the rhythm of life/expectations—these are what matter to most people.
(*Jonathan Gershuny*)

Time-management will become a crucial economic issue as well as the individual one of shaping time so as to be able to meet the demands on it. Since managerial jobs will by then be able to be done more at home with standardised problem-solving being assisted by artificial intelligence, the recognition of increased home-based output will lead to more management time being spent there too. Thus, much of the time which was previously wasted on commuting will be released for both work and leisure purposes.

In his lecture, 'Lifestyle, Innovation and the Future of Work', given to the Royal Society of Arts in February 1987, Professor Jonathan Gershuny pointed out how the reduction in the working week and the diffusion of time-saving household gadgets has combined to increase the leisure portion of the average British adult day by 45 minutes between 1961 and 1985, creating 57,000 extra jobs per minute of this extra available time. Gershuny's findings are that two-thirds of this time is spent on recreational, educational, medical and social activities outside the home, employment in which has increased by 1.7 million over the period in consequence.

Information technology is thus going to be the key to a double wave of innovation and a boom in the world economy in the early years of the next century, claims Gershuny, in an extension of the Kondratieff and Marchetti cycle theories—once creation of the new infrastructure enables people to shop, learn and work from home, releases even more discretionary time, and in the process gives another fantastic boost to the recreational/social sector. Thus the homeworking revolution will not only enhance personal time-management and operational effectiveness, but at the same stroke release more time for all manner of self-developmental activity—an inner-directed stimulus both to the individual and to the economy.

Thus, high technology need not be job-displacing as long as

- there is investment in the communications infrastructure appropriate to the new paradigm, and
- public policy is targeted towards the creation of this free time by releasing people so that they can employ others indirectly in this way.

Gershuny is optimistic that by 2020 both these conditions will pertain. Roy Dibble of the Central Computer Telecommunications Agency (the agency providing advice and support on IT matters in the UK Civil Service) agrees, adding that government will lead in establishing a universal networking system.

> For the home/remote operation to work, all the elements of the current systems must come together. This will certainly have happened by 2020. The basic infrastructure will be there to handle and manipulate all information—there is distinct and widespread recognition of this within government even now. Government departments now see their future role as capturing and disseminating information from/to the public as communicators—and the implication is that by this date they will be able to do so to every dwelling, though first individual people must be happy about the security/privacy issues.
> (*Roy Dibble*)

## THE NEW TELECOMMUNITY

One serious discontinuity caused by one-third of all work being done at home will be the impact of this on the old existing infrastructure. Alvin Toffler in *Future Shock* described the uniquely extensive and rapid urbanisation process he saw in 1970, with the world's urban population locked into an eleven-year doubling time. Alongside this is the fact that urbanities maintained only superficial contact with their many fellows, and hardly ever became involved with the whole personality of the individuals they met. Instead, they picked and chose the modules of each person with which they wished to interact.

Hence the post-industrial nightmare of tomorrow's city, teeming with skyscrapers, soulless and heartless, populated by throwaway people living non-stick, oven-ready lives. All very plausible; except that the way things are beginning to look, it will not be like that at all.

> People's interest and involvement in their neighbourhood is increasing. They are more aware of local problems than ever before and have a feeling they are able to contribute more to solving them—the scale seems more relevant and at this level everyone can be allowed to sing. The new sense of community is very powerful.
> (*Sir Peter Parker quoted in Francis Kinsman, The New Agenda,* 1983)

> Near me in Essex there are already a number of people working from home. Electronics is being used to break down the barriers but we need also to use it to bolster the local community and the local economy, so that a vibrant socio-economic way of life grows up through the roots of the old formal economy. Homeworking ensures that people become part of where they live, as the 'mine and move' mentality gives way to the 'stay and cultivate'.
> (*Denis Pym*)

David Boyle, writing in *The Sunday Times,* drew attention to the views of leading geographer Professor Peter Hall of Reading University, who believes that all over Europe we are going back to the settlement patterns of the Middle Ages as today's maps of population change take on a pattern almost precisely opposite to those of a hundred years ago. Cities no longer have a military significance , they have largely lost their manufacturing base, and as individual buyers no longer need frequent face-to-face contact with the sellers of goods and services, they are beginning to lose their service base as well. Many of the City of London's financial monoliths have even pushed staff outside the Square Mile; while big manufacturing and service enterprises are likely to continue their break-up into smaller and more local federated units.

The new image is that of the 'spread city', in London's case stretching across the whole south-east of the country, from Cambridge and Northampton in the north to Oxford and Southampton to the west and south, curving round from the Solent almost to the Wash. It will burst out into a whole rainbow of environments, from urban through small town to rural, embracing high-tech/light industry, science parks, art and craft centres, computerised superstores, neighbourhood work centres, diverse areas of recreation, telecommuters' homes and—with the incipient deep and prolonged agricultural crisis—part-time farmers, whose salvation could prove to be the provision of locally-grown organic food to the increasing number of people working at home. According to Boyle, the last two major economic upheavals, of a hundred years and of fifty years ago, were both based on new uses of land due to an agricultural depression near the major cities, and each led to a totally new pattern of development. The Telecommunity will be the next new pattern, the germination of which is happening already, notwithstanding protests and rearguard actions.

Of course, some people will still want to live in city centres, and these may well also remain financial centres for some while, at least. But increasingly the trick will be seen to be to green them too, by improving their vacated spaces so as to make them more attractive to those who want to stay there or even move there, and for the large shopping and recreation ventures that are at present being developed on out-of-town sites. The crisis in the cities will only be reversed by making them more pleasant, but the fear is that this process will be highly selective, with some areas becoming playgrounds for the rich, the tourists and the yuppies; while others degenerate into no-go ghettoes, left to rot with their rotting populations, their crumbling high-rise flats and office blocks that serve only as kennels for guard-dogs.

The Telecommunity can work, as long as it is not spread too unevenly. To work, it has to be, and can have become by then, what Ivan Illich called a 'convivial society', designed so as to allow all its members the greatest scope for their autonomous action, through means as little as possible controlled by others, towards the design of machinery for eliminating slavery without enslaving them to the machine. A society where telecommuting was a significant feature could well be such a convivial one, and for that very reason. David Boyle's piece expounds this Telecommunity as not so much *rus in urbe* as *rus plus urbs*, the secret of which is a combination of both, with some areas whose most attractive features are still those of pure city and pure country.

## THE NEIGHBOURHOOD WORK-CENTRE

As one element of this perception, the neighbourhood work-centre evinced great support from the homeworkers who formed the survey's panel.

> In a recent trip to the United States I found that nobody knows anyone in the community or walks about to meet anyone. You can see the whole world on TV, but you lose the sense of what's under your nose. On the other hand the neighbourhood work-centre could increase the feeling of community, which would be wonderful. I certainly have interacted much more with my immediate surroundings since I have been homeworking, and this could be also a by-product of the neighbourhood work-centre in future.
> (*CPS homeworker*)

With a pleasant ambience, it could straddle the best of both worlds—a convivial link between the 'office-as-core' of Robert Reck and the productive loneliness of the home work-station; which would provide the self-discipline and support that some could only derive from having others work in close proximity. They could be combined with distance training/open learning centres for both adults and children, and equipped with crêches for the younger ones. Older children would have their educational needs fulfilled at home, at the neighbourhood centre and at school, just as their parents' working needs would be fulfilled at home (equipped with fully integrated work-station) at the neighbourhood centre and at the office. There would, of course, be a boom in the sale of soundproofing building materials. . .

The neighbourhood centre could be of two types, as James Martin sees it in *The Wired Society*. The first is effectively the main office split down into many local satellites which are situated closer to where the employees actually live with total communications facilities eliminating the necessity of much of the travelling between them. Employees would work in these decentralised out-stations regardless of what department they belonged to, but would sometimes need to meet together with their close working colleagues from other locations for team-building sessions.

The other type of centre would be shared between several organisations, rather on the Swedish and French models outlined in Chapter 7. Though at present technical problems of employee control and information security inhibit managements from experimenting along these lines, it is safe to assume that by 2020 many of these fears will have been found to be imaginary, and other genuine problems will have been overcome by technological improvement. Social change will also have enhanced the process, for this is a truly inner-directed work-style. Clearly the technique would also defuse some of the difficulties surrounding the dedicated work-centre; for example, it would not be as practical for organisational units to keep changing location in step with the way that these more independent workers of the future are likely to change jobs, move house or retire. The shared centre would provide scope to absorb these fluctuations and the vagaries of business life through the flexibility introduced by the shedding of fixed overheads.

Of course, for a long time yet there will be a residual of traditional office activity, though the forecast is that it will be considerably lessened by the year 2020. Some of the outer-directed men who are still around will still want to be seen performing and may resist the idea of a work-style where no one else knows how clever they are being; further, some key functions will always need to be undertaken on site. But there will still be a gradual drift towards telecommuting, both in the neighbourhood and homeworking modes, nudged along by changes both in the types of job concerned and in the means of performing them.

The neighbourhood work-centre will provide a sense of bonding, of loyalty and mutual culture, and a means for people to test out their confidence in themselves by interacting with others, in the way that work has always played a major role in fulfilling this need. It cannot be too outlandish to suggest that by this date, then, on average one-third of work will be carried out on site or in satellite offices, one-third in shared neighbourhood centres of some kind, and the final third at or from home, the aggregate majority of workers having made the psychological leap from a white-collar existence to a green-sweater one.

## THE CONSEQUENCES FOR SOCIAL LIFE

Martin labels commuting as the greatest waste of energy that exists today, with expensive equipment of all kinds lying idle because transportation facilities must be available in sufficient quantity to meet the rush-hour demand. But not only is energy wasted, he points out, so also is the even more precious resource of human time, which unlike other economic resources cannot be accumulated. Staffan Linder (*The Harried Leisure Class*) argues that because time is limited, it has a cost—cheap when productivity is low but more expensive when productivity is high. Normally, therefore, economic growth entails a greater scarcity of time. By abolishing commuting, or reducing it, however, a whole block of time is freed for further economic growth—or for the channelling of more effort into socially productive activity without depressing the economy—another way of stating Jonathan Gershuny's positive point.

Time is money, but it can also be enjoyment, too, and both will be available if planners at the national, local and corporate levels combine to focus on moving information to people rather than people to places where they work with information. In summary, the indirect consequences of this transformation would be as follows:

- More community stability, as employees could stay put when they changed jobs, simply by plugging into a different computer. The result would be less stress, less forced mobility, more deep and lasting relationships, more community participation.
- A better and more attractive environment to live and work in, but better also because of reduced energy requirements and their decentralisation, making feasible the application of alternative energy technologies, and hence a decline in pollution because of this switch to renewable resources. And an environment where though more people may own cars, they will use them less.
- A varied economic impact on different businesses—the expansion of the electronics and communications industries but also all manner of small-scale local business and household consultancies and cooperative

> services; the contraction of oil, coal, rail, the motor industry and the post office. Commercial property interests would obviously switch the focus of their direction from central monoliths to local, flexible and comfortable units.

James Robertson's *The Sane Alternative* gives us an ultimate taste of this kind of societal change where managing the breakdown of the old system is seen as a task of decolonisation; while creating the breakthrough to a new one is seen as a task of liberation, both of which enable people to become more fully themselves as they move from dependence through independence to interdependence. He carries the theme further in *Future Work*, where the change of direction brought about by a combination of social and technological pressures will take us out of what he calls the Age of Employment towards 'ownwork', the next stage of the historical progression from slavery through serfdom and traditional employment to beyond.

Ownwork he defines as purposeful and important, organised and controlled by people for themselves, and either paid or unpaid—in the form of self-employment, essential household and family activities, productive leisure activities such as DIY or grow-your-own, or participation in voluntary work. This is a very different model from the ultimately pessimistic one where homeworking accelerates the descent into a worker/drone future divided between a few highly paid meritocrats and a mass of epsilon semi-morons who have to be provided with free curried chips and video-feelies to keep them quiet.

Robertson holds that the industrial system, by driving work out of the home and into the factory, brought not only a loss of independence at work but also a split between men's and women's work. However, the old attribution of higher status to men's work than to women's work is increasingly becoming inappropriate. Tasks which have typically fallen to women begin to seem more important than many of those which have traditionally fallen to men, which are now frequently perceived as more damaging, less useful and less attractive. Furthermore the conventional pattern of male working life is changing, as we have seen, into a flexible mixture of part-time employment, family work-at-home and voluntary work, combined with spells of full-time employment—a mixture, in fact, that has been more typical of women's lives in recent decades.

It must be highly significant that one growing-tip of this broad change is situated in two organisations of telecommuting women, managed by women, enthusiastically succeeding in a man's world. The shape of work to come will owe a lot to this shift in approach, releasing the potential for what E.F. Schumacher has called Buddhist economics, where the function of work is, as in these two main examples:

- to give the individual a chance to utilise and develop his/her own faculties
- to enable him/her to overcome ego-centredness by joining with other people in a common task
- to bring forth the goods and services needed for a becoming existence.

The new work ethic heralded by Robertson and in accordance with the principles expressed in the teleworking movement, will be based on the principle of enabling all people to become more self-reliant in this way, echoing aspects of both the Charles Handy model of the increasing contractual fringe and the Taylor Nelson/Stanford Research Institute one of growing inner-directedness.

## THE OTHER NEW GENERATION

One major reason why acceptance of the new telecommuting culture will be more evidently on the cards 33 years from now is that there will then be a complete new generation of people around to accept it. This cohort will be today's children—not so much today's teenagers, some of whom will already be on the way to their early retirement by then, but today's primary schoolchildren, at that.

Whatever shortcomings may now be perceived in the educational system and its current end-product, these should be by then more or less over and done with. Fears of the inadequacy of these people to cope with technological and social change will either have been justified or they will not. The slate will be clean and we shall now be dealing with a totally different group. They will not have gone through the unemployment and job traumas of their seniors by ten or fifteen years, who are now just beginning to enter the labour market with nervous foreboding. In contrast, the generation which will be coming to professional and occupational maturity by the year 2020 will have had a very different experience. Having never known a world without computers, electronics and information technology, they will be in a position to cross the frontiers of the information society and harvest the first vastness of its opportunity.

The survey's homeworking panelists had some revealing comments to make about their own young children in this connection. According to their view, there will by this time be a complete shift of perception. Some children are now growing up with the technology and accept computers absolutely. Although some teenagers show reluctance with them, particularly the girls (though certainly there seem to be many teenage girls who are extraordinarily keen), with little children there is already a complete sense of familiarity. For them it is normal to have terminals around the house and though computer-literacy varies enormously from school to school, some teachers feeling themselves threatened by it and therefore playing it down, to the disadvantage of their pupils, computers are a part of these children's lives. Many may be doing nothing particularly relevant with them at the moment, admittedly, but by playing with them they are growing in awareness, and will latch on to them more easily when the time comes for serious work application. Education has in common with information technology the fact that it is knowledge shared among people leading to their interaction with it.

This is an extension of the experience at the underwriting room at Lloyd's, when it was first supplied with a new telephone system whereby one could transfer calls from one extension to another. People larked around, ringing 'Dial-a-Fairy-Story' on their own set and then re-routing it to their least favourite underwriters for a giggle. The older and stuffier brigade complained to the technical wizard who had installed the system. His reply was, 'Good, they're playing about—that means they'll all learn how to use it properly more quickly.' This sense of playful experimentation is an important key to the acceptance of any kind of new technology. Meanwhile, in a more formal sense, the educational system is trying to expose children to computers in every way, not only directly but also indirectly in helping them to learn both on site and at a distance about other subjects. NEDO notes that at 62 per 10,000 of the UK population, the number of personal computers in use in education was about half as much again as for any other nation in 1984.

Relevant here are the small children who become strongly attached to the computer as a toy, and are desolated when it is taken away by an adult. Phillip Judkins of Rank Xerox tells the related story of his secretary's four-year-old who went to playgroup for the first time. The fubsy, middle-aged playgroup leader read them a lovely adventure of a mouse in a red velvet coat with brass buttons. The child looked at her as if she was certifiable—as far as he was concerned a 'mouse' was something on his mother's computer and all this talk of velvety fur and shiny black eyes was in another language. There is liable to be almost as wide a computer culture gap between him and a senior manager when he starts his first job, aged 21, in 16½ years' time. But another 16½ years after that, and the scene will have changed irrevocably—in his favour.

By then, Alvin Toffler suggests that in many cases the family will have gained from this trend in other respects, with shared working at home enriching the variety and quality of many relationships (though perhaps not all, he is prepared to admit). Some couples would divide the action up conventionally, he suggests, with one doing the 'job work' and the other looking after the domestic side. Others would each hold a separate part-time job but learn their partner's vocabulary and be able to share their concerns in conversation and mutual support, parallel to current experience in neighbourhood work centres. In yet other cases, the couple could share a single job, and even gradually involve the children in it too. Finally there is the possibility of what Toffler calls the expanded family, which invites an outsider or two to join the electronic homestead—a colleague, customer, supplier or apprentice. By this stage the family has also become a business, just as it was for the medieval farmer and the eighteenth-century handloom weaver.

There are still one or two possible hang-ups, however, the most important of which is that sexist stereotyping remains strong among today's children—witness the already quoted homeworking respondent whose son teased his younger sister as inferior because she 'wouldn't have to work for a living'.

> I have seen films of children interacting with micros. At eight or ten it's absolutely fine, but then at puberty girls get self-conscious and want to please—and when boys elbow them out of the way they step back. There is probably a need for single-sex classes in computing in mixed-sex schools. In the United States, two-thirds of women in computer literacy classes dropped out after three weeks until they arranged classes for women alone.
> (*Steve Shirley*)

In consequence, F International in its jubilee year of 1987 has focused a great deal of time and energy in supporting the girls of St Paul's School in their computer studies. As FI sees it, the problem also relates to the current difficulties of many women managers who have arrived through the secretarial route—they have keyboard skills, but in order not to be shunted into a siding, their motto has had to be 'never let them know you type'. By 2020, however, we ought to be shot of these distortions, once more successful role models of both genders have come out into the open as balanced human beings.

There was only one other tentatively negative aspect raised by the survey panel, besides the possible fear that human nature would not have moved that far by then. The technology was going to be there, it was agreed, but could the very universality of it induce a retreat to older values—particularly if the information revolution was blamed for the destruction of the developed world's manufacturing base, or if the moral misuse of the system connected with the inability to protect personal data brought about a backlash of opinion? Brushing these thoughts aside, however, the panel reckoned that by 2020 telecommuting would be a wholly accepted feature of the commercial scene. The homeworkers and the managers made 75 positive points (many of them in common, of course) as against 30 negative ones as to whether homeworking would represent one third of all work by this date. This compared with only 97 positive as against 113 negative in their group assessment of the position ten years ahead, in 1997. As Chapter 8 also suggests, full acceptance of the mode is unlikely by then; but their 2020 endorsement of it is perhaps the more significant for that reason.

The next century may thus see our release from the pains of a geriatric industrial society—the unemployment, the monotony, the dehumanisation, the divisiveness—into the reincarnation of a new system where the old debates and the dying issues have no longer a part. The experience of these first homeworkers depicted here can serve to form one pouring of the foundation of this new order, where the holistic view prevails and work is not as in the First Law of Thermodynamics, merely the equivalent of heat, but an activity nourishing to the body, the mind, the heart and the spirit of each individual within each group. That indeed is the '2020 Vision'.

## BIBLIOGRAPHY AND REFERENCES

Bell, Daniel, *The Coming of Post-industrial Society*, Heinemann, 1974
Boyle, Davis, 'Cities of the future look set to spread', *The Sunday Times*, 17 May 1987
Clarke, Arthur C., *Profiles of the Future*, Gollancz, 1962
Council for Science and Society, *Access for All? Technology and Urban Movement*, 1986
Gershuny, Jonathan, 'Lifestyle, Innovation and the Future of Work', Presentation to the Royal Society of Arts, 9 February 1987
Handy, Charles, *The Future of Work*, Basil Blackwell, 1984
Illich, Ivan, *Tools for Conviviality*, Calder and Boyers, 1973
Kinsman, Francis, *The New Agenda*, Spencer Stuart and Associates, 1983
Linder, Staffan, *The Harried Leisure Class*, New York, 1970
Martin, James, *The Wired Society*, Prentice-Hall, 1978
Martin, James, *Future Developments in Tele-Communications*, Prentice-Hall, 1977
NEDO, *IT Futures ... It Can Work*, Long-term Perspectives Group, 1987
Robertson, J. *The Sane Alternative: A Choice of Futures*, revised edn, 1983
Robertson, J. *Future Work*, Gower, 1985
Schumacher, E.F., *Small is Beautiful*, Blond and Briggs, 1973
Toffler, Alvin, *Future Shock*, Bodley Head, 1970
Toffler, Alvin, *The Third Wave*, Collins, 1980
Malik, Rex, 'Beyond the exponential cascade: on the reduction of complexity', *Intermedia Magazine*, March 1986

# 11
# What Do We Do On Monday Morning?

Let us come down again with a bump from our vision of the future, back to the pressing details of the here and now. What this is about, after all, is persuading managements that it is worth looking at telecommuting for a solution to some of their immediate and incipient problems. Here, then, is a checklist for you, the far-sighted manager, who have decided to give the idea some elbow-room. What, as a matter of practical urgency, do you do on Monday morning, having come to a state of theoretical acceptance over the weekend?

## THE VISION

First, quantify the actual and/or potential overheads that are associated with employing your workforce in offices but would be eliminated by remote working—not only the costs you might reduce but also those you might not even have to carry, should you expand. Aggregate this with the value of the control of flexible costs; the increased productivity of committed people; the attraction and retention of scarce skills; and the necessary management discipline that will permeate the organisation as a result of telecommuting practice. Use this equation to enthuse yourself and your colleagues.

Accepting the opportunities of change, create a vision of this for yourself and translate it into practical terms in the form of a mission, a strategy and a set of values, to be known and recognised by your whole workforce—core workers and homeworkers—so that they and you share it and are committed to it. As a first step, develop a cult of efficiency to compensate for some of the difficulties of remote working you are inevitably going to meet.

Experiment, admit that you are experimenting and be prepared for mistakes. Acknowledge that this is a learning process and enlist your work force into it. Seek advice from other managements that have successfully introduced the method—they are keen to offer encouragement and spread the word. If possible, also engage your own clients and customers in the development of a remote working network. It can provide an excellent sales tool with boundless application.

## THE TECHNOLOGY

Be familiar with the details of new information technology—not only all the new features of the extended telephone, but of cable, cellular radio and pagers, too. Keep continuously abreast with what is about to happen as well as what is already here today, and incorporate this into your strategic plan. Be innovative and demand that your workforce is innovative, encouraging people to play with the concept and the equipment with the aim of solving problems, some of which you may not even know you have. Reward them directly or indirectly for their contributions. Naturally, all involved will need to be trained to the necessary technological standard, but also use distance networking techniques on an office-to-office basis so that employees of all levels get used to it and the idea of home teleworking becomes less daunting to them.

## THE STRUCTURE AND ORGANISATION

Arrange that one person is responsible for the success of the whole telecommuting operation—or of each integral part of it if clearly divisible—whose job stands or falls by its performance.

Decide how to graft the teleworking concept onto your organisation. How many of your workforce will work remotely? Will they be full-time or part-time? Salaried or freelance? Existing workers or new recruits? Will the operation be best conducted on a mobile basis, from home, in a shared or dedicated work-centre, or in a combination of all of these?

Define each job in respect of its 'continuity' aspects to be performed in some recognisable centre, and its 'output' aspects which can (and should where possible) be performed remotely, whether 'service' or 'nomadic' in nature. The latter require contact during mobility; the former are static and primarily concerned with the processing, analysis, interpretation and presentation of information—where few direct personal transactions are involved and peace and quiet are at a premium. Devise accurate estimating, monitoring and quality control procedures with well set aims and targets for this remote 'output' work.

Some core staff will not be able to work remotely at all under the above definition, but most others will to a greater or lesser extent. Encourage them to do so; for example, by taking terminals home with them, in order that as many as possible recognise both the value of the working mode and the difficulties that it can involve—this will help them to appreciate the position of those colleagues who work largely on a distance basis when they communicate with them in future. Make sure that the latter also work part of the time on site and/or with their teams.

Create a flexible, non-hierarchical organisation structure with project teams forming and reforming according to the demands of each organisational task. If your workforce, or part of it, is freelance, maintain human utilisation levels as high as possible—both as regards quantity (i.e. time) and quality (i.e. intellectual stimulation). Break the work down into short chunks both for reasons of interest and variety, and for ease of quality control.

Create very formal but simple procedures, fully and clearly explained in a procedures manual, which are supported by well-designed documentation from telecommuter to centre (reporting), and back (instructing/informing/supporting).

## THE WORKING CONTRACT

The nature of the contract between you and your telecommuters will depend entirely on your own circumstances. There are no hard-and-fast rules, and plenty of alternatives to choose from as exemplified here. Naturally the contract must be fair and non-exploitative, with adequate financial rewards. These and other conditions, fringe benefits and reimbursement details must also be fair in relation to core or on-site staff. Where there are differences these must be valid and accepted by all as such.

With a workforce that is partly or wholly freelance, encourage people to take up additional outside work in order that new ideas and principles may be introduced. However, in this connection, consider the limitations you need to impose on working for competitors and on the security of in-house data.

Ensure that the ambience and the circumstances of the homeworker are suitable for telecommuting needs; that the equipment, office furniture and environment are appropriate; and that health and safety provisions are being met. Where required, train freelancers in the skills they will need to run their own businesses and, in any event, keep them abreast of the tax and legal implications of their status.

## RECRUITMENT

Managers must be trained not only to recruit the right kind of people for this remote working mode but to read them fast and accurately, since they will from then on be in less face-to-face contact with them than in traditional working practice. As regards selection, those who have good reason to want to work from home (mothers with small children, the disabled, and others mentioned in Chapter 5) are liable to be committed in their approach to it. More essential, however, is that potential telecommuters should have the right psychological, attitudinal and entrepreneurial characteristics (also see Chapter 5) and where possible that these qualities should be confirmed after interview assessment by means of professional testing methods.

When extending telecommuting to an existing workforce, undertake a pilot scheme with those such as maternity or disabled workers whose skills you wish to retain, and with volunteers for the new system—subject to your assessment of their stability and appropriateness, as above. Only once the scheme has been shown to be successful and the pioneers enthusiastic should you extend it to others in the organisation who will pick up the positive message. In any event, be most careful in the selection of young unmarried people who are liable to find the experience insufficiently broadening in terms of human contact.

Arrange for recruitment to be followed by a full and carefully structured induction programme, and for communication with these new recruits to be extremely supportive. Consider whether at first they might advantageously spend more time on site/in the branch office/in the business support centre so as to get to know personally other members of the network and of the support staff. Once used to each other, and having crossed the language barrier, they will then interact better in an electronic mode.

## TRAINING AND DEVELOPMENT

More formal training than normal is needed for distributed workers since they miss much of the informal training on the job that is involved in picking up hints, tips and knowledge from others (the somewhat maligned 'sitting-next-to-Nellie' system). However, training for training's sake or as a substitute for productive work must be avoided—all training should be followed as soon as possible with application in the new skill.

Remote workers must be kept up-to-date in the technological aspects of their work, especially where their current skills are to be retained but on a remote rather than a traditional basis. However, they must also be taught both general and particular business skills, including workload and time-management, and how to ameliorate the physical and mental impact of their working mode on their home and family. Above all, they need to acquire 'people' and communications skills—as also do their managers, especially.

Though much training can be undertaken on a distance learning basis particularly where individuals are house-bound, joint training sessions are particularly valuable to remote workers as providing the sense of a shared and common purpose and of the membership of a team. Where distance learning methods are used, trainers must communicate more with their trainees than usual, and provide a 'hotline' for psychological as well as for technical support besides encouraging trainees in the same geographical locality to engage in a relationship of mutual help.

Managers themselves particularly need to know what it is like to work from a home or remote base, so that they grasp the importance of these communications and 'people' skills. When starting they should also be trained in part with the telecommuting homeworkers they will be managing, so as to experience the reality of their circumstances. They also need skills in estimating and defining output; in quality control and monitoring; in negotiating and in contract purchasing; and finally, in motivating their teams at a distance, for which there are a number of prerequisites.

It will thus be necessary for individual teleworkers to be allowed to grow, through managers leaving space for their self-development and self-expression around the solid core of the practical and definable requirements of each job. The motivation of people towards this end should be based on the encouragement of the entrepreneurship and the non-conformity of individuals: by enabling them to be themselves to the full; and by creating a sense of shared values and interdependent trust within the team. For this to happen, managers have to be trained to understand both individual and group role psychology, so that they treat and care for their team as whole people, each of whom has something of value to give, and who are collectively happy, confident and effective as a result.

## TEAM-BUILDING AND COMMUNICATION

Much of the foregoing clearly involves the skills of team-building and of fostering communications within the team. Contact between telecommuters must be encouraged so that they are freely prepared to ask for and to give help in problem-solving—not only technologically but as regards the very process of working from home within a family space. This especially applies, as in the Rank Xerox case, where networks do not often work on a team basis—here local peer groups or business support centres can prove an answer, but only if well organised and with an excellent and human organiser or administrator.

Remote workers must be given the opportunity to socialise with each other if they so wish, besides being regularly engaged in projects, training, creative brainstorming, or strategic meetings. The sense of team spirit will be engendered in all these ways, but it is also important that there is opportunity for them to voice their collective, participatory opinions on broader issues.

At the same time, teleworkers must also be helped to move from the position of dependence to that of independence before they can conceptualise the full advantages of interdependence. They must unbundle their previous experience of traditional work and obtain from additional or other sources its pyschologically positive side-effects, such as status, companionship, visible performance or time-structuring. Meanwhile, as above, on-site, core or support colleagues must learn to accept the telecommuters as they are and absorb the difficulties and misunderstandings that they may bring in their train, and vice versa.

Managers should also consider encouraging (in the absence of any trade union understanding) a possible new Guild of Telecommuters, able to negotiate with employers or contractors more effectively than today's unions and whose members could derive mutual support from each other in ways described above.

Communication is paramount—up, down and sideways—managers in particular must ensure that the channels are free between themselves and their team, between telecommuting colleagues and between networking and core support workers. Remote workers must feel they are part of the action—on circulation lists, on organisation charts, invited to social events, and so forth. They must be kept in touch with company, regional, area and team developments—by word of mouth, newsletter, technical bulletins, chatty circulars, electronic mail and group meetings of various types which have a social content as well as an informative one.

All telecommuters and their managers should be equipped with answering machines and with pagers so that they can be contacted in the field. They should also inform colleagues of their movements and ensure in advance that they can be physically and technologically accommodated when they need to visit the local or central office.

## MANAGEMENT AND CONTROL

Because of the increased demands on management, it will be necessary to have more managers, and possibly more tiers of management. However, managers must act heterarchically rather than hierarchically, and be prepared to perform in different capacities for different projects.

The management emphasis must be on the quality, rather than the quantity of control and supervision—managers must not breathe down telecommuters' necks, but rather leave them to their own individuality while at the same time making themselves available, approachable and supportive. They must listen for the cry for help, but also be awake to unspoken things. They must be conscious of the worker as a whole person, adopting a counselling role where appropriate but also moving fast when technical and human problems occur, in order to limit damage as far as possible. They must foster morale, balancing consideration with firmness, appreciating the special circumstances of each worker as well as the general difficulties of remote working—an experience which they should make a point of sharing.

They must give immediate, accurate and understanding feedback about workers' performance. They should encourage the free admission of errors in order that both they and their team can learn from mistakes in a non-threatening way. Feedback must relate to the output of each job, but also workers should have the benefit of regular (at least annual) assessments in respect of their career paths, to pinpoint where they fit into the grand strategy of the organisation.

In short, they must obey all the recognised rules of good management, in the realisation that in order to succeed, the distributed organisation needs a higher degree of all round performance than the traditional one - but given that, it will outstrip it.

This is an excellent note on which to leave our prosaic though necessary checklist of managerial requirements, and end with a short burst of enthusiasm for this whole exciting concept. It has all been said. The distributed organisation will indeed outstrip the traditional one in future. And as the facts become increasingly self-evident, more and more of them will be doing just that. Today's pioneer telecommuters, who have been represented in detail here, will be the pathfinders for a whole range of experiments over the coming years, the end results of which will be higher productivity, better management, greater job fulfilment, the blossoming of neighbourhood communities, and the silencing forever of those drear Dickensian footsteps with which we began. Praise be.

# Appendix A Homeworkers' and Managers' Surveys: The Panel of Respondents

*CPS*

Ninian Eadie
Diana Hill
Janet Davies

Sue Chesser
Carole Cox
Paul Drage
Carol Fallon
Jane Finlayson
Fiona Flower
Jacqui Gerrard
Kathy Gilbert
Linda Hammond
Beverley Hubbard
Chris Mayne
Diana Potter
John Shepherd
Jenny Turner
Karen Walker
Sally Weymouth

*DTI/IT World*

Frits Janssen
Pamela Grice
Breda Robertson

*F International*

Steve Shirley
Hilary Cropper
Penny Tutt

Chris Burrows
Rita Clifford
Helen Ellis
Linda English
Pam Evans
Linda Handley
Chris Harpham
Maralyn Harris
Rosemary Hewitt
Hilary Holman
Ray Lloyd
Kath Lucass
George Lupton
Gay Marks
Pearl Murphy
Vivienne Steele
Mary Smith
Eileen Wallace
Jenny Williams

*Rank Xerox*

Phillip Judkins
Roger Walker

# Appendix B Homeworkers' Survey Questionnaire

1 (a) When and how did you start working from home?
What are the practical details of your work?

*Prompts*
1. Type of work
2. Amount of work
3. Work patterns
4. Basis of contract
5. Employer/clients
6. Payment
7. Technology/equipment

(b) Do you do any freelance work in addition to that for your employer? If so, in about what proportion? Is the work of the same type? Does it affect your relationship with your employer?

2 (a) What are your broad views about your experience of homeworking?
(b) How does it compare for you with other more conventional types of work?
(c) What are its advantages and disadvantages for you?

3 (a) What do you have to supply/pay for yourself and what is supplied/reimbursed by your employer? Does this seem fair and reasonable to you?
(b) Are you registered for VAT? Are you given any tax/financial/pensions advice by your employer? Or any other kind of counselling?

4 (a) How do your work-life and your home-life fit in together? Have you a family and how do they feel about it? How do your friends regard this way of working?
(b) Are there any common or occasional circumstances that make this work/home relationship particularly easier or more difficult?
(c) Could you ever envisage members of your family helping you in your actual work?

5 (a) What kind of a person makes a good homeworker?
(b) What kind of employer would run a good homeworking network?
(c) How do you feel that you and your employer measure up to this?
(d) Is there anything about your circumstances that makes your own story untypical in any way? What other views do your colleagues express?

6 (a) What kind of relationship do you have with your employer at both the managerial and the human levels? How does this differ from your experience of conventional employment?

*Prompts*
1. Communication
2. Motivation
3. Control/supervision
4. Contact/support
5. Training
6. Fulfilment/development
7. Manipulation/exploitation

(b) What is your relationship with other members of your network — both as colleagues and socially? How does this differ from your experience of conventional employment?
(c) What is your relationship with clients? How does this differ from your experience of conventional employment?

7 (a) What are the main changes that have occurred for you during the time you have been homeworking? Who or what instituted them? How do you feel about them?
(b) Do you anticipate any likely changes within the next three years? What would you feel about them?
(c) Other than that, what changes would you like to see within the next three years?

8 (a) How do you view the ten-year outlook for your own career as a homeworker? And your network's development?
(b) What do you see as the ten-year outlook for homeworking in general in the UK, and in the rest of the world — bearing in mind technological and social change?
(c) What might be the constraints that hold up its progress, and the positive factors that could accelerate it?
(d) Finally, what do you imagine might be happening in and around the world of homeworking a long time ahead, say 33 years from now in the year 2020?

# Appendix C
# Commentators' Survey: The Panel of Respondents

Dr Jim Cowie, Director for Strategic Issues, British Telecom
Roy Dibble, Head of Advanced Technology and Telecommunications, Central Computer Telecommunications Agency
Ken Edwards, Consultant, Strategic Information Technology, Imperial Chemical Industries
Dr David Firnberg, Managing Director, Eosys
Professor Jonathan Gershuny, Professor of Sociology, University of Bath
Professor Charles Handy, Visiting Professor, London Business School
Frits Janssen, Managing Director, IT World
Michael Josephs, Director, Point Consulting
Christine MacNulty, Managing Director, Taylor Nelson Applied Futures
Rex Malik, Contributing Editor, *Intermedia*
Dr Graham Milborrow, Director of Professional Development, British Institute of Management
Joe Miller, Managing Director, Miller Research Associates
Bob Pell, Director, Conran Roche
Professor Denis Pym, London Business School
Dr Robert Reck, Managing Director, Index Group
James Robertson, independent writer, lecturer and consultant
Sheila Rothwell, Director, Centre for Employment Studies, Henley Management College
Barrie Sherman, freelance consultant
Professor Tom Stonier, Chairman, The School of Science in Society, University of Bradford
Michel Syrett, Editor, *Manpower Policy and Practice*
Peter Templer, management and organisation development consultant

# Index

*Note*: This index does not include the names of those who are listed only in the Introduction and Acknowledgements, the Bibliography and References sections of the various Chapters, or the Appendices.